EVERYDAY EATING

"A fascinating book on food, meals and taste which is bound to become a classic in this field."
Christel Lane, University of Cambridge

"A unique revelatory analysis that disrupts common assumptions and identifies continuities and changes in the 'what, when and why' of British everyday eating in the post-war era."
Julia Brannen, Professor Emerita, UCL

"Illustrates the reassuring familiarity in our everyday eating amid social, cultural and historic change and offers us a way to better understand historical shifts and contemporary challenges."
David Marshall, University of Edinburgh Business School

EVERYDAY EATING

Food, Taste and Trends in
Britain since the 1950s

Alan Warde

First published in Great Britain in 2024 by

Bristol University Press
University of Bristol
1–9 Old Park Hill
Bristol
BS2 8BB
UK
t: +44 (0)117 374 6645
e: bup-info@bristol.ac.uk

Details of international sales and distribution partners are available at bristoluniversitypress.co.uk

© Bristol University Press 2024

British Library Cataloguing in Publication Data
A catalogue record for this book is available from the British Library

ISBN 978-1-5292-2412-2 hardcover
ISBN 978-1-5292-2413-9 paperback
ISBN 978-1-5292-2414-6 ePub
ISBN 978-1-5292-2415-3 ePdf

The right of Alan Warde to be identified as author of this work has been asserted by him in accordance with the Copyright, Designs and Patents Act 1988.

All rights reserved: no part of this publication may be reproduced, stored in a retrieval system, or transmitted in any form or by any means, electronic, mechanical, photocopying, recording, or otherwise without the prior permission of Bristol University Press.

Every reasonable effort has been made to obtain permission to reproduce copyrighted material. If, however, anyone knows of an oversight, please contact the publisher.

The statements and opinions contained within this publication are solely those of the author and not of the University of Bristol or Bristol University Press. The University of Bristol and Bristol University Press disclaim responsibility for any injury to persons or property resulting from any material published in this publication.

Bristol University Press works to counter discrimination on grounds of gender, race, disability, age and sexuality.

Cover design: riverdesignbooks.com
Front cover image: Shutterstock/Enmler

In memory of my parents Nancy
and Ernie who fed me so well
for years

Contents

List of Figures, Tables and Boxes	viii
List of Abbreviations	x
Acknowledgements	xi
Preface	xii
1 Changing Eating Habits	1
2 Meals: Occasions and Arrangements	17
3 Acquisition and Diversity	39
4 Tasting: Embracing Foreign Flavours	64
5 Meal Preparation	84
6 Eating with Style	102
7 Anxious Pleasures: Eating and Happiness	123
8 An Unfinished Revolution?	149
Notes	166
References	181
Index	192

List of Figures, Tables and Boxes

Figures

2.1	Changing times of meal events in Britain, 1961 and 2001	27
3.1	Clusters of food preferences, adults aged 18+, Great Britain, 2018	43
6.1	Percentage of respondents visiting restaurants with different cuisine styles within the last year and on the last occasion, 2015	110
7.1	EAT-Lancet Commission reference diet for a sustainable planet	145

Tables

3.1	Frequency of consumption of selected foodstuffs, adults aged 18+, Great Britain, 2018. All adults, lowest income quartile and highest income quartile	41
6.1	The growth of interest in food, 1995–2015	108
6.2	The hierarchical ranking of cuisines served in restaurants in England, 2015	111
6.3	Comparison of distinctive features of omnivorous and restricted behaviour, 2015	113
7.1	Enjoyment of last occasion dining out at commercial establishment and someone else's home	125

Boxes

1.1	Ordinary household menus from 1901	3
3.1	Trussell Trust's single food box three-day menu	48

4.1	A typical menu of an English pub's 'Classic Main Courses' in 2023	71
4.2	A tasting menu (Aizle, Edinburgh)	81
6.1	Are you a Foodie?	103

List of Abbreviations

BMI	Body Mass Index
DEFRA	Department for Environment, Food and Rural Affairs
EMP	Everyday Meals Project
FYS	Food and You Survey
GFG	*Good Food Guide*
OFH	*Official Foodie Handbook*
TCP	Three Cities Project
UPF	ultra-processed food

Acknowledgements

If I were to acknowledge all the help that I have received over several decades to make this book possible the list would be very long. Suffice instead to offer my profound and sincere thanks to the collaborators and co-authors with whom I conducted recent research projects upon which the text draws heavily: Isabelle Darmon, Steffen Hirth, Lydia Martens, Jess Paddock, Dan Welch, Jen Whillans and Luke Yates. I would also like to thank Dale Southerton and Sue Scott for reading drafts of the manuscript and offering advice about its improvement, and to Sue in addition for her patient encouragement throughout the process. Thanks also to Jukka Gronow and Lotte Holm for allowing me to borrow the main title of this book from their *Everyday Eating in Denmark, Finland, Norway and Sweden*. I am very grateful to Bristol University Press for the exceptional quality of its support, to Anna Richardson and especially to my editor Victoria Pittman who could not have been more helpful in seeing the book through to completion. I also want to record my gratitude to the Economic and Social Research Council and to the Sustainable Consumption Institute at the University of Manchester for grants to undertake much of the research.

Preface

The preparation of this book, long in gestation, was revived in earnest during the COVID-19 pandemic and completed in its aftermath. The pandemic will remain in the collective memory for many reasons, among them its effect on eating habits. Many routines were disrupted, most notably, shopping, dining out, use of takeaway foods and sharing meals with others beyond the household. Government instructions reduced personal mobility and prescribed a tiny number of admissible companions as catering outlets were closed and visits to other people's homes prohibited. To be compelled to eat only at home, and only with household members, constituted a major and abrupt transformation of habits and routines. No restaurant visits. No drinking coffee in cafes. No sharing meals with non-resident parents, siblings or children. COVID-19 severely interfered with established arrangements by eliminating many regular social events. Not insignificantly, a bizarre government initiative at the end of the first period of total lockdown was to introduce a policy called 'eat out to help out', acknowledging both the importance of the catering trades and their role in providing settings for convivial social interaction.

COVID-19 was a potential moment for behaviour change, a natural experiment in the reorientation of everyday practices. It seemed possible that some of the adjustments, required in an emergency, would become permanent. Given trenchant critiques of the British food system of production and consumption the experience of COVID-19 (along with Brexit and climate change) encouraged some citizens of a radical disposition to envisage significant positive change. By contrast, many others, not only the powerful in government and the business community, apparently could not wait for the reinstatement of prior routines. The frequently expressed wish 'to get back to normal' meant for most people a return to their own *personal* previously established habits of 2019, their usual ways of arranging events, their regular companions, menus, and so on.

At the point of completion of the draft of this book Britain was experiencing the most severe inflation of food prices for over 50 years. Prices rose by about 18 per cent in the year to February 2023. That caused consternation, its adverse effects affecting disproportionately those on low to moderate incomes. Whereas the COVID-19 pandemic apparently showed the supply chain to be robust and resilient, as food got through from the beginning of 2022, spurred by the actual implementation of post-Brexit arrangements with the European Union (EU) and war in Ukraine, dependence on international trade seemed precarious. Changing circumstances disrupted habits and threatened food insecurity in the form of unpredictable supply and high prices.

Maybe in the longer term these two extended disruptive episodes will be seen as unremarkable examples of turbulence, typical of cycles of capitalist accumulation and geopolitical instability. On the other hand, they might contain the seeds of a transition to a new stage of food production and consumption. Such questions could have been asked of many developments over the last century, and the answer is, probably, that it depends, and that predictions are unreliable.

Normal refers to both norms and regularities. Although we prefer not to think of ourselves as creatures of habit, we mostly assume and depend on the fact that others are; other people being consistent in temperament and predictable in their reactions means that we can rely on them to behave in ways to which we can relate. Occasionally we stop to evaluate the motivations and strategic intentions of others, but mostly we anticipate, based on stereotypes or derived from previous direct experience, how others will behave in particular situations relevant to us. Sociologists call the processes underlying regular or habitual action, by organisations and people, institutionalisation. From any individual's point of view, institutions are other people's behaviour – modes of conduct carried out in appropriate circumstances by a significant proportion, often a majority, of other people.

Individuals and groups adjust specific practices in response to changes in environment and context, from which emanate both continuity – as people try to protect or preserve their sense of normality by retaining their established habits – and discontinuity, as some ways of proceeding dissolve as they become subject to disapproval or practically ineffective. Food habits change in just such a manner. To live in normal times means to be subject to the forces of orderly, though not entirely predictable, development. Normal is a matter of currently established routines, but is rarely a permanent or stationary condition. Retrospective examination of processes reveals trends. Acknowledgement of the longevity of the most prevalent trends emphasises how difficult it is to change habits, a not inconsiderable matter in the face of a climate emergency which requires radical shifts in food production and consumption. Social processes typically generate a high level of *continuity*.

This book is an examination of continuities and discontinuities in British eating habits as they have been conditioned by broad cultural and economic processes since the mid-1950s. It offers a thematic review of changes in British culinary practice. The spur to writing arose from being asked, fairly frequently, by journalists and marketers to express a view about trends in British eating habits. Often those requests arose in the context of either reports identifying problems or fashionable developments in British alimentation. Sometimes inquiries were in the context of scares and anxieties – about the safety of food, the fate of the family meal, or the population's capacity to cook. Sometimes they arose from intrigued surprise at the novel and strange behaviours of fellow citizens; a confusion with food labelling when asked about supermarket dating comes to mind.

A culture of the new is strong in modern societies. Innovation is lauded and fashion followed. However, the fascination of the media with the new, both new events and new things, diverts attention away from continuities and gives a distorted impression of the rate of change. In the field of food that diversion is problematic because much remains the same, anchored in personal habits and institutional arrangements. Mass media news coverage also tends to sever events from their wider context. Long-term trends are not news. Background forces are not news. Explanation is not the journalist's first priority. Often a satisfactory explanation of events requires more elaborate contextualisation of the new and fragmentary evidence than attracts the journalist's attention. That is the space for social science, to provide explanations in terms of the social, economic and cultural structures and processes which are preconditions of the events to be explained. Social science aims to give explanations using carefully defined concepts, for the complexity of which the indulgence of the reader is craved. My sociological eye alights upon the constraints on the action of individuals and the ways in which people act together by making arrangements for managing their social interdependence. I focus on patterns of interaction and group differentiation in knowledge and behaviour. Such an approach usually produces less startling and less opinionated conclusions, preferring an analytic story to declarations of delight, disgust or disapproval.

There already exists a rather magnificent literature on eating in Britain in both the past and the recent present. I draw extensively upon it. However, I try to provide evidence of everyday practices – what ordinary people say and do – rather than what scholars have written. In the text I depend particularly on sources containing reliable data for capturing institutional and collective change over time. I draw heavily on several of my research projects which were explicitly designed to examine change systematically. One study examined expenditure on food between 1968 and 1992. Another looked at time and money spent in eating and cooking between 1975 and 2000. A third analysed changes in recommendations in the recipe columns of the most popular women's interest magazines between 1968 and 1992. The sequence was subsequently extended to 2016. A fourth investigation analysed changes in the *Good Food Guide* (*GFG*) between 1951 and 2006. A fifth, and the most recent and elaborate, was a re-study of dining out in England. Surveys and interviews were employed to dissect patterns of eating out and their relationship to eating at home in 1995. The same methods and an identical questionnaire were employed again in 2015 with the specific aim of identifying change and continuity. I will refer to it as the Three Cities Project (TCP), which I carried out with Lydia Martens, Jessica Paddock and Jennifer Whillans, and will have frequent recourse to its findings. Several other projects have collected data on eating in Britain at single points in time on cultural consumption and participation in 2003, trust in food in 2003, and everyday meals in 2012. The last of these, the Everyday Meals Project (EMP), conducted with Luke Yates, is also referred to often. The studies cover a wide range of topics, tapping key dimensions of stability and change. They are valuable because systematic comparison over time is uncommon. Also, being aware of the strengths and limitations of the data collected and their analysis gives me confidence in its reliability.

I also make extensive use of a book published in 1958, *The Foods We Eat*, by Geoffrey C. Warren, whose account of ordinary eating practices in Britain in the years 1955–1956 serves as a yardstick for comparison. It is a simple description of how a sample of the English population across six cities organised their eating behaviour – meals, times of day, locale, food and drinks consumed, by season and day of the week, gender and social grade. It is little more than a book of tables of data summarising what respondents reported doing and in what proportions. A market research report, it is driven neither by nutrition nor aesthetics, the two main poles of more recent discussion and controversy about British habits. Although far from perfect from a social scientific point of view its extended frequency count of arrangements and consumption by categories of item paints a basic picture of everyday eating in the 1950s. Sadly there were no periodic repeat studies giving evidence of scales and rates of change in everyday behaviour over time. The more varied and sophisticated subsequent literature addresses more specialised topics and does not have the simple descriptive and non-judgemental orientation of Warren, although it makes for more interesting reading!

In Chapter 1 I sketch a general outline of how UK eating habits have changed since the late 19th century. The next five chapters give more detailed and elaborate accounts of change after 1960 in sub-domains of the practice of eating – the social arrangements for meals, the acquisition of foodstuffs, their palatability in terms of taste and flavour, food preparation, and style. I describe continuity and discontinuity in ways of going about organising meals, shopping, cooking, and experiences and expressions of taste. These I explain in relation to broad social, economic and cultural processes. I consider how people in different social positions adjust their behaviour in response to cultural cues and economic conditions. Chapter 7 examines how the combination of activity leads to pleasures and anxieties. The final chapter gives a summary audit of change and continuity in the practice of eating in Britain since the 1950s.

Major changes can be observed in how and what people in Britain have eaten since the middle of the 20th century, but the book argues that the key trends developed over several decades and that change was slow and uneven. Trends originating in the 1970s continued to hold sway and determine the direction of travel well into the 21st century. Some changes are striking and pervasive. The book returns to them intermittently to consider their origins and effects. Greater informality of manners and social arrangements has affected almost all aspects of food consumption. Unresolved controversy about the mass production and consumption of heavily manufactured and globally transported foodstuffs has continuously shaped dominant understandings of what it means to eat well. Eating out has underpinned transformations of taste since the 1960s, not least through the normalisation of foreign cuisines. Changes in household composition and organisation have slowly modified the routines of food preparation and the domestic division of labour to reduce dependence on the work of housewives. These developments have all been subject to variation by class, gender and ethnicity, the intersections of which have structured emergent patterns. In consequence, both pleasure and anxiety have intensified. The book paints a big picture of the diversification of eating patterns, emphasising neglected social and cultural forces and processes behind emergent trends in British eating habits. Close scrutiny of long-term trends puts the current situation in context, permitting consideration of the nature and rate of social change and unravelling the complexity of practices in a society where eating is weakly regulated and weakly coordinated.

1

Changing Eating Habits

The origins of the mid-20th century British diet

The quality of eating in Britain is controversial but the balance of opinion has been that Britain's culinary culture is woeful. Foreign observers are in no doubt about its inadequacies. As a passing remark from the Dutch historian Wintle put it: 'The Netherlands has an atrocious reputation for its cuisine and food: it is almost as bad as that of the British, except that at least the Dutch diet is considered "wholesome".'[1]

Chris Otter's concise review of historical scholarship of the modern period attributes Britain's deficiencies to its extended and pioneering path through 'the nutrition transition'. The nutrition transition, a 'shift to a diet rich in carbohydrates, fats and animal proteins', has now occurred throughout many parts of the world, but it was early in Britain 'as a result of precocious industrialization, rapid urbanization, expansive empire and conscious outsourcing of food production'.[2] The transition, which began in the 18th century and matured during the 19th and early 20th, 'slowly radiated across the British Isles, producing a recognizably "British diet" which was more geographically uniform and standardized than previously'.[3] A high energy diet, it was devoted to maximising calories rather than culinary taste or optimal nutrition. According to Avner Offer, the predominance of white flour, refined sugar, processed fats and frozen meat in the diet in 1900 'gave Britain the worst dietary heritage in Europe'.[4] In archetypal form it was 'primarily a working-class diet', characterised by 'sugary tea, white bread, margarine, condensed milk, fish and chips and Sunday dinner'.[5] This urban-industrial working-class diet persisted throughout the mid-20th century and affected a majority of the population.

Otter found four other distinctive forces shaping developments in Britain besides its early industrialisation – prevailing standards of living, public health regulation, two world wars, and the way in which imperial domination inserted Britain into the system of international trade. British distinctiveness emerged as part of the White settler-colonialist system between 1850 and 1930. Imports were no longer primarily luxury items, like spices typical of the mercantilist era. Instead, the production of staple foods, 'wheat, sugar, cheese, bacon, mutton and beef', was outsourced at an unprecedented level: 'a settler-colonialists regime produced the sugars, starches, fats and caffeine which energized an industrial workforce'.[6] The scale of imports was huge:

> [B]y the end of the 1930s Britain imported 88 per cent of her flour, 93 per cent of her butter, lard and margarine, 82 per cent of her sugar, 55 per cent of her meat, 40 per cent of her 'eggs and egg products', 76 per cent of her cheese and 74 per cent of her fruit.[7]

These were the foundations of popular consumption in the late 1930s, 'a high point of the stereotypical British meal' according to Panayi.[8] He observed that in the years to 1945 'the staples of bread, potatoes and meat did not alter greatly so that in the middle of the twentieth century they made up the classic British meal of meat, potatoes, veg, bread and pudding'.[9] While not everyone followed the 'British diet', it was the predominant mode of eating and probably justifiably responsible for its negative reputation abroad.

Class and the British diet

British food history is deeply and indelibly imprinted by class divisions.[10] Eating has always been a class issue. The discrepancies between the nutritional composition and the menus of the affluent and the poor have long been apparent. Elites and the upper middle classes always ate more varied, better quality, more nutritious and more interesting food. However, dealing with hunger and malnutrition among the most impoverished section of the working class had required state intervention for centuries, since at least the time of the Elizabethan Poor Laws. The industrial revolution may have made matters worse.

John Burnett in *Plenty and Want: A Social History of Food in England from 1815 to the Present Day* describes the impact of cumulative social processes and political reforms on nutrition, and on health more generally. Burnett illustrates significant differences around 1900 within the lower classes by contrasting weekly menus of households from the moderately comfortable lower middle class, the skilled and the unskilled working class (see Box 1.1). What a family might eat,

---

Box 1.1: Ordinary household menus from 1901

John Burnett (1989) offered examples of weekly menus to illustrate differences between households in different non-elite class positions around 1900. For reasons of space only Sundays, Tuesdays and Thursdays are reproduced here.

Burnett draws his examples from Rowntree's survey of York in 1901, noting that no detailed budgets were obtained from the very poorest households, earning less than 18 shillings per week. A typical menu for a household with an income of between 18 and 21 shillings per week was that of a carter with a small family, which Burnett describes as 'starchy and monotonous, deficient in protein value by 18 per cent' (see Menu A).[11] Menu B, where the husband was a polisher, earning 25 shillings per week, was a little more varied and there was still enough food for supper by the Thursday. Menu C exemplifies the category of skilled manual workers earning over 30 shillings per week (only 32 per cent of people living in York earned that amount or more) and was a foreman earning 38 shillings per week. Menu D was for a family of the lower middle class (occupations like tradesmen, managers, cashiers, chief clerks) earning £2 10s 6d, in a household of five adults and three children.

Menu A

	Breakfast	Dinner	Tea	Supper
Sunday	Bread, butter, shortcake, coffee	Pork, onions, potatoes, Yorkshire pudding	Bread, butter, shortcake, tea	Bread and meat

EVERYDAY EATING

	Breakfast	Dinner	Tea	Supper
Tuesday	Bread, bacon, butter, coffee	Pork, bread, tea	Bread, butter, eggs, tea	Bread, boiled bacon, butter, tea
Thursday	Bread, butter, coffee	Bread, bacon, tea	Bread, butter, tea	

Source: Burnett, 1989: 182

Menu B

	Breakfast	Dinner	Tea	Supper
Sunday	Light cake, butter, tea	Roast beef, potatoes, cabbage, Yorkshire pudding	Bread, butter, jam, tea	Jam, bread
Tuesday	Bread, butter, jam, tea	Meat pie, potatoes	Bread, butter, jam pie, tea	Shortcake
Thursday	Bread, butter, tea	Bacon, bread, potatoes	Bread, butter, tea	Bread, butter

Source: Burnett, 1989: 183

Menu C

	Breakfast	Dinner	Tea	Supper
Sunday	Ham, bacon, mushrooms, porridge, bread, coffee	Roast beef, Yorkshire pudding, potatoes, beer	Bread, butter, pastry, tea	Bread and milk, meat, fried potatoes
Tuesday	Bacon bread, porridge, tea	Hashed beef, potatoes, rice pudding	Bread, butter, pastry, tea	Bread and milk, fried fish
Thursday	Bacon, bread, butter, mushrooms, tea	Meat, potatoes, sop, cheese, bread, rice pudding	Bread, butter, pastry, tea	Sheep's 'reed' with sage and onions, potatoes

Source: Burnett, 1989: 184–185

Menu D

	Breakfast	**Dinner**	**Tea**	**Supper**
Sunday	Porridge, eggs, bread, butter, milk, coffee, tea, cream	Mutton, cauliflower, bread sauce, potatoes, rhubarb, custard, blancmange, oranges, biscuits, tea	Potted meat sandwiches, bread, butter, cake, marmalade, tea, milk	Potted meat cornflour mould, bread, butter, cake, rhubarb custard, cheese, hot milk
Tuesday	Porridge, fried bacon and eggs, bread, butter, toast, marmalade, coffee, tea, milk, cream	Mutton, carrots, turnips, caper sauce, potatoes, hayrick pudding, lemon sauce, tapioca, tea	Bread, butter, Frame food,[12] marmalade, milk, cream, tea	Cutlets, stewed plums, bread, biscuits, cheese, cocoa
Thursday	Frame food, fried eggs, bacon and bread, toast, white and brown bread, butter, marmalade, coffee, tea, milk, cream	Roast mutton, greens, potatoes, chocolate mould, rhubarb and orange tart, bananas, coffee, cream	Bread, butter, tea-cake, seed-cake, Frame food, marmalade, milk, tea	Fish cakes, stewed rhubarb, biscuits, bread, butter, hot milk

Source: Burnett, 1989: 212–213

in quantity and in variety, was directly associated with its income and its access to different types of employment. For all sections of the lower classes the repertoire was comparatively limited, and for many it was monotonously repetitive.

Some features of the diets are revealing. The carter's household had no supper on Thursday, meals becoming very limited, presumably as money ran out before pay day. The menu of the foreman was sufficiently varied to provide interest but hardly distinctive or distinguished. The menu of the middle-class family was much more varied; Burnett observes that its diet 'was somewhat heavy and deficient in fresh vegetables, though otherwise not unnutritious; it provided 4,009 kilocalories per man a day'.[13]

The sharp differences between elites and the upper middle classes and the rest reduced during the 20th century with hunger and malnutrition disappearing towards its end. Elites ate sumptuously throughout. Burnett devotes one chapter, 'High living',[14] to the rich in the hundred years before the outbreak of the First World War. Meals were elaborate and lavish. A meal for the aristocracy, the bourgeoisie and the higher professionals might include a dozen or more dishes with a wide variety of meat, game, fish and desserts.

The dinners of the upper classes from the 16th century onwards are discussed in many books by a succession of food writers who have tried to persuade their readers that Britain has a noble and distinguished culinary tradition.[15] Accounts of the meals of monarchs or of celebratory dinners during the London season are remarkable in the number and the range of the dishes served and the quality of the cooking was probably high. However, according to Stephen Mennell, they were probably not typical of the everyday meals of even the highest echelons of the dominant classes nor of the non-metropolitan landowners and industrial bourgeoisie whose dishes were mostly rather plain. His classic study, *All Manners of Food: Eating and Taste in England and France from the Middle Ages to the Present*, attributes the divergence in quality of the meals of dominant classes in the two countries to the formation of their upper classes. In France, upper-class life was concentrated around the Court in the environs of Paris where eating was a formal, highly mannered affair accessible to only a small and tightly defined social circle. In Britain, the upper classes were more differentiated, much of activity of the landed aristocracy and the gentry occurred in the provinces and rural areas, and the emergent bourgeoisie was more influential.[16] However, by the end of the 19th century the British upper classes were converted admirers of French haute cuisine which had become a watchword for culinary excellence. The upper classes, and the most prestigious restaurants, employed French chefs from early in the 19th century and many upmarket restaurants continued to print their menus in French into the 1970s. The deference to French cuisine may be partly responsible for Britain's undistinguished culinary culture.

The two world wars proved to be critical events for changing patterns of food distribution and consumption. The First World War was followed by a period of inflation and rising taxes for the wealthy. Subsequently, recession and the Slump negatively affected both the elites and the middle classes, for whom the 'servant crisis' had a significant effect upon household organisation of food provision. For the working classes, the period delivered some improvement, though unevenly; some sections of the working class prospered, while others, especially in the regions of traditional heavy industry, suffered dreadfully during the Hungry Thirties. Overall, conditions improved during the first half of the 20th century, but the gradual hesitant convergence in class experience in the first half of the century might have been insignificant were it not for the Second World War.

The Second World War and post-war reconstruction

The Second World War imposed great restrictions on elites and the professional classes. The war was a period of emergency calling forth radical policy reactions by government in order to feed the population adequately for the purposes of waging total war. It involved intensive state intervention in the distribution of foodstuffs in the form of rationing ensuring a broadly equal distribution of essential and nutritious items which were in short supply. Vulnerable sections of the population, children and pregnant women, received additional rations of strategic items. Interruption in supply also resulted in radical modification to the foods that were eaten. Among the notorious novelties were 'mock goose', 'mock cream', snoek, Woolton pie and powdered egg, all intended to provide substitutes for conventional foodstuffs no longer available.[17] Also notable was the scanty size of rations; in 1941 the weekly allocation for an adult was

2oz butter, 2oz cooking fat, 4oz margarine, 2oz cheese, 4oz bacon, 8oz sugar, 2oz tea and one or two small portions of meat.[18] The entire population more or less willingly adjusted its eating behaviour to prevailing circumstances in support of 'the war effort'. Ironically, it seems to have been a diet which produced the most healthily fed generation ever.[19]

The experiences of the war accelerated the consolidation of state welfare provision, which, in its concern with adequate standards of living of all citizens, was the culmination of over 50 years of fitful liberal social reform. The post-war settlement emphasised minimum standards of welfare for all, free healthcare, collective insurance against unemployment, extended universal education and an expansion of social housing. The reformed state services reduced hardship and moderated inequalities. A progressive taxation regime promoted social equality. The redistribution of income and wealth during the middle of the 20th century meant that Britain was at its most equal in 1976.[20]

It took some years of reconstruction to re-establish previously 'normal' eating practices. Shortages and rationing of some key items persisted. Not until 1954 did rationing cease completely. However, people had begun to get restless and by 1950 many resented rationing.[21] Common practices, or at least aspirations, ideals and preferences regarding food consumption, were not much different to the immediate pre-war years and most people were eager to 'get back to normal'.

Post-war reconstruction re-established the 'urban-industrial working class diet'. Its common features were widely shared. That there was a common diet is now increasingly accepted wisdom and implicitly underpins two of the most authoritative interpretations of changing British habits, those of Burnett and Mennell. Both took a long view of developments and from their vantage point of the 1980s they viewed the 20th century as a period of increasing similarity in diets. Generally, class differences diminished, although they certainly didn't disappear.

The mid-century witnessed widely shared ordinary and popular consumption which was heavily stamped by the staple foods of the urban-industrial diet. As a small child in the 1950s I ate a recognisable though nuanced version of it. Living in a lower-middle-class suburb of Newcastle upon Tyne, my mother bought food from the local

Co-op and from the nearest independent butcher, baker, greengrocer and fishmonger. She was a very efficient and competent ordinary cook, very good at pastry, cakes and preserves, although inclined to cook meat and boil vegetables for longer times than is now recommended. We ate three meals a day, with breakfast almost always bacon and eggs, toast and tea. Dinner was in the middle of the day (12.15 on the dot!), as my father was mostly able to return home from work for that meal. A rough schedule saw similar dishes appearing on the dinner table on particular days of the week. Leftovers from the regular Sunday roast appeared on Mondays and Tuesdays. Less prime butcher's meat appeared later in the week, with savoury pies or boiled fish and parsley sauce occasionally. Puddings – wonderful puddings – almost always featured. Tea (as we would call it) occurred around 6pm and might be scrambled eggs, beans or cheese on toast, tinned fish perhaps, and always bread and jam and cake. Supper was mostly cornflakes or crackers and cheese. Brought up with the conventions of the lower middle class, I ate a 'respectable' version of the core diet, avoiding fish and chips and an excess of fried foods, no offal or condensed milk, no shop-bought cakes, though a lot of chocolate and confectionery, and not *very* much golden syrup. This version of the 'British diet' was in no way unusual or eccentric. A report of the eating habits of Britons in 1955–1956, Warren's *The Foods We Eat*, confirms that my memory is not playing tricks on me.

Warren's report is not about nutrition but rather records which food items appeared regularly at different meals at the end of the period of reconstruction. It gives a description of eating patterns of the urban English population, meal by meal.[22] It portrays the broad contours of how the ideals and preferences inscribed in the urban-industrial diet were implemented. The report indicates not just what was eaten but also social arrangements for eating meals which are regular and similar in patterns across the whole society. There are differences of gender, class and season. For example, men ate more meat, vegetables and potatoes, women more cake. The upper class had a main course in the evening more often than the lower class (a difference of about 8 per cent in the summer). So homogeneity should not be exaggerated. The better-off sections of society, as always, ate sufficient food of better quality and in greater variety than the working poor. Nevertheless, the overall impression is of a period of limited class differentiation in routines, in norms and preferences, and consequently in the foodstuffs appearing on the plate. Warren shows that most ate meals with a similar structure, using the same categories of ingredients, and in keeping with a similar timetable.

The relatively homogeneous British diet of the mid-20th century should be considered an achievement rather than a catastrophe. Working-class preferences – or rather the regularities resulting from the working class consuming both what was readily available to them and also that which had also passed the test of tasting good – were central. The late 1950s witnessed its zenith. The staple items that had produced Britain's 'awful reputation' (sugar, white bread, tea, and so on) featured heavily but were enlivened and enhanced by more meat, some luxuries, like imported fruits, and greater variety. It eliminated hunger and malnutrition. It was a national diet in the sense that its main elements appeared frequently and regularly and its appropriateness was not normatively contested. The urban-industrial diet of the mid-1950s provides my benchmark for examining continuity and discontinuity and for estimating the direction and rate of subsequent change.

Modification of the urban-industrial diet: the later 20th century

Perceptions of quality are always contestable. Merit is ineffable and a constant source of controversy. Nevertheless, if we look at the evidence about practice generally in the mid-20th century, there is substance in the accusations that the urban-industrial diet was not wholesome. Otter's account of the period from 1780 to 1950 presages the contribution to the contemporary crisis of obesity of over-refined and highly processed foods.[23] For most of the 20th century the diets and eating opportunities for the majority of the population were inadequate. Critics regarded it as monotonous and rather bland. Mennell's extended discussion of domestic cookery as reflected in recipe books and other printed material characterises the advice about domestic food preparation from the middle of the 19th century as limited, lacking imagination, overly concerned with economy – of sourcing cheap food and the use of leftovers – and prone to encourage the overcooking of meat and vegetables. British consumption lacked style and aesthetic refinement.[24]

Almost as soon as it had been thoroughly re-established during post-war reconstruction the urban-industrial diet underwent modification. By the late 1970s it was no longer so pervasive or dominant. It faded, partly because it was losing legitimacy. Interpretations vary. Most scholars writing about changing habits agree that diversification of ingredients and increased real incomes were central factors behind a significant modification of diets in the years after post-war reconstruction. Further details are contested. Some see the subsequent history as a progressive continuation of long run trends. Mennell, for example, elaborated on Norbert Elias's view of the European civilising process as one of 'diminishing contrasts, increasing variety'. John Burnett offered another, evolutionary, account. Arguably, though, when they were writing in the 1980s, the most radical aspects of a new cultural formation were insufficiently pronounced to conclude that the post-war settlement was coming to an end.

By contrast, writing 20 years later, Panikos Panayi declared that a 'culinary revolution' had occurred. Panayi sees the period from the 1960s as transformative, not because it signified the maturation of the welfare state in its effects on nutrition and health as Burnett would suggest, but for its cultural characteristics. Panayi explained the supersession of a regime of monotonous plain fare by three key forces: migration, restaurants selling foreign cuisine, and affluence. The introduction of foreign foodstuffs and foreign cuisines – through small migrant businesses in particular, and the catering industry more generally – resulted in a multicultural foodscape which was well cemented by 2000. It involved some radical changes and a redefinition of national traditions. No doubt a growing familiarity with a great many dishes with foreign origins, discussed in the mass media and made available through commercial outlets, constituted a major development. Burnett, while struck striking an evolutionary note regarding household meals, for foreign dishes were only gradually incorporated into domestic provision, also used the term 'revolution' in his companion volume on eating out.[25] He was especially impressed by the range of foreign restaurants and takeaway outlets that emerged to educate British palates. The lagged effect of commercial catering on domestic cookery in the period is difficult to assess.

Panayi's intriguing claim, that Britain experienced a culinary 'revolution' which transformed British food habits in the second half of the 20th century, will be examined by inquiring about the degree to which the commonly shared core 'British' diet disappeared. From the vantage point of the present, and with the benefits of hindsight, the food regime of 2020 is very different to that of 1955. Although many meals eaten in Britain in 2020 could have been put on the table in 1955, a great many others could not. However, the former are as worthy of note as the latter. Against contemporary proponents of the view that change is constant, accelerating and progressive, I will argue that most of the significant change occurred in the third quarter of the 20th century. The period since can best be understood in the light of the *continuation* of trends originating and coalescing in the years after post-war reconstruction. I also maintain that the *rate of change* has been relatively slow. Diversification of the food supply and taste generated processes of gradual adjustment. In addition, some of the developments of the previous half century slowed, ceased or were put into reverse, as older problems recurred when welfare provision was dismantled. It remains an open question as to whether these developments justify being called a revolution.

A related question is whether the urban-industrial formula gave way to a coherent alternative regime. That view has found little support, diagnoses of pluralisation, fragmentation or specialisation being more common. The range of specific items and dishes consumed grew enormously such that it is difficult to pin specific preferences and tastes to tightly bounded social groups. However, I will argue that new dominant *principles* can be detected, championed by a section of the middle class rich in cultural capital – the new middle class – and underpinned by general orientations towards health and taste.[26] The injunctions and recommendations articulated by 'sociocultural specialists', employed professionals engaged in cultural intermediation and the culture industries, are widely endorsed.[27] No best culinary regime is prescribed, but dominant standards are recognisable. For instance, when eating out one should pursue varied experiences, in comfortable circumstances, paying close attention to meals and contexts.[28] This is a dominant paradigm acknowledged and reiterated by people in all classes. Parallel principles echo through domestic contexts. Kate Gibson shows widespread agreement among the university-educated middle class around critical individual judgement, conscientious selection in the face of options and the exercise of self-control.[29] Of course, principles are often only spasmodically applied, put into practice systematically by the few rather than the many, and held dear more by some groups than others. The gap between aspiration and practice is often yawningly wide. Nevertheless, a general understanding about good and bad eating practices, revolving around a distinction between mass-processed and tenderly nurtured products, has emerged to compromise the legitimacy and popularity of the urban-industrial diet.

The practice of eating

Painting a picture of continuity and change is complicated because eating is a multifaceted type of practice. At first glance eating is a simple physiological activity associated with ingestion. However, reflection suggests that it is a highly elaborate domain of everyday life, unintelligible without reference to its social embeddedness. Eating is a compound practice.[30] Any account of eating will necessarily refer to selecting foodstuffs, preparing dishes, making social arrangements for meals and making judgements about taste. Contemporary eating presupposes the integration of at least four distinct but intersecting activities: obtaining a supply of food, cooking, the organisation of meal occasions, and aesthetic judgements of taste. These are formalised and discussed in terms of practices of nutrition, food preparation, etiquette and gastronomy. Each of these has its own logic, its own different coordinating agents, and therefore its own distinct history. The practices associated with each are also differentiated by social origin, age, gender and class position.

As a result, eating is loosely framed, more a matter of convention than authoritative regulation. Eating is a weakly coordinated and weakly regulated practice.[31] It is neither formally taught nor accredited and, because occurring mostly in private, does not require constant coordination with strangers. Nor is it subject to direction and control by powerful organisations or regulatory agencies. For most it is held together by routine and habit, observance of which is never mandatory. Therefore, individuals have much discretion. Their many degrees of freedom are sometimes troubling and a cause of anxiety. Uncertainty is exacerbated by the belief in the primacy of individual agency which holds people accountable for their own successes and errors of judgement. At the same time, however, people are reassured, their anxieties alleviated by mechanisms of habit, membership of social networks, and by adaptation and adjustment to their social and material environment.

This poses problems for describing and analysing continuity and discontinuity in individual and collective experience given the strong cultural and cognitive bias towards emphasising change and ignoring continuity. It is salutary to recall that public health concerns and interventions to regulate food have their origins in the 1840s. A concern with obesity, initially among the well-off in Victorian times, had become widespread enough to instigate a craze for dieting by the 1920s. Vegetarianism had its origins in the mid-19th century, as did campaigns against white bread. These should give pause for thought when diagnosing a revolution. Stories of continuity and discontinuity are delicately balanced and vary with temporal perspective, for institutions change relatively slowly. Garry Runciman in *Very Different, But Much the Same: The Evolution of English Society since 1714*, writes a history of underlying continuities in English history, emphasising 'path development' in the way that institutional arrangements dominant at earlier times continue to have effects in the long-term.[32] From such a perspective, much of what energises the social and political controversies of the moment is nothing more than 'noise and clutter'. Structural and institutional continuities run alongside the events and trends that attract more attention and emotion. Danny Dorling, also taking a long view by contrasting the speed of change on very many fronts from the 1930s, finds that despite popular perception and much commentary to the contrary, the pace of life is *not* accelerating.[33] In his view, with only a very few exceptions (carbon emissions, air travel and university education) the *rate* of change of the most important institutionalised processes in modern societies is slowing rather than gathering speed.

Individuals, practices and the slow pace of cultural change

It is always difficult to identify and understand recent tendencies and current trends. Distance facilitates confidence when analysing the past. Isolating the most significant movements from the constant churn of activity and media publicity is daunting. Commercial innovation, driven by the restless logic of capitalist accumulation, constantly introduces new ingredients, new preparations and new equipment, generating new fads and fashions of which a few will stick. Commercial culture encourages constant renovation. It encourages people to regard themselves as consumers, autonomous individuals making personal and meaningful choices in market situations which will have consequences for their health, happiness and wellbeing. Cultural intermediaries, both professional food writers and academics, publicise options and offer advice. Under conditions of uncertainty these may boost confidence or intensify anxiety.

Habits adapt to changes in the external institutional environment. Institutional developments in the practices surrounding eating are underpinned by a range of cultural and social processes. In this examination of continuities and discontinuities the focus is not upon individuals in charge of their own personal fates but on broad social, cultural and economic processes since the mid-1950s which frame the socioeconomic and cultural contexts of action. The cultural processes playing a big part in an explanation of institutional adjustment since the 1950s include: the reactions to mass, and increasingly global, production and consumption; an intensification of the impact of commodification and markets; aestheticisation and marketing; global trade, migration and the dissemination of foreign cuisines; and the disintegration of working-class culture.

Change in consumption patterns are driven as much by transformations in social structure and social relations as by cultural innovation. As already discussed, the social base for the urban-industrial diet dissipated. The manual working class diminished in size and influence. The middle classes grew in numbers and became more differentiated in composition and activity. Their recomposition into different fractions, harbouring competing dispositions, accentuated social and cultural diversity. A 'new middle class' stamped its imprint on popular and culinary culture. In addition, ethnic minorities, themselves distributed across class groupings, influenced tastes and altered the aggregate patterns of consumption. Other social processes with profound impacts on eating included population replacement, a result of both migration and cohort succession, household restructuring following the demise of the male breadwinner wage system, the reconstitution of family arrangements, and the restructuring of temporal rhythms of everyday life.

Political mismanagement and commercial avarice in the early 21st century raised new challenges. State action and intervention beyond agriculture – decolonisation, joining and leaving the EU, encouragement of international tourism – have uncertain consequences for eating patterns. Adverse economic conditions and political neglect have resulted in a return to hunger, and to greater deprivation and ill health in the decade to 2023. Overshadowing these matters is the spectre of climate change, and the fear that the political will to resolve the ensuing problems is absent, which puts seriously into question the viability of currently normal eating habits. Radical change is required. Yet political projects to change eating habits are hard to agree upon and difficult to implement. The intransigent problem of behaviour change requires a thorough grasp of how cultural, social and economic processes affect eating practices.

In sum, this book is a story of the restructuring of social divisions and their interplay with cultural processes. It examines the retreat of the urban-industrial diet and looks for the bases of shared experiences, tastes and practices in Britain. Explanation is in terms of processes and trends, their timing and speed, and the forces behind them. Elements of culinary culture change at different speeds and their combined effect is a complex cultural formation supporting different experiences of eating for different sections of the population.

2

Meals: Occasions and Arrangements

Meal occasions

Meals are the organisational backbone of western eating habits. Meals form a sequence of distinct eating occasions, usually at very regular intervals, with different types of food content, which are often consumed in a social context usually with other people. In most societies events have annual, seasonal, weekly and daily rhythms. Religious and national festivals, Sunday lunch and weekday breakfast carry different expectations about what will be eaten, with whom, how long the meal will last, and so on. Throughout the modern period in Europe the number of daily meals has varied from place to place, as has their timing. What sorts of people would be present also varies. Landowners shared their meals with close and distant co-resident kin, and with workers and servants. As households increasingly came to contain only the elementary family – comprising solely parents and their children – the normal range of companions reduced markedly. With the passage of time, meals change their meanings, their content varies, and arrangements are revised and restructured – *slowly*.

The decline of Sunday lunch

Until a little over 50 years ago most of the British population sat down on Sunday to eat 'dinner', as I did as a child, usually between 1 and 3 o'clock in the afternoon, the centre-piece of which was a joint of roast meat. Beef had the highest status, but pork and lamb were suitable and popular equivalents. As yet, chicken was not a likely centre-piece, because those were the days before cheap industrialised chickens and it was therefore an expensive item. The joint came with potatoes, roasted and sometimes boiled, vegetables, perhaps Yorkshire pudding, gravy, and each type of meat was accompanied by its more or less traditional special sauce or stuffing. The Sunday dinner usually comprised more than one course, with perhaps soup first and usually some form of pudding or dessert afterwards. It tended to be a family event in which all members of the household participated, often with extended kin alongside, but rarely friends. For several generations of Britons Sunday dinners were sources of food memories, probably more good than bad. The food itself was popular – people liked to buy it in restaurants, as they still do – and it was of a better quality than that available during the rest of the week. It was the landmark in the weekly round of eating. Some people subsequently reflected that they didn't much like the food, especially the routinely overcooked vegetables. Others disliked the social occasion for its repetitiveness, formality, pomposity or tedium. The anthropologist Mary Douglas argued that its structure was reflected in other lesser meals, each with fewer of its elements.[1] Weekday dinners had fewer courses and fewer components to the main course. Lesser meals like lunch, tea or breakfast were even simpler.

Douglas exposed rules governing the degree of complexity of food content that was appropriate to the social relationship in which companions stand in relation to one another. People offer their neighbours drinks, usually with something to nibble, like tea and biscuits, but they reserve meals for those with whom they are most closely related and/or intimate. Her scheme offers one yardstick for estimating change in the social and symbolic aspects of eating.

Some relevant basic facts regarding frequency and timing of eating events in the post-war years, and their content, were recorded by Warren.[2] Then, 'Sunday Dinner' occurred between 12 and 3pm, and involved roast beef, roast lamb or roast pork (pork replacing lamb during the winter).[3] Sunday lunches are now fewer and more unevenly distributed across the population. In reply to the EMP survey of 2012,[4] addressing the fate of Sunday dinner, 16 per cent of respondents explicitly said that they ate a roast dinner last weekend, almost exclusively on Sundays, and given the description of component ingredients, up to 30 per cent of people may have done.[5] During the weekend older people are more likely to eat roasts and other meat-focused dishes in the middle of the day. Of those who progressed no further than secondary education, 23 per cent recorded explicitly a roast dinner at the weekend, twice as many as those with degrees.[6] Household structure also has a significant effect on consumption; 19 per cent of nuclear families with children, 17 per cent of adult-only households and 13 per cent of solo dwellers eat roasts for lunch at the weekend. However, the majority of roasts now occur after 5pm on Sundays. Some are eaten mid-week too. On aggregate, the symbolic significance of the Sunday roast is receding and, alongside, its contribution to weekly food intake. Once crucial ingredients for meals at the beginning of the following week, the leftovers from Sunday dinner, are less important. Sunday lunch is no longer the fulcrum of a weekly cycle.

The explanation lies not in the distaste for the food, which remains popular at restaurant visits and when entertaining. Nor probably do the reservations indicate a wish to avoid eating commensally with family. Rather, the role of Sundays in the weekly cycle has changed. Sunday in the 1950s was a very quiet and rather dull day, almost exclusively domestic, where the collective social schedule usually prescribed church attendance, often in the morning, followed by lunch at home, and then assorted domestic activities, or at most exciting, taking a walk, a drive in a car for the more affluent, or visiting non-resident kin or friends. Sunday was private.[7] From the 1960s people began to use Sundays for entertainment and engagement in more public activities. A more multicultural Britain shifted the character and timing of religious observance and established different religious festivals; a more varied population by religious affiliation holds Friday or Saturday rather than Sunday as their most sacred day. More recreational opportunities included professional sports events increasingly scheduled on Sundays, many more shops opened, and going out for Sunday lunch – often with the family and to eat roast meat – became more common. Also the restrictions on the opening hours of pubs and bars in the decades after the Second World War, especially tight on Sundays, with some closed entirely in the 'dry' counties of Wales and Scotland, were relaxed. By 2012 it had become much more like any other day of the week.

After lunch, dinner

As the pivotal role of the midday Sunday dinner diminished, evening meals gained a more elevated place in the culinary hierarchy. In mid-20th century, the schedules of northern Britain and of the lower classes placed 'dinner' in the middle of the day and made it the major meal. Now evening meals provide the biggest and most structured daily eating event both on weekdays and at weekends. The more diverse and adventurous dishes and menus appear at night, and they reveal most about increasing variety in domestic alimentation.[8] Midday meals, except on Sundays, are mostly minor affairs.

Lunch is a meal whose arrangements vary enormously between countries. The Norwegians take their *Matpakke* (meal pack) to school or the workplace where they eat it in company. Germans return home, as do rather a lot of Spaniards. The French tend to eat proper meals, if in a more simplified format than earlier, in canteens, cafeterias and restaurants, often subsidised by their employer. Finnish workers eat their major meal in the middle of the day in some public establishment, although not subsidised. In Britain, by contrast, people eat a remarkable volume of sandwiches, at home, in a shop close to the workplace, in the office, or in the street.

The EMP study shows that meals eaten in Britain between 12pm and 5pm, 'midday meals' or 'lunches', are less substantial, less intricate and require less preparation than evening meals. They are very brief, with 75 per cent eaten in under 20 minutes on weekdays and 59 per cent at weekends. Three-quarters of weekday lunches are composed of simple dishes like sandwiches, soups and salads. These items, by contrast, feature in only 10 per cent of dinners. All indicators of size and complexity suggest that weekday lunches are smaller and less complex meals than dinners, although with exceptions at weekends. The five most popular British lunches on weekdays are all different types of sandwich – with fillings, in order of popularity, ham, cheese, vegetables, fish and chicken. Even at the weekend sandwiches fill the first two slots, the other three being dishes of meat and potatoes.[9]

Comparison with the 1950s reveals a dramatic simplification of midday meals. Warren reports that working men took six out of ten midday meals at home. Only 13 per cent reported eating sandwiches. Almost everyone else ate some type of 'main dish', which, Warren writes, included 'roasts, stews, ham, bacon, sausages, offal, cold meats, fish, cheese and egg dishes' – nearly all hot foods.[10] Potatoes appeared in two-thirds and other vegetables were present in around half. Also, over half of Warren's respondents ate a 'sweet', one in ten ate cakes and biscuits too, and in winter up to 20 per cent started their meal with soup. The comparison with 2012 could not be more stark; 74 per cent report minor dishes on weekdays (and 53 per cent on weekends), the vast majority of which are cold and based around bread, and where the vast majority of 'desserts' comprise fruit, biscuits or confectionery. The primary victor from this change has been the sandwich – manufactured or prepared at home – which dominates midday meals on weekdays and has crept into the weekend.

The prevalence of the minor dish captures a most important change in recent years. As in 1955, of the two principal eating events of the day (everyone agrees that breakfast is a 'meal', but it is never a 'main meal') one is typically heavier and more elaborate than the other. In the 1950s, a light lunch referred primarily to the habit of middle-class households preparing meals which contained fewer heavy ingredients and were smaller in size but not otherwise fundamentally different from dinner. In the 1950s evening meals on all days were generally lighter than midday meals – 'the figures for heavier meats, roasts and stews go down, and ham, bacon and corned beef, spam and other cooked meats go up'.[11] Still some ate more than one course, with 'sweets' – complex desserts generally requiring additional plates or utensils – appearing at around one-third of evening meals, and with simpler desserts of cakes and biscuits at another third. In the north of Britain this would be called 'tea' and would typically be followed by a snack before going to bed.[12]

When I was a child growing up in the 1950s to have 'dinner at night' was a mark of elevated social class.[13] Now, most people have their dinner, the main meal event of the day, in the evening on weekdays. While not all dinners are large nor lunches light, main meals became more diverse in form and content than was recorded by Warren. Main meals are, however, mostly simpler than in the 1950s. They have fewer courses; 79 per cent of reported domestic dinners in 2012 comprised only one course.[14] They are also less routinised as timing is less closely synchronised with other households.

Breakfast

Breakfast is another instructive site of simplification. Breakfast now requires almost no labour and mostly comes directly from the fridge or store cupboard. This is a clear process of simplification and also marks a reduction in variety. It is a meal often eaten alone, rushed, and of little culinary significance. The demise of shared collective practices in the later 20th century was considerable but protracted and slow, as is demonstrated by evidence about the British breakfast. Importantly, this is an institutional form which has changed faster than almost any other, yet it still retains many recognisable features of mid-20th-century practice.

The first eating event of each new day is conventionally referred to as 'breakfast', an event which breaks the 'fast' attendant upon sleeping and occurs most usually therefore in the morning. The form and content of such episodes vary markedly between countries. Despite some convergence, with mass manufactured cereals playing an increasing role, southern Europe still favours light and sweet items, northern Europe cheese, ham and bread. In Britain, according to O'Connor in *The English Breakfast: The Biography of a National Meal*,[15] breakfast was promoted to the status of a *meal* by the gentry in the 18th century. Previously insignificant, when often two meals per day was normal, it became an occasion to which guests might be invited to share a profusion of elaborate cooked dishes including curry (and kedgeree), many kinds of fish, devilled meats and offal, cold roast meats, as well as bread and porridge.

Subsequently breakfast became more widely recognised and observed in practice. By the middle of the 19th century there were specialised cookbooks devoted to breakfast dishes and domestic economy manuals, like *Mrs Beeton's Book of Household Management*,[16] included advice about what to prepare. Observance of breakfast spread from the country house to the urban industrial working class, for whom it was a much more simple and frugal affair. Bread, porridge and treacle, and sweetened tea were the primary staple elements for the industrial proletariat.[17] The deficient dietary regimes common among the mass of the population – as revealed notoriously by the number of men found unfit to fight in the Boer War – were reflected in breakfasts. The occasional egg or piece of bacon was a supplement for better off artisans, although mostly only as a treat at the weekend. The onset of more compassionate and pragmatic social reforms from the beginning of the 20th century saw some improvements to diet – with the biggest improvements from the point of view of health coming probably (inadvertently) from the rationing of the Second World War. More nutritious and varied breakfasts for most of the population were in evidence in Warren's *The Foods We Eat*.

Warren reported that 'over 92% of all adults in the country take breakfast and of these more than half the men and over a third of the women have a cooked course, with eggs and bacon high in favour!' Comparing the inter-war years he noted more cold cereals and fruit, but 'not enough to give significant percentages'.[18] Bacon was singled out as 'essentially an English dish' and much coveted:

> [R]eferring to the Crawford and Broadley survey *The People's Food* (1938) it was found that 'in spite of its cost every housewife strives to provide her family with fried bacon for breakfast if it can possibly be squeezed out of the housekeeping allowance. Bacon is the hallmark of a "proper" breakfast'.[19]

Warren describes breakfasts comprising several items, often cooked, although with much less variety than the country house version. He noted differences between men and women, summer and winter, weekdays and weekends, age, region and class. Most differentiation was limited and there was little difference by class. Warren recorded that at breakfast on weekdays in 1956 about 45 per cent of English urban dwellers ate a cooked course, around 30 per cent cereals or porridge, 56 per cent bread or toast, 5 per cent fruit or fruit juice.[20]

The recent EMP sample of weekday eating habits in 2012 showed that for breakfast over half the population (54 per cent) eats cereal, almost all of them with milk, a quarter (27 per cent) eat toast, and just over a fifth (22 per cent) eat fruit.[21] The other most popular items were yoghurt (7 per cent) and porridge (7 per cent). Croissants, bagels and muffins got a few mentions. Only 6 per cent reported anything cooked, examples being bacon sandwiches, cheese on toast, poached eggs, scrambled eggs, beans on toast. Although it is difficult to date precisely, the very pronounced decline in cooked dishes at breakfast, from 45 per cent to 6 per cent, is, viewed from the perspective of typical rates of change in habits, enormous.

Given publicity proclaiming the high international reputation of a distinctive British breakfast, it is ironic that so few regularly eat it.[22] Such divergence between the symbolic representation of national cuisine and the actual practice of the British population is a recurrent feature in accounts of habits. Appearing a little more often at the weekend, the 'iconic' vaunted and celebrated British breakfast once common across a wide swathe of the population does still exist. The 3,500 breakfasts reported in 2012 did include sausages, bacon and eggs. The difference lies not in the items themselves, but rather their relative prevalence. I was given bacon and eggs, followed by bread and marmalade, more or less everyday throughout my childhood – a substantial meal prepared by my mother to send me to school and my father to work. The disappearance of the English breakfast from the domestic dining table, which is one of the greatest measurable shifts over the period, results from changes in material and social environment rather than transformation in tastes. The changed pattern of British breakfast behaviour might be explained as a conjunctural consequence of material and social factors. The domestic circumstances in which the meal occurs have changed: family members leave home for work and school at different times and few are prepared to cook and clear up early in the morning before engaging in other activities. In 2015, 55 per cent of those in couple-only households ate alone (an increase of 14 per cent on 1995) and among couples with children 41 per cent had no company (11 per cent more than 1995).[23] Behind that lies very limited obligation or expectation that family members will eat breakfast together.[24] Women spending more time in the labour market, more flexible working hours, less energetic manual labour, corporations robustly promoting branded cereals and dairy products, ever greater acceptability of supermarkets' pre-prepared foods, near universal ownership of a refrigerator, perhaps the learning of new tastes from travel abroad, and exposure to multiple commercial substitutes outside the home, conspire to make breakfast a short, unsociable, routinised and disappointing apology for a meal. The evolutionary path of breakfast is thus a crossroads where household reorganisation, temporal restructuring, commercial provision and conditions of employment mutually interact. Habits certainly have been reshaped, but it has taken more than 50 years and previous preferences have still not been eliminated.

Arrangements

Meal times and coordination

The simplification of breakfast is often seen as a problem of coordination and timing. Meal arrangements depend crucially upon time and timing. The simplification of lunch and also of dinner is partly a function of temporal coordination. Timing involves coordinating diners around the table and now people often struggle to get to eat together.[25] In the past, and still in other countries, the timing of meals in modern societies was broadly similar across the whole population, although always with some variation by class in the UK.[26]

Mass Observation reports from 1937 make clear that meal times were regular and predictable, calibrated to the working hours of factory and office, around which meal times were set for all household members.[27] The coordination of participation in household meals was more difficult by 2000; as Dale Southerton notes, interviewees in Bristol in 2000 'were acutely aware of a need to coordinate and schedule their everyday activities and do so in a way that aligns with others in their households and social networks'.[28] At present, the decline in eating together arises from the impracticability of getting families round a table, rather than any general or reasoned aversion to eating with co-habitees.[29] Since the middle of the 20th century, several factors have increased the difficulties of intra-household coordination. People travel further to work and are more likely to live in dual-earner households. Smaller workplaces with more flexible hours of employment mean less uniform collective schedules; since many people go home to eat soon after work, heterogeneity produces more variable meal times. Half-day work on Saturdays and weekday half-days have disappeared, while 24/7 shopping and the expansion of service sector employment reduce collective temporal constraints. Also, as noted earlier, Sundays are less subject to religious observance. These changes reflect a weakening of society-wide temporal rhythms.

Nevertheless, the 2012 EMP survey results suggest a still considerable commonality of pattern, a significant degree of collective order, and much routinised behaviour. A very large majority of people (approaching 90 per cent) claim to have a regular pattern, mostly of three meals per day. Only one person in ten report that on the days of the survey they had diverged from their normal practice. At population level there are still pronounced peaks in the day when a substantial proportion of people are eating, although the pattern is less homogeneous than in many other European countries or in 1961 (see Figure 2.1).[30] Relatively regular mealtimes are interspersed with predictable times for snacks. At both individual and population levels a sense remains that eating regularly punctuates and gives temporal order to daily life.

As a general rule, the more important the occasion, the longer it takes and the more it requires appropriate companions. Yet eating events in Britain are remarkably brief. Of all meals reported in the 2012 survey, 71 per cent are eaten in under 20 minutes. Meals increase in average length over the course of the day. Nine out of ten breakfasts are eaten in less than 20 minutes, but only half of evening meals are so quick. Dinners now last longer than lunch; half last over 20 minutes although only 15 per cent are longer than 30 minutes. Dinner is the time for 'major' dishes, ones which are more complex and take time to prepare. However, one 'major' dish per day, taken at the third of three meals is the common pattern. The vast majority of dinners have only one course. Just over 20 per cent have two courses and only 1 per cent has three.[31] Weekends are slightly more leisurely. The biggest difference is for lunches: on weekdays only 6 per cent took longer than half an hour, compared with 17 per cent at weekends.[32]

Britain is probably ahead of most European countries in casualising its eating arrangements. Ceremonial aspects of eating are increasingly reserved for very special occasions. Opportunities for meals are foregone. Events are more hurried, the format abridged, and the content less symbolically significant. Eating in the street, much more prevalent than 50 years ago, is perhaps the ultimate example of the lack of ceremony. Characteristics of what French scholars describe as the 'de-structuration' of meals can be found in British practice. The changing arrangements for a formalised and organised sequence of meals has caused more disquiet in France than in the UK; French scholars seem particularly concerned about decorum and commensality. Herpin identified

Figure 2.1: Changing times of meal events in Britain, 1961 and 2001

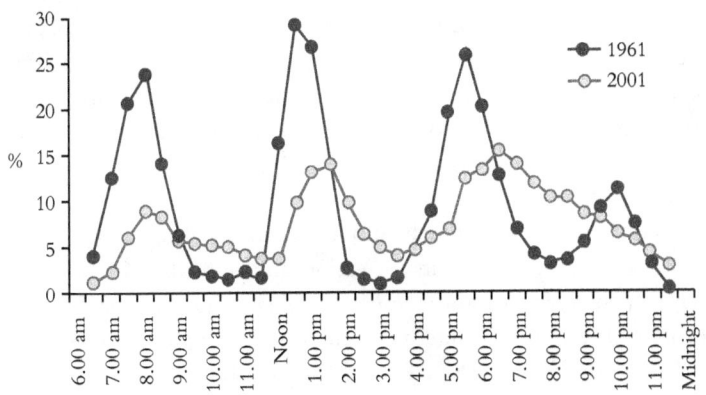

Source: Cabinet Office (2008)

several dimensions – disimplantation, de-synchronisation, de-localisation, de-concentration and de-ritualisation.[33] Surely similar and parallel trends occurred in the UK, but how common they are, and whether they are part of a secular trend towards greater disorganisation is less clear. People eat at different times, sometimes eat different dishes, while watching television and consulting mobile phones. The exact extent of de-structuration is uncertain, although practices contrast oddly with the reverence expressed for the family meal.

Snacks

In Britain, where more concern is usually expressed about nutrition than conviviality, evidence about de-structuration has often focused upon snacks. The snack is the smallest type of event in the vocabulary of British eating habits. It is hard to define, but its characteristics typically include small portions of portable foods, easily prepared, and consumed casually at simple and quick events.[34] Eating other than at appointed meals times has an ambiguous status. I was always told by my mother that eating between meals would spoil my appetite, not so much I suspect as a matter of health than of economy because throwing away food was unaffordable. So ice cream, biscuits and cake were viewed as both a treat and a problem, slightly naughty. Their moral status has not much altered. The late 20th century saw a moral panic around 'grazing', a practice where instead of eating three meals people were thought to be having smaller portions of food throughout the day at unnamed events. This offended the nutritionists, the protectors of the sanctity of the family meal and the defenders of the virtues of commensality. Shown to affect scarcely anyone, concern about grazing transmogrified into one about snacking. Snacking is a rather ugly term which implicitly conveys the impression of frequently recurring events for eating unhealthy, highly processed items, primarily as a supplement to meals. They are seen as one cause of the obesity epidemic, which is one reason for observing a distinction between 'snacks' and 'snack foods'.[35]

Snacks, qua small events involving small amounts of food, often accompanied by a beverage, have been a fixed element in eating patterns for a long time. Warren in the 1950s took for granted the existence of, and reported on, seven victualling occasions: early morning tea, breakfast, the mid-morning break, the midday meal, the mid-afternoon break, the principal evening meal, and late supper.[36] Britons did not avail themselves of all these opportunities to eat every day, but all were common and legitimate options.[37] Mid-morning and mid-afternoon breaks were taken by more than half the population. Around half were at home (more for women, fewer for men) and half at work, in a cafe, or in a few instances at the houses of friends or relatives. Almost all involved a beverage, mostly tea, but with more tea than coffee in the afternoon, and were accompanied by food on about half of all occasions. The food items were predictable. These events did not seem to cause alarm, rather the opposite as they were recognisable and easily interpretable.

The EMP study of daily habits in 2012 show similar time patterns, snacks concentrating mid-morning, mid-afternoon and at late supper time.[38] Forty-three per cent of respondents on weekdays and 27 per cent at the weekend reported eating at least one snack; and 51 per cent of all respondents report at least one snack across the two surveyed days. The snack occasions fit into a wider picture in which people generally eat three meals a day on both weekdays and weekends (79 per cent and 63 per cent respectively).[39] People who eat fewer than three meals are only very marginally more likely to report snacking. The findings imply that snacking in the UK is largely scheduled and episodic rather than continual as predicted by the grazing hypothesis. Snacks have a rhythm, occurring midway between main meals and supplementing rather than substituting for meals. Also, the most commonly reported snack foods are not much different from those in 1955 and many of them cannot be considered harmful. The most common snack food items in 2012 were, in order of frequency, fruit, biscuits, chocolate, crisps, cake, bread, cheese, ices/ice creams, nuts and cereal.[40] Mostly, these items were not bought and eaten spontaneously but sourced from household food stocks.

Snacks may sometimes be problematic for they can encourage over-indulgence, contain excessive amounts of sugar, salt and fat, and suppress appetite at more nutritious main meals. A great many cultural cues in public space encourage eating, with snack foods and highly calorific and sweetened beverages ubiquitous. Greater daily mobility offers more time and more places to purchase ready-to-eat food. Also commercially sold snacks – just like plates, cups and glasses – got bigger. However the evidence shows that the concern about snacks, which escalated in the 1990s, is exaggerated.

The fate of the family meal

The roast dinner on Sunday is the prototype of the 'proper' and 'family' meal. The family meal attracted increasing interest in the 1970s when it was thought to be both endangered and oppressive. The post-war settlement generated a mixed economy where welfare state provision and public enterprises oiled the wheels of capitalist organisations, many of which were engaged in the mass production of consumer goods. Household economies were sustained through the 'male breadwinner wage'. Earnings for men were sufficient in many households to support a family, making it an option for women to stay at home at least while their children were growing up. Such a housewife did the vast majority of indoor domestic chores. While an understandable division of household labour where a full-time home-maker existed, the arrangement firmly coded many tasks as female with a knock-on effect on other women, married or single, who were in employment. They were required to continue being responsible for domestic matters including housework and the organisation of household activities like the family meal.

Marjorie DeVault, in *Feeding the Family*, gave a classic description of the complex contradictory feelings associated with food preparation. Her study was of Canada, but the findings are probably equally applicable to the UK. As she argues, women made families and family life through the love, care, consideration and planning associated with meal provision. The experiences she described were consistent with the supposed virtues of family meals. Meals provide opportunities to converse, swap news and be sociable at home. Meals teach children about food, manners, relationships and conversation. Meals maintain health and vitality. Meals provide opportunities for giving special treats and rewards. Meals are occasions of gift giving. Meals express love through applying effort and thought to please the diner. Meals create bonds of solidarity.

Given its positive functions, and recognising its contradictions, fears have been recurrently expressed that the family meal may lose its vitality and integrity. Anne Murcott notes that ever since its establishment in the Victorian era as the preferred ideal mode of restauration of the middle class, its imminent demise has been forecasted.[41] Moral panic has ensued because in Britain the meal symbolises the family itself. For while the French are equally disturbed by the 'de-structuration' of meals, they are more worried about the loss of perceived virtues of commensality and companionship than of family values. Consequently, in Britain the family meal has frequently been an object of scrutiny when examining changes in eating habits.

So far, the accumulated evidence suggests that the family meal survives. Anne Murcott concludes that there is 'little support for the actual decline of family meals, much more evidence of fears of their imminent demise'.[42] Shu-Li and colleagues suggest that the time spent in family dinners was constant between 1975 and 2000. Popular public concern is more evidence of its symbolic esteem than decline in frequency. Certainly the template of the family meal continues to glisten brightly and people try very hard to conform.[43] For example, an English woman in Paris told us that she couldn't wait for her baby daughter to grow up enough to eat with them at table.[44] Many times interviewees have told me regretfully why their family meal is less frequent and less perfect than it should be. Constraints of the external environment and social adverse circumstances are invoked to explain sub-standard performances. Managing everyday life gets in the way of eating together.[45] The barriers are many and genuine.[46] Many family meal occasions will be imperfect and will be rare occurrences for some households. Coordinating co-presence is difficult and improvisation is often required to approximate to the ideal. Nevertheless, the 2012 EMP survey showed that those living in family households mostly eat the main meal of the day in the evening with other family members. Other surveys give rather similar estimates.[47] However, TCP data for 2015 suggested some reduction recently. In couple-only households 20 per cent of respondents had eaten the previous day's dinner alone, compared with 11 per cent in 1995, and couples with children had both partners and children together in only 57 per cent of occasions (compared with 76 per cent in 1995). This may be some indication that acceptance of greater flexibility in arrangements and increasing disruption to routines are having an effect. Sadly, it is not possible to obtain precise estimates at population level for much earlier periods.

Despite the disruptive potential of dual careers, more flexible working hours, greater out-of-home leisure activity and much increased opportunities to eat out, the evidence testifies to the continuing joint strength of custom, preference and necessity surrounding the domestic family meal arrangement. Work schedules and household composition remain the basic structuring features of the eating timetable. It appears that the more control a household (or its members collectively) has over its work obligations, the more frequently it will eat together. Also, the fewer the hours spent in employment and in extra-domestic leisure activities, the greater the personal and collective time devoted to domestic eating. Meals are not only subject to the institutional constraints and local conventions of eating, but also constrained by how other practices are organised and scheduled, as eating is slotted into the spaces between work, sleep, personal maintenance and leisure.

Eating out

A potential reason for fewer domestic family meals is the expansion of eating out on commercial premises. One emergent and novel form of recreation in the later 20th century involved dining away from home. Although modern urban life demands that meals be eaten away from home sometimes, the rise in eating out since the 1970s is mostly a matter of discretion rather than necessity. While moderately common in earlier centuries and increasingly necessary in urban industrial settings, dining out on commercial premises for pleasure was mostly an upper-middle-class activity.[48] The use of restaurants and cafes is now much greater than 50 years ago. The proportion of household expenditure on food devoted to eating away from home rose fairly steadily from 10 per cent in 1960, to 17 per cent in 1980, to 27 per cent in 1995 and 32 per cent in 2015.[49] Most people's weeks are now punctuated by eating events outside the home. A Department for Environment, Food and Rural Affairs (DEFRA) survey of 2014 estimates that one in six meals are eaten outside the home, although that includes breakfasts and lunches during the working week. Nevertheless, almost everyone eats dinner out sometimes, and many do so very frequently. An adult of working age ate a *main* meal out on average about once in every three weeks in 2015, only a modest increase on 1995.[50]

The attractions of the restaurant are many. At interviews women express their appreciation of eating out because it relieves them of domestic labour, even though it is primarily recreational rather than functional benefits that it offers. Eating out is also source of immense gratification because it facilitates commensality and conviviality with family and friends and is a means to maintain social connections.[51] Company is the principal source of gratification. Eating out without company is mostly avoided, especially by women, although about 6 per cent of meals out reported in the TCP survey in 2015 were alone.[52]

The restaurant provides the setting for many family members to eat together. Partners eat out together. Parents take their children with them along fairly often also, although having children reduces the frequency of eating out. Sixty-nine per cent of main meals reported in 2015 had a member of family present. The growth of eating out has many interesting features to be returned to in later chapters. Restaurants have played a key role in the commercialisation of provision and the commodification of eating. They are a nexus for the impact of consumer culture on domestic arrangements. Overall, dining out could play a much greater role than it does, as in the

United States. However, an increasing majority of people say they would not like to eat out more often than currently.

Restaurants come in many shapes and sizes, with many different formats and menus. Most are classified both by the primary cuisine on offer and by type of establishment (restaurant, pub, hotel, and so on). Establishments vary in the type of service they offer, menus are variously structured and some are more formal than others (some are referred to as 'casual dining' in market research circles). Eating out has been subject to informalisation, casualisation and simplification. In the 1970s it was a formal and sometimes frightening activity. Nevertheless, social conduct is rather similar in all. The practice of dining out is very orderly. Scripts impose discipline. Diners start and finish at the same time, they sit at a table, select from a menu. Interactions occur in accordance with conventions sufficiently common between restaurants for customers to anticipate how they and others will behave. By and large, behaviour is fairly restrained, remaining seated at tables only with the companions one arrived with, food arriving in sequence in accordance with understandings about course progression and the order of savoury and sweet food, and accepted arrangements for payment, and so on. Basic procedures appropriate to different venues are widely recognised and followed, the distinctiveness of an event marked by type of occasion, dishes presented and price.

Eating alone: meals and companionship

Given the ideological power of the family meal (and the overwhelming preference for company when eating out), what does an increase in numbers eating alone signify? Is it a major problem? Eating alone, according to Claude Fischler, is a practice which 'in many or most cultures ... is frowned upon',[53] and is obviously a threat to dominant norms of commensality. Around one-third of meals taken in Britain in 2012 were eaten alone, about four in ten weekday meals and around one in four weekend meals. Almost certainly this has increased since the mid-20th century, although shortage of historical data prevents precise measurement. Companionship also has a temporal pattern. Overall, evening meals are shared twice as often as breakfasts or lunches on weekdays. At weekends, both afternoon and evening meals are generally eaten with others present; fewer than one in ten who live with others eat their weekday evening, or weekend afternoon or weekend evening meals without companions.[54]

Where companions are readily available, to eat alone is highly unusual, particularly at meals taken later in the day. This suggests that change in living arrangements is the most important factor explaining reduction in family meals. One reason why people eat alone is that they live alone. The increase in the number of single-person households is one of the most prominent demographic shifts of the last century, part of a wider trend of households becoming smaller. Today in the UK some 29 per cent of private households have only a single occupant, compared with 12 per cent in 1961.[55] This has consequences for behaviour. Those living alone eat alone three times more often than do those living with others; 74 per cent of all the meals reported by people living alone are eaten alone, compared to only 27 per cent of those reported by people living with others. Men living alone report more meals alone (76 per cent compared with 70 per cent of women). Elderly respondents living alone are least likely to eat with others and are especially reliant on household members if meals are to be shared. Members of the professional-managerial class who live alone find more non-household commensal companions. Solos compensate somewhat by eating with friends and non-co-resident family slightly more often than others. The most sociable meals for those living alone are weekday lunches, where they are particularly likely to eat with work colleagues. Those living alone also eat more quickly on average (apparently because they eat alone more often). Meal content is somewhat distinct but similar meal times are observed. Few foods are rigidly associated with sociability, although cereals for breakfast and sandwiches for lunch tend to figure among the least sociable occasions. Eating alone involves less cooking. More lone meals are sourced directly from commercial outlets outside the household, require less complicated preparation, and occur in short eating episodes. The dish least likely to be eaten alone is the roast; 94 per cent of people who reported eating a roast dinner had companions.

There is no necessary or compelling reason for dismay about the evidence on eating alone. No doubt, most people prefer to eat with others, but not eating always with family members may be welcome relief. For those who live alone, the absence of company at meals may well be preferable to having to share a domicile with others in order to find companions. There is a difference between loneliness and solitude. Nevertheless, if eating with others has the positive functions usually ascribed to it, then Britons miss out on some of the simpler pleasures of life. For they eat alone more often than populations of most other European countries. For example, in striking contrast, the sociable Spanish share 62 per cent of morning meals, 82 per cent of afternoon meals and 82 per cent of evening meals.[56] Problems of coordination are not the only explanation. Smaller and more determinedly nuclear families, divorce and separation, and widowhood mean that companions are less easily or inevitably available. That, in turn, however, reflects a wider social process – hard to pin down – of individualisation that became more prominent and pervasive during post-war reconstruction and was accentuated by cultural developments in the 1960s.[57]

Informality: the end of ceremony

Britain is probably ahead of most European countries in casualising its eating arrangements. Ceremonial aspects of eating are increasingly reserved for very special occasions. Opportunities for elaborate and protracted meals are few. Events are more hurried, the format abridged and the content less symbolically significant. Eating in the street, much more prevalent than 50 years ago, is perhaps the ultimate example of lack of ceremony. Most sections of the population share elements of what used to be referred to in the 20th century as a working-class approach to everyday life and consumption, one which emphasised immediate over deferred pleasure, homeliness and boisterous fun rather than pomp and self-control, corporeal rather than cerebral appreciation.[58] The sense of occasion reflected in ordered ritual has diminished. The dinner table, the dining room, the setting of tables, starting and finishing eating at the same time as companions – symbolic and material properties of commensal ceremony – are less prevalent. For example, when asked about specific food chores at home, 11 per cent fewer respondents reported laying the table as a routine task in 2015 than in 1995.[59] Concomitantly, activity is less centred upon the table, with fewer households having dining tables, and more reporting watching television while eating, and the use of mobile phones during meals is undoubtedly becoming more frequent.

The conjuncture of forces of casualisation, individualisation and informalisation have impacted most areas of eating behaviour. What once was a significant publishing activity, the sale of books devoted to etiquette and table manners more or less ceased. The mode of address of much advice about eating has shifted from instruction in the rules of best behaviour to recommendations about options. Decisions are left to the discretion of the reader.

Another instance might be the operation of restaurant regimes. Professional waiting staff and the infrastructural features of the white tablecloth restaurant and its conventional distribution of cutlery, plates and glasses used to intimidate customers, particularly those from lower social classes who had very limited experience of eating in restaurants. Dress codes, for example men having to wear a tie, were a subject of complaint in the *GFG* in the 1970s. Now very few outlets object to informal attire. Fewer people in 2015 than in 1995 changed their clothes for a dining out occasion. Formality can no longer be insisted upon, but rather is a matter of discretion, to be determined by consumers in the light of their definition of the importance of the occasion. Not that all customers on every occasion are averse to formal arrangements and settings; in 2015, 28 per cent of survey respondents agreed that they 'liked to go to places where the other diners are smartly dressed'.[60]

Informalisation is not a process specific to the field of eating. Rather it is a general social process which has affected many fields of activity since the 1950s. Clothing is an obvious example. People are at liberty to dress up smartly in suits for work or to attend the theatre or the races, but they are not compelled to and will be looked askance only if appearing in casual clothes at the most ritualistic of occasions like weddings, funerals and banquets. Other examples include modes of address where the use of first names rather than titles is almost ubiquitous, interactions between sales assistants and customers, and expectations of how to behave as a guest.

Informalisation is not an acceptance that 'anything goes'.[61] In some ways it is easier to follow explicit rules in a disciplined manner than to have to work out what is or is not acceptable once discretion is introduced. Informalisation carries a veneer of mutual tolerance and respect which may also mask, and certainly does not eliminate, social inequality and hierarchy. Informalisation of manners should not be confused with democratisation; a change in manners guarantees neither everyone equal access nor parity of prestige. Neither does a regime of informality necessarily avoid shame and embarrassment resulting from social *faux pas*. When best practice is not prescribed and defined in advance, knowing what to do, or especially what not to do, in specific social settings just becomes more difficult, and the outcomes more uncertain.

The meanings of occasions, routines and manners

A perceptible and dominant national rhythm of eating events has gradually evolved and now differs from the 1950s. On weekdays the majority of breakfasts are quick, rudimentary and taken alone, followed by a brief and simple lunch, and with dinner in the evening comprising more complex and substantial dishes mostly eaten with household members. Weekends are a little different. Most people normally participate in three eating events per day, and in a manner that they describe as routine, two small events (breakfast and lunch) followed by one larger (dinner). If they eat snacks they do so mostly at predictable times and not as replacement for meals. The pattern is less rigid, predictable and collectively shared than 70 years ago. Arrangements are more flexible and fitted to changing settings. Yet while the tendencies towards informalisation have affected arrangements and manners, they have not eliminated order. Gradual modification of the meal pattern has occurred, but without any sign of radical transformation or collapse. Despite a great deal of publicly expressed angst and evidence of modification, the meal retains its integral place in eating arrangements.

Changes in meals and meal patterns are at least as much a consequence of shifting social contexts as personal preferences or ideals. Ritualised family meals remain powerful as an ideal, prone to inspire disappointment or regret when not achievable. Even if less prevalent than in the 1950s, my grandmother would recognise the rhythms and the meanings, and would have condoned exceptions due to contingencies. That might suggest that the remodelling of the distribution of practices throughout the week accounts for the major shifts in meal format and timing as much as changes in men's and women's roles, the most common explanation.

3

Acquisition and Diversity

What people buy and eat

Everyone must eat, and often. Lack of regular access to food is a mark of severe deprivation, causing misery, desperation, illness and possible death. Nowadays in the global North obtaining an adequate sufficiency is almost entirely mediated by markets. Functioning markets require the integration of processes of production, distribution and exchange involving the harmonisation of foodstuffs, firms, machinery, human labour and shopping. The metaphor of the food chain captures the complexity of the sequential arrangements for getting food from farm to fork. Items pass through many hands and many markets before reaching the table.

The public encounters food mostly at a late stage on its journey along the supply chain, at the point of retail purchase. At that juncture, ingredients and pre-prepared dishes are taken home for domestic processing, or prepared dishes are consumed immediately at the point of delivery in catering outlets. Spending money from the household budget is the key mechanism; in 2015 the contribution of food grown in gardens and allotments was a mere 4 per cent of the total.[1]

Official statistical sources stretching back to the 1940s offer historical perspective on how relative costs and household expenditure of items and categories of food have changed. In 2018, the average household allocated 10.5 per cent of its expenditure to food and non-alcoholic drinks.[2] As Engel's Law maintains, as incomes rise relative expenditure on food falls. Accordingly, the average British household devoted 40 per cent of its expenditure to food in 1952, just before the end of rationing, 20 per cent by 1985 and just 11 per cent to domestic supplies in 2015. Food itself is neither more nor less expensive in real terms compared with 70 years ago,[3] its diminished proportion of budgets resulting primarily from increases in incomes which give greater spending power.[4] Annual household expenditure per capita quadrupled between 1955 and 2019, the sharpest rate of increase occurring in the final quarter of the 20th century. Averages, of course, mask levels of inequality; the very rich have increased their wealth massively in the last four decades while the real wages of the majority have stagnated since 2000.[5]

The extent of the decline in the value of food purchased to eat at home is perhaps a little less significant when the changing incidence of eating out is taken into account. Such spending was negligible in the 1950s, appearing in the records rather belatedly; only in 1994 did eating out figure in any detail in official statistics. Catering, of all kinds, absorbed 40 per cent of all household food expenditure in the first two decades of the 21st century.[6] The proportion of the household food expenditure devoted to eating out trebled between 1960 and 2020.[7]

Food items purchased and consumed have changed in type and volume since the 1950s. Celebrating its 75th anniversary in 2015 by reviewing trends, *Family Food*, a DEFRA publication, identified some symbolic and substantial changes in household consumption. Between 1952 and 2014 the contribution of bread and butter to energy intake reduced from 30 to 10 per cent, consumption reducing from 1,700 grams per week per person to 540. Chickens were reared almost solely for their eggs and rarely eaten in the 1950s, but are now the most popular meat. Over the period consumption of pig meat fluctuated, beef remained constant and lamb declined. Potatoes also declined, partly replaced by rice and pasta. Meanwhile previously rare vegetables and fruits, like avocado pears, capsicums and aubergines, mangoes and melons, became common items on domestic dining tables.

Conducted every second year since 2010, DEFRA's Food and You Survey (FYS) focuses on everyday activities of households and asks about dietary restrictions, food security, purchase and preparation of food, and frequency of eating core categories of foodstuffs. Table 3.1 selects a few strategic food items to show how often respondents in

Table 3.1: Frequency of consumption of selected foodstuffs, adults aged 18+, Great Britain, 2018. All adults, lowest income quartile and highest income quartile (percentages by column)

	Times per week	All adults	Low household income: <£10,399	High household income: >£52,000
Meat (beef, pork, lamb)	5+	3	1	3
	1–4	52	60	56
	Never	11	11	8
Pre-cooked meats (ham, pate)	5+	9	9	8
	1–4	54	38	43
	Never	22	24	22
Poultry (chicken, turkey)	5+	10	6	10
	1–4	72	71	75
	Never	7	8	8
Cooked veg	5+	57	45	65
	1–4	39	50	33
	Never	1	1	0
Raw fruit	5+	65	65	69
	1–4	25	23	25
	Never	3	4	1
Cooked fish (not seafood)	5+	1	2	1
	1–4	40	36	39
	Never	20	26	16
Duck, goose	5+	–	–	–
	1–4	1	1	1
	Never	60	73	51
Raw oysters	5+	–	–	–
	1–4	–	–	–
	Never	90	95	84

Note: In answer to the question: 'At the moment how often do you eat …'. Columns do not sum to 100 per cent because items consumed less often than weekly are omitted.

Source: FSA (2018), tables 1.4, 1.6, 1.7

2018 eat specific foods. It shows that in any given week in 2018, 96 per cent of adults ate cooked vegetables, 90 per cent raw fruit, 82 per cent chicken, 63 per cent pre-cooked meats, 55 per cent carcase meats and 1 per cent duck or goose.

The table also shows the extent to which behaviour varies between households with the highest and the lowest incomes. The poor spend a significantly greater proportion of their disposable income on food than do affluent households; in 2018 households in the top decile (tenth) spent 7 per cent of their budgets on domestic food supplies while the lowest decile spent 14 per cent.[8]

Despite the pressure of high prices being more intense for poorer households, there are not vast differences in the *categories* of item purchased. As was the case in the 1950s, households mostly buy the same basic items, suggesting that the poor and the rich are not much different in their tastes for the core items gracing British dinner tables. The rich probably have diets a little more compliant with current national dietary guidelines, primarily because they eat a wider variety of items. They are less likely to say that they never eat the items listed. They also, and distinctively, eat luxurious items like duck and oysters more frequently. Poor households are not totally denied any of the foodstuffs, but rather eat the more healthy and more prestigious items marginally less frequently. Chicken and turkey, for example, appear at least weekly for 85 per cent of rich households but only 77 per cent of poor households, although the proportion who never eat chicken is the same.

Why then do the rich spend a great deal more money in absolute terms than do the poor? They buy better quality produce; free range and intensively reared chickens vary in price and flavour. They shop in retail outlets with higher prices – in accordance with class-based brand loyalty to different supermarkets. They buy larger quantities of expensive produce. By purchasing a wider variety of items they include miscellaneous, non-staple and therefore relatively expensive foodstuffs. Perhaps, cushioned by their greater disposable income, they may overstock and waste more. When asked in 2022 whether any changes had been made recently for financial reasons – for example by eating out less, buying cheaper alternatives, using leftovers more, or eating food past its use-by date more – 53 per cent of the total population said 'no'. Differences by income were negligible, although more of the rich cut back on eating out while the poor resorted to using out-of-date food more frequently.

Will Atkinson used the same FYS data to describe aggregate patterns of consumption and identify sources of social differentiation other than income.[9] The coincidence of foods purchased for domestic consumption shows how tastes cluster. For example, while most people (81 per cent) ate a burger sometime in the last year, the relatively few who did so weekly also tend to eat ready meals and pre-packaged sandwiches very often but fish and fresh fruit very infrequently. Atkinson maps the concurrences of actual food preferences, characteristics of social position (income, age, gender, ethnicity, educational qualifications) and cultural and culinary orientations and dispositions. What, following the French sociologist Pierre Bourdieu, he calls 'the food space' can be represented on a diagram with two axes, one contrasting abundance and scarcity, the other the fat and the lean. This produces four quadrants where the superimposing of preferences, social attributes and dispositions upon each other show how preferences cluster. Figure 3.1 is a very much

Figure 3.1: Clusters of food preferences, adults aged 18+, Great Britain, 2018

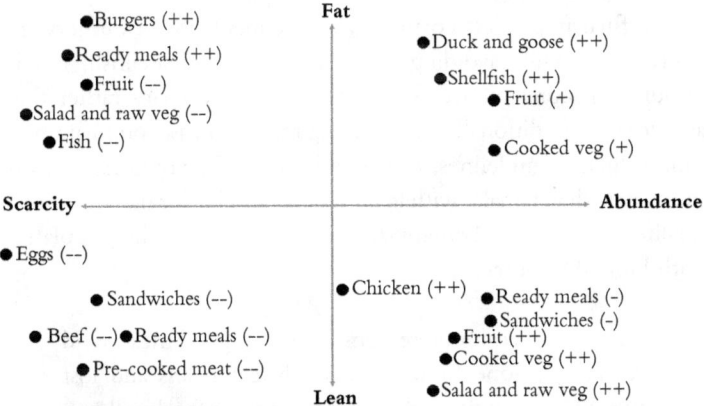

Note: This identifies items most prominent by their presence (++) or absence (--) in clusters of foods that define the food space. It is a highly selective and simplified version of the description in Atkinson (2021: 903, figure 1).

simplified and selective chart locating some especially significant features of the two axes.

In the bottom right corner are situated frequent (+) consumption of salad and raw vegetables, cooked vegetables, fruit and chicken, and infrequent (−) use of ready meals and pre-packed sandwiches. This zone contains more women, more couples and more affluent and educationally qualified individuals, with higher education a more defining characteristic than high income. To this quadrant, which encompasses abundant and lean foods, Atkinson attributes culinary principles of healthy and ethical eating.

In the top right corner there are more men who, while also well qualified, are richer, their high incomes more determinant than higher education. In Bourdieu's terminology this is a segment with high overall levels of capital but more economic in composition than cultural. Preferences include frequent consumption of richer foods like duck and goose, shellfish and cured meats, but not to the exclusion of raw and cooked vegetables and raw fruit. The orientation is towards rich and pleasurable eating.

The whole of the left half of the diagram is a zone of relative scarcity which 'corresponds with fewer resources'.[10] Atkinson says of the bottom left zone: 'The austere/ascetic/traditionalist quadrant, where consumption of meat and convenience foods is limited, eating out rare and those with special dietary requirements typically located, is closely associated with ethnic and religious minorities.'[11] The majority of vegetarians in the sample inhabit this quadrant.

The final upper left corner makes frequent use of burgers and ready meals while avoiding fruit, vegetables and shellfish. For its population 'convenience is paramount and necessity rather than asceticism or traditionalism the driving force'.[12] Least compliant with official dietary guidelines, it is populated by the youngest cohorts, more male than female, with low incomes and low or no educational qualifications. It also contains the (small) section of the population with limited resources

> who – for economic reasons – have skipped meals (and regularly), gone hungry, generally eaten less and lost weight as a result, and who worry their food will run out before their next pay packet, whose food has in fact

not lasted from one pay cheque to the next and who explicitly state they cannot afford to buy healthy food all gather in this zone.[13]

Unsurprisingly, those to whom these measures of food deprivation apply also report poor health and have greatest likelihood of suffering '*existential* pain: to feel unhappy, unsatisfied with their life and, ultimately, that life is not worthwhile'.[14]

Atkinson shows how preferences, identified by the frequency with which key items are consumed, cluster and are associated with social position and social attitudes. The food space is primarily structured by the distributions of economic and cultural capital. People with the highest incomes eat richer and also varied foods. Those with high educational qualifications and lower incomes – likely to be cultural intermediaries, state-employed professionals, and so on – tend to be more abstemious, for example eating duck less frequently and salads and vegetables more often. Those positioned closer to 'the pole of scarcity' have lower incomes, few qualifications and are more likely to come from ethnic minority households. Atkinson thus demonstrates a persisting systematic class basis to food habits. Gender and age are most influential social sources of variation on the second (vertical) axis which opposes lean and rich foods. Ethnicity registers on both axes.

Affordability: poverty, deprivation and inequality

For much of the past many people went short of food, impelling religious institutions, charitable bodies, political authorities and communal associations to play a part in relieving hunger. A mix of ethical concern and fear of insurrection made insufficient food a public and political concern; the food riot was one of the most common emotive and contentious episodes in European history. Governments, or rather the local representatives of central political authorities, faced popular protests when food stocks were insufficient. E.P. Thompson's famous essay on the moral economy of the crowd pointed out that it was felt as particularly egregious when, upon the expansion of the geographic range of markets, food produced in rural areas was put on sale at highly inflated prices unaffordable to local populations, or not put on sale locally at all.[15] Residents of Dorset felt very aggrieved when food was denied to them in order to supply richer populations in Bristol or London.

The circumstances of 18th-century England are long gone, although the same logic still applies in other parts of the world. The market for food has only continued to grow in scope and scale. Britain, like the rest of Europe, North America and the rest of the affluent countries in the orbit of the world economy, no longer face problems of famine – whether induced naturally or, much more usually, institutionally[16] – for large swathes of the population. Now deprivation and insufficiency are problems concentrated in pockets, where some people find it impossible to access a sufficient amount of adequately nutritious food. In Europe – though not in the United States – this has until recently affected a tiny proportion of the population who are likely to be suffering from other deprivations – the homeless, asylum seekers, those ineligible for assistance or whose social security benefits have been suspended. The precariousness of the availability of food reappeared in Britain early in the 21st century. The arrival of COVID-19 exacerbated an already endemic level of food insecurity most obviously manifested in the spread of food banks after 2010.

Alison Garthwaite, in a prize-winning book on the emergence and rapid expansion of food banks after 2010, describes in painful detail the demeaning experiences of those compelled to have recourse to a particularly distressing form of charitable aid.[17] Based on a detailed study of a church-based food bank in the northeast of England, *Hunger Pains* charts both the dedication and generosity of the volunteer workers and the distress of their clients. Although emergency soup kitchens have existed for decades, they played a minor role in relieving destitution. Food banks have multiplied – a recent estimate for 2021 was 2,200 – to deal with a substantial number of people.[18] The clientele are mostly victims of the predictable misfortunes of contemporary Britain – debt, divorce, inadequate housing, mental illness and unemployment. That a significant number of people who are in employment also now rely on them is an indictment of the failure of the contemporary economy. These misfortunes had met with greater compassion in the heyday of the social democratic welfare state than under the neoliberal policies of Conservative governments from the 1980s onwards. Precarious employment and low wages, and political arrangements which exhibit a diminished sense of collective responsibility for insuring against the predictable insecurities of the 21st-century capitalist economy,[19] confront many respectable ordinary folk with risks which they cannot offset. Betrayed by the ideological injunctions to exercise individual responsibility, those in precarious circumstances face problems beyond their own powers to resolve.

Garthwaite acknowledges that a few of the clients are not in dire straits, but the overwhelming majority face insuperable obstacles to feeding their households. Receipt of this form of charitable support is a source of strong feelings of embarrassment, shame and depression. Scarcely anyone *wants* to use a food bank. Rather, it has become a necessary humiliation for a substantial number of Britons, the COVID-19 pandemic only serving to increase the number of claimants under even more difficult circumstances for the charitable organisations. Food becomes insufficient, monotonous and unadaptable to personal tastes. While attempts are made to accommodate personal preferences and circumstances – 'cold boxes' are made up for applicants who lack electricity, a cooker or a means of heating food, for example[20] – the contents of the emergency food parcel issued by the Trussell Trust to last three days indicate the limitations of acquiring food through these channels: 'The Trussell Trust guidelines specify exactly what each food parcel should contain: cereal; juice; soup; tea/coffee; tinned tomato; pasta sauce; tinned vegetables; tinned fruit; rice/pasta; tinned fish; tinned meat; biscuits; long-life milk; sugar; and extra treats (where available) of jam, chocolate and sauces.'[21] The parcel also includes a proposed menu for the three days (see Box 3.1); having followed it religiously, once only I am pleased to say, without questioning its nutritional adequacy I can confirm that it does nothing to lift the spirits.

A significant proportion of poor people in Britain are now subject to shortages of food. As Sen might observe, lack of access to decent food for some sections of the British population is the result not of the unavailability of food, for neither Brexit nor COVID-19 precipitated a situation of serious shortage, but of the distribution of income. The failings of political management are laid bare when households with two members in paid employment have recourse to food banks because their wages are insufficient to provide enough food for themselves and their families.

The last period when food shortages were common in Britain was during and in the immediate aftermath of the Second World War. Basic items were rationed to ensure an acceptably fair distribution

---

Box 3.1: Trussell Trust's single food box three-day menu

DAY 1

Breakfast   **Cereal, fruit juice, tea**
Lunch   **Soup with pasta**

Empty 1 tin of soup into a pan and heat through. Cook 75g of dry pasta (approximately 2 handfuls) in boiling water for 10–12 minutes, drain off water, and add to soup.

Dinner   **Ham hash (or tinned meat) with beans, potatoes/
             or vegetables
             Rice pudding and tinned fruit**

Cut up the ham (or meat) and the potatoes/or vegetables into small chunks. Heat up 1 tin of baked beans and add the meat and potatoes/vegetables.

Serve the rice pudding (hot or cold) on top of 1 tin of fruit.

DAY 2

Breakfast   **Cereal, fruit juice, tea**
Lunch   **Corned beef (or tinned meat) and pasta, with tomatoes**

Empty 1 tin of tomatoes into a pan and heat through. Cut the corned beef (or meat) into chunks and add to the tomatoes. Cook 75g of dry pasta (approximately 2 handfuls) in boiling water for 10–12 minutes and add to the tomato and meat mixture.

Dinner   **Tuna pasta with vegetables
             Tinned fruit**

Mash up the tuna with a fork and add 1 tin of vegetables. Heat this through. Cook 75g of dry pasta (approximately 2 handfuls) in boiling water for 10–12 minutes. Mix together.

DAY 3
Breakfast Cereal, fruit juice, tea
Lunch Soup with pasta

Empty 1 tin of soup into a pan and heat through. Cook 75g of dry pasta (approximately 2 handfuls) in boiling water for 10–12 minutes, drain off water, and add to soup.

Dinner Pasta with tomatoes and beans

Open 1 tin of tomatoes and add these to a pan and add 1 tin of baked beans. Mix up with a fork and heat through. Cook 75g of dry pasta (approximately 2 handfuls) in boiling water for 10–12 minutes. Serve with tomato and bean sauce on top.

Note: The Trussell Trust delivered 2,537,198 such parcels in the year 2020–2021. *Food Banks in the UK*, House of Commons Library Research Briefing, 14 July 2021.

Source: Garthwaite (2016: 50, box 2.1).

---

of food; pain was shared. The response included the circulation of recipes for unusual ingredients like snoek, substitute ingredients like powdered egg for items rationed or unobtainable, and encouragement to grow vegetables in flower beds.[22] Pride arose from cobbling together ingenious new adaptations to deal with a shared predicament. Such levels of deprivation, disappointment and discomfort have not been experienced since, although the outbreak of the COVID-19 pandemic saw mild reverberations when despite government assurances, panic buying occurred as households sought private remediation for anticipated food shortages. In retrospect, the overstocking of kitchen cupboards with dried pasta and tins of tomatoes and beans seems a little ridiculous but also oddly reminiscent of charitable rations.

Origins of diversity

COVID-19 did not disrupt the industrialised food chain, despite supermarkets restricting customers for a brief period to small amounts of a few products like flour and pasta. Subsequently, though, during 2022, food prices increased significantly in the face of inflation following the outbreak of war between Ukraine and Russia. This fuels concern about the resilience of the food system. Tim Lang, a vocal advocate of the need to ensure food security in the UK, identifies climate change, obesity and declining biodiversity as fundamental systemic problems. They underlie a system which is institutionally enormous, complex and deeply entrenched. The extent of lock-in to established, entrenched and complicated arrangements makes reform very difficult. Immediate and specific problems include misdirection of resources, diet-related illness, over-concentration of ownership of land and industrial production and circulation, shortage of labour consequent upon restriction of inward migration after Brexit, waste, public misperception of the most significant problems, and poor governance. All deserve consideration (and are dealt with in other parts of this book) but here I concentrate on the supply of the foodstuffs which, circulating as commodities, provide the basis for the diversity of produce available.

Britain has imported more than it exports since the end of the 18th century. France, by contrast, is almost entirely self-sufficient in agricultural produce, where, Lang says, 'trade is marginal in meeting the population's nutritional needs'.[23] The extent of the imbalance of trade raises concern. In 1914, food self-sufficiency was around 40 per cent. The economic exchanges associated with free trade and imperial extraction in the later 19th century meant that less than half of all food consumed by Britain's increasingly urbanised population was produced in the UK. In the 1950s it was 40–50 per cent, rising to 80 per cent in the early 1980s and declining again to 50–60 per cent by 2018.[24] Membership of the EU initially increased self-sufficiency through its extensive subsidy arrangement but subsequently levels gradually reduced. Immediately prior to Brexit, Britain was producing about half of its foods, 30 per cent coming from the EU, with Africa, Asia, North and South America each supplying 4 per cent.[25] In some sectors a substantial majority of consumption is supplied from British producers, for example, dairy, cereals and red meat, but only 23 per cent of fruit and vegetables are grown in the UK. Although a substantial proportion of imports could be grown in the UK, cheaper food can be obtained from overseas producers. The established economic and logistics system means that both the volume and the diversity of foodstuffs depend heavily on global trade and world commodity prices, the security of which cannot be guaranteed in times of crisis.

Availability

Global trade and new ingredients

Producers, retailers and restaurateurs tailor their offers to impressions of conventional preferences and past experience of aggregate levels of demand. Their anticipation is based on recent experience. A huge range of edible items are omitted from the roster. Which raw ingredients or manufactured preparations are present is sifted through calculations about cost of production, availability of products, uniformity of appearance, shelf-life and potential wastage, popularity among the local customers, but also the weather and the seasons. These qualities, condensed into the selling price, act as a filter through which pass loss of biodiversity, non-availability of varietals, air-freight to deliver counter-seasonal produce, animal welfare standards, and many other concerns which emerge as problems of environmental sustainability. British agricultural policy prioritised cheap food for the urban industrial working class for 200 years and the consequences are increasingly apparent.

Globalisation in the later 20th century expanded international trade and delivered an unprecedented volume of diverse commodities. It is hard to specify when the process of globalisation began. Sidney Mintz shows that the transportation of foodstuffs across national boundaries occurred over centuries, from transporting new plants, trading spices, extraction of staples from colonies overseas, to the integrated transnational regime orchestrated by the industrialised food corporations of the 21st century.[26] 'Ingredients, recipes, dishes, meals and cuisines circulate, not to mention cooks, capital and broadcast images.'[27] Globalisation entails that more of these entities move more frequently, further and faster than in earlier times with major consequences for other practices besides eating. The effects are disputed. In one view, globalisation reduces differences between countries and within populations. The ubiquity of the internationally standardised offerings of McDonald's is a prototypical example of homogenisation, industrialisation and rationalisation. Exemplifying mass production in the service sector, it is efficient and profitable but brings with it uniformity. Hence, people on different continents eat the same foods from almost identical menus in similar surroundings. What Appadurai calls 'instruments of homogenization' do exist.[28] However, they call forth counter-trends like movements for localisation, reiteration of national distinctiveness and revaluation of *terroir*. National cultural diversity persists and is deliberately cultivated. Globalisation both introduces new foreign elements and reinvigorates local specialisation.[29]

Repertoires of dishes popular within, and said to belong to, particular countries or social groups are never entirely stable. From the early modern period onwards novel ingredients were introduced into Europe from other continents, steadily refreshing and augmenting local materials. Novelty has many sources. Long-distance trade is one. Technologies of preservation is a second, making more items available through smoking, salting, pickling and canning, altering the taste of the same raw ingredients. Rapid refrigerated transportation is a third. Another comes from the manipulation of foodstuffs, of animals and plants, by breeders and laboratories. Items with the same name cease to have their original chemical or organoleptic properties, as for instance with the tomato which is now bred for colour, perfect shape and long shelf-life. Its initial introduction to Europe is often commented upon, but its genetic and biological transformation is rarely observed.[30] The mass manufacture of foods for the market also augments the range, as companies aspire to manufacture saleable products. And finally, professional chefs make their reputations by inventing new dishes using arcane ingredients in unlikely combinations as they refine restaurant menus.[31] Novelty is an artifice, often faddish, usually a commercial rather than a gastronomic imperative. The corporate promotion of new products opens innovative paths to greater variety. The histories of the potato, the tomato, the avocado and kimchi reflect a mixture of scientific and biological curiosity, technological change, imperialist state aggrandisement and pursuit of private profit and wealth. By the 21st century accumulation involving the operations and organisation of more powerful global corporations has created a highly complex system of international trade serving the residents of gigantic cities. This has been accompanied by ever greater delocalisation of production and more mobile populations. All facilitate a market for diverse ingredients and new forms of manufactured foodstuffs.

Mass markets, niche markets and supermarkets

Supermarkets make available and visible ever more novel ingredients and prepared meals. Imitating earlier developments in the United States, the self-service supermarket became common after the mid-1960s and is now the principal channel for the purchase of food. The largest five chains command a majority (60 per cent in 2018) of all grocery sales.[32] They coordinate British food provision.

The supermarket raised the baseline for standards of food for much of the population. It exhibits some of the positive features of mass consumption. Ordinary members of the population have access to clean, hygienic, fresh and preserved food of fair quality, in great variety, from wide geographical sources, and at moderate prices which most can afford. They also provide a steady and reliable supply, including of items partly or wholly prepared which obviate irksome labour and compensate for lack of cooking skills.

Making foodstuffs abundantly available is a social and institutional achievement. Security of supply for the last 50 years has been orchestrated by supermarkets. They are competitive and not oligopolistic.[33] Cheap food can be attributed to the competitiveness of food markets and the strategies of the supermarkets. They stock what they can sell at a profit, permitting plentiful product lines. They are increasingly powerful, the balance of power in the food chain having moved against both growers and manufacturers. From the point of view of putting palatable and clean food on a domestic table, supermarkets are highly efficient economic organisations.

Their social, political and environmental record is more problematic. The supermarket formula of moderate and acceptable quality at prices low enough to eliminate competition from small retail businesses but high enough to maintain viable levels of profit has meant that the supermarket regime established its own future with major consequences for the quality of British eating. The principal costs of supermarkets are to the earth, due to the farming techniques required to guarantee this form of supply. Application of fertilisers to the land is gradually exhausting the soil; the uprooting of hedges reduces biodiversity of species and plants; field size and the size of farming operations get larger to facilitate the use of heavy machinery; pharmaceuticals are given to livestock and transmitted on into the human food chain, polluting waterways on the way; pesticides kill the bees critical to food production.

The social and infrastructural effects of supermarkets create additional urban environmental problems. The large out-of-town sites create dependence on the automobile, roads from city centres and suburbs attracting more traffic. Air freight is a major means for importing fresh produce. The energy costs of counter-cyclical production to put out of season fresh items on the shelves all year round are formidable. Items serving specialised tastes or marginal foods (like eels and sweetbreads) are eliminated thereby reducing the range of possible sources of tasty, sustainable and nutritious foods. Mendacious contractual relationships reduce the profitability and viability of suppliers. While supermarkets do not preclude the operation of smaller producers they make it more difficult for them, as niche products are relegated from the high street to box schemes, farmers' markets and local speciality suppliers.

Supermarkets, at the same time, are neither irresponsible nor unresponsive. They react to adverse criticism to maintain brand reputation. Their hygiene arrangements are fastidious, not only because of government regulation but also for reputational reasons; for example, an E. coli outbreak not only requires the destruction of large stocks and the withdrawal of popular products but also raises public concern about food safety procedures associated with other products. They demonstrate some corporate responsibility, including for instance some innovative responses to the problem of food waste with transfers of surplus produce to food banks. Much of this is not inconsistent with their own self-interest; corporations in mature market sectors do little without reference to rational calculations of costs and profits.

Supermarkets eagerly grasp fresh and creative opportunities for expanding the range of foods available. They are awake to the gains from stocking new items, sometimes those which are sought by minority social groups – providing customers exist in sufficient numbers. Currently, supermarket shelves and aisles are devoted to gluten-free, organic and vegan produce, testimony to the possibilities of large organisations carrying extensive stock. Nevertheless, industrial scale techniques mostly compromise the viability of more specialised production; the number of types of apples and potatoes on general sale have fallen dramatically.[34] For the other major consequence of supermarket organisation is standardisation. That involves a great deal of branding and packaging which also serves to sanitise the less appealing aspects of food production methods.

For many people who take pleasure in food and eating uniform produce proves disappointing, especially to the food enthusiasts who turn necessity into art, making a transcendent virtue of the human need for daily bread. Many people express distaste for visits to the supermarket per se – perhaps a reason for declining use of gigantic out-of-town superstores and a shift to more frequent purchasing and buying online. Smaller retail outlets provide a more intimate experience of shopping. Small specialist outlets may also offer a wider variety of items – health food shops, fishmongers who purchase their wares daily at a local harbour, organic vegetable communes, specialist cheesemongers, farm shops, places to pick your own fruit. The number of independent businesses is not great: it is estimated that in 2020 there were 6,000 independent butchers (a 60 per cent decline since the mid-1990s), 950 independent fishmongers and about 1,000 farm shops.[35] Taken together they have a small but significant share of the market for food and offer precisely non-standardised experience. Of course, absence of standardisation may mean unpredictable variation in quality. Small shops polarise between those selling high price, reliable and distinctive products and those which deal with products on the boundaries of imminent deterioration, of less reliable provenance, but cheap. It is important to remember that most foodstuffs are highly perishable and require timely sales. Sometimes this results in food being both cheap and very good, as in seasonal gluts. Other times it is valued because it is rare and hard to source, resulting in high prices for specialised, new or fashionable items. The local artisan can provide small batch, hand-crafted produce with distinguishing overtones of *terroir*, tradition or authenticity. It is no accident that foodies buy local produce and use specialist outlets more frequently than others.

Shopping opportunities are dynamic. If supermarkets still do most of the provisioning, the once-a-week or once-a-fortnight large shopping expedition is declining, replaced by both more smaller branch outlets of the major supermarkets and by the growing use of home delivery. The COVID-19 pandemic saw an increase in customers for online delivery of groceries and meals. Levels of usage of such services show no sign of reduction and market analysts predict further expansion. Organisations like Just Eat, UberEats and Deliveroo thrive, with younger people especially using mobile phone apps to order meals for home delivery. In the 2020s all the major supermarket chains offer doorstep deliveries, as do their new competitors like Ocado and Amazon which use their logistical capabilities to deliver an even greater range of products. Other new commercial enterprises offer competition by way of digital food platforms and third party delivery services for takeaway shops and cooked dishes. In addition, other smaller specialist ventures emerge, like urban gardening and the Incredible Edible movement which are embraced by food enthusiasts and those of radical persuasion who see potential for other ways of feeding populations.

Alternatives to the market: critique of commodification

Retail sale is the final stage in an often long series of economic transactions which get food onto the table. The clichéd route from farm to fork conceals a long series of economic activities which are linked together by market exchanges. Retail sales via shops and restaurants are the culmination of multiple specific market transactions during a process of production involving not just farmers and fisherfolk, but also seed merchandising, fertiliser manufacturing, boat building, industrial food processing, refrigerated storage, bulk transportation, wholesale marketing, advertising and shop fitting and design. Shops and restaurants provide the junction between these multiple production activities and final consumers. The process is complex and requires coordination across many local and specific product markets, each with their own contingent and instituted features.[36] Much of what is eaten is stamped by the market system and economic organisations whose fundamental *raison d'être* is to sell food profitably with access governed, directly and immediately, by the financial resources of the purchaser. In a commodified, market-centric system those with the most resources, typically money in the case of the consumer but many other assets for producers, have the strongest negotiating hand. Hence, the weak and the poor find that markets treat them badly. Alternative movements and practices testify to the fact that markets don't necessarily serve everyone well.

Alternative sources of provision exist which, although limited and compromised by the depth of penetration of commercial culture, do not require the diner to engage personally in a market transaction. Reliance on retail markets can be reduced by recourse to self-provisioning, institutional catering (prison, hospital and works canteens), state provision, charity, mutual aid (including communal exchange and domestic hospitality) and various forms of unregulated acquisition (including foraging, freegan appropriation and shoplifting). They variously permutate forms of labour, social obligation and property rights which contest market valuation. The state when involved tends to subsidise rather than directly deliver food to its citizens, school meals being a current example and British restaurants a wartime anomaly. Institutional catering is substantial: in barracks, boarding schools, hospitals, prisons and merchant navy vessels food is allocated to in-mates as part of a package of other activities with any payment involved indirect or non-instantaneous. However, the food service sector for institutional catering is also populated by large multinational corporations with many branches and remains subject to the logic of commodity exchange even if payment is waived or offset by subsidies or tax relief.

Nevertheless, not all transfers of food items involve exchange at a market-determined price. Some transactions resulting in a final consumer acquiring the food required for dinner do not involve money at all. Household self-provisioning, gifts and barter – the principal means for supplying food before the capitalist era – persist in various evolved forms. In total they make a substantial contribution to feeding Britain. Dave Elder-Vass, for instance, claims that 'the contemporary gift economy remains larger than the market economy, on some measures at least'.[37] Although only a small amount of food is grown by households for their own consumption, a vast amount of labour is added through domestic preparation activities. Charities and the communal sector offer models for more radical alternatives. The amount of charitable provision ebbs and flows according to circumstances, but no cash changes hands and the market is kept at arm's length. Food banks, for example, dole out free the proceeds from donations of food and money.

So too with forms of mutual and communal cooperation. Initiatives for reviving supplementary collective provision have emerged. Radical hopes are founded on transition towns, community gardens, communal orchards, and other forms of local cooperation and mutual exchange.[38] In some instances volunteers undertake to garden public plots of land to cultivate fruit and vegetables which can be freely harvested by other local people, for which Todmorden in West Yorkshire became famous.[39] Also undergoing recent revival is foraging for wild foods (although foraged foods seem to be increasingly appropriated by small businesses supplying upmarket restaurants).

Some people are strongly committed to these alternatives, seeing them as socially necessary, good for the planet and politically progressive, as well as providing better quality food and a greater appreciation of the natural world. Such people may align themselves with the communal sector because expressly critical of commodification, advocating instead mutual aid, sharing and giving of gifts. For many people have reservations about markets and seek to minimise their engagement, not only the poor who are not well served practically, but on the basis of a broader moral critique of markets. One version points out that workers subject to employment relation are themselves treated as commodities; it is not just a matter of fair or just distribution, but also of the types of social relationships which market exchange encourages.

Collective preparation of meals is not common, and perhaps now restricted to households in multiple occupancy shared accommodation and whose members by agreement cook in rotation. However, a much more common way to receive free food and labour lies in the much overlooked practices of domestic hospitality.

Most people eat out occasionally at the houses of family or friends and some do so very regularly.[40] The hosted meal is widespread, resistant to displacement by commercial alternatives and is highly appreciated.[41] Domestic hospitality makes for a distinctive type of eating event. It deems that hosts shall provide and prepare food in their own home, invite guests, serve a comparatively elaborate meal, in suitable surroundings, explicitly requiring nothing in return other than companionable conversation around the table and an expression of gratitude at the close of the event. Provided on a voluntary and non-pecuniary basis, such meals display generosity towards non-household members. Although ostensibly a gift, hosts usually receive return invitations from their guests. This arrangement avoids both labour and expense for the guests, although the ingredients themselves are mostly sourced via market exchange. One of its most pronounced features is that such events maximise the enjoyment associated with eating with others – of commensality. In 2015, 94 per cent of survey respondents said that they 'liked a lot' the last occasion when they were guests, whereas only 77 per cent of respondents were equally pleased with their last meal in a restaurant.[42] This is a form of provision which is not diminishing: many fewer people said that they never ate with friends in 2015 than in 1995. On the face of it this might be a basis for a sharing (and caring) economy. The hosted meal supplies a template for alternatives to capitalist economic relations based on exclusive property rights, alienated labour, market modes of distribution and severe inequalities in the distribution of goods and satisfactions. Like other forms of the communal economy it has limits, for it is also not independent of commodity exchange to source the food to be served or the equipment required for its preparation, and nor is it easily immediately scaled up to replace other modes of provision.

A rather different but pertinent critique of the commodification of the food supply is that it is wasteful. Capitalism, industrial and post-industrial, is an engine for the creation of waste. The critique of mass production and consumption has long pointed to mechanisms like a desire for the new, the planned obsolescence of goods and machines, that malfunctioning machines are no longer repaired, and that ordinary households overstock goods just in case exceptional circumstances require them. In relation to food, excess material items include kitchen equipment, overstocked cupboards, all those jars of herbs and spices that become out of date long before even a fraction of their content has been used, the amount of packaged salad that ends up in the kitchen bin, and the ineffective use of leftovers.

The Waste and Resources Action Programme, a campaigning organisation with some claim to success, estimates that in the UK one-fifth of edible food and drink brought into the home in 2012 was sent to the rubbish tip.[43] This amounts to 4.2 million tonnes of avoidable waste which would 'fill Wembley stadium nine times over'. Reducing waste could, in principle, both feed some of the billion or so under-nourished people in the world and reduce the quantity of greenhouse gases being emitted in the more affluent parts of the world.

David Evans explores this matter sympathetically, showing that people inadvertently, reluctantly and unavoidably throw away food which they had previously purchased.[44] They recognise and regret waste. They hold leftovers and otherwise unused ingredients in their refrigerators until the last possible moment, hoping that they will not have to be discarded. The imaginary rational consumer would ensure that exactly the amount of food required by a household during a week would be purchased, cooked and eaten. But obstacles crop up and other priorities like keeping children healthy, responding to the needs of friends, flexible working hours and unanticipated opportunities for social entertainment take precedence. Evans finds an explanation of the mismatch in the portions which supermarkets sell, the ethic of generosity which means that it is disrespectful to leave people hungry at the end of a meal, the ideology of family care which requires mothers both to give their children new foods to try while still ensuring that they eat sufficiently, and in the location of retail outlets. Waste might be reduced if food shops were just around the corner and food purchase occurred daily, but suburban living arrangements and the dominance of food distribution through supermarkets make adaptation to immediate and unforeseen needs very difficult, almost guaranteeing waste.

Freeganism, or dumpster diving as it is known in the United States, where it is more common, is a strategy for food procurement directly opposed to market supremacy. It is premised on an ingenious, radical and disruptive response to waste, and to the fact that most food is perishable. Its rationale lies in the wastefulness of dominant production arrangements. The practice involves locating discarded food, typically from skips outside restaurants and supermarkets, and rescuing it for household consumption. Retrieving cheese, bread, pizza and lettuce from a skip highlights, by contravening, several prominent conventions around food provisioning. That it is not paid for and that it has already seen the inside of a rubbish bin marks it out as very different. Not the British penchant for clean and cheap food but a valorisation of the dirty and free. It is primarily presented as a form of political protest against the waste of valuable resources, but is also often associated with a strong practical critique of the capitalist organisation of the food system. It can, however, provide a sufficient, if often imperfect, source of food for individuals and households. As Mourad and Barnard observe, the diets of dumpster divers are subject to the vagaries of what on any given day shops have failed to sell. They recount interviewees telling of gluts of pastry, pizzas and doughnuts. Constructing meals from a random set of foodstuffs may make for engaging television programmes but is a serious challenge as a mode of everyday survival. However, dumpster divers become very knowledgeable about what items of food are usually available, where and at what times of the day. They develop favourites; one informant travels a considerable distance to obtain a preferred brand of pizza. This urban equivalent of hunting and gathering takes time and requires knowledge. It has its imperfections, generating, as Mourad and Barnard note, practical and ethical quandaries. Poor personal nutrition is a constant danger. This is amplified by the worry about whether it is ethical to throw away any of the food that has been salvaged. There is always a residue. Moreover, an element of the despised consumer attitude creeps in once a map of where the best pickings can be found steers behaviour. Nevertheless, it is a thrifty practice with the honourable intention of reducing the quantities of food sent to landfill. Retailers sometimes try to hinder the practice but in other cases cooperate. It brings fresh attention to the public and political issue of waste in a way that composting domestic detritus never will. Incidentally, the dishes I was served through this mode of provision proved safe and delicious.

To sum up, new food movements conduct valuable and brave experiments. They pursue intrinsic rather than monetary value (sometimes in pursuit of internal rather than external goods). They may advance full-blown critiques of capitalism as a mode of production and recommend its abolition, or simply note that the social relations associated with alternative modes are preferable because kinder and more human(e). However, most are forced to operate in the interstices of multiple markets which constantly threaten to obliterate the good intentions and overwhelm non-market alternatives of supply. In addition, they are reluctant to acknowledge Lane's argument that markets bring diversity, and shopping gives a sense of control and self-determination which is beneficial to self-assurance and wellbeing.[45]

Availability, affordability and acceptability

Most people in most societies most of the time learn as children to eat what others in their social circle eat. That may be very restricted. Economic and ecological forces, and social barriers and facilitators determine the scope of acceptable foodstuffs. Accessibility, local ecology, religious allegiance, income and social status all bear upon the formation of menus. Affluent populations served by corporate retailers have greatly diversified options. Availability, affordability and acceptability were the principal constraints on the eating habits of the working class in the period of the urban-industrial diet. These probably remain major determinants of the acquisition of foodstuffs.

The period since the Second World War has seen a more diverse range of items generally available, although for the poorest sections of the population and those living in food deserts, access is restricted. Real prices have remained static over a 70-year period; although prices inflated rapidly in 2022 the expectation is that they will revert to the long-term average soon. That may not be wholly welcome as it can be argued that food has been both too cheap and inappropriately valued given levels of waste and the environmental burden of its production on an industrial scale. Richer households have easy access to a vast range of products for which they could be expected to pay more. Overall, poorer households can afford, and do purchase, a wider range of items than in the 1950s. The narrow range of acceptable products and tastes inscribed in the urban-industrial diet widened as more items became commonplace although the rate was slower for the working class than other classes.

Income alone does not determine differences in access, and except at the lowest levels is not very distinguishing. Taste is equally important and intricately linked to what we buy, but not directly determined by it. Economics pays little attention to taste and overestimates income as a determining factor. As Atkinson shows, preferences cluster in relation to other social factors besides income, including age, religious affiliation and in particular education. The coincidence of social position and social attitudes towards food and food preferences are the reasons why taste matters. Together they explain how some social classes and groups come to eat in symbolically different, though not entirely different, patterns. Taste is both a matter of sensory and social classification, as is revealed by the doings and sayings of people in different class positions.

4

Tasting: Embracing Foreign Flavours

Expanding tastes

The availability of a vast range of comestibles is both a privilege and a challenge. Diversity creates new opportunities but also creates problems of selection; mark the oft-repeated refrain, 'there's too much choice'. It expands taste by introducing new and unfamiliar items with strange flavours combined in previously unrecognisable dishes. Novel, and mostly foreign, foods were widely adopted in the second half of the 20th century, becoming important symbols of good taste and culinary pedigree. In tandem with non-customary items came styles of cooking from outside Europe, often referred to as 'ethnic cuisine'. Associated with the growth of takeaway outlets, modest restaurants and food shops in the urban centres hosting migrant communities, 'ethnic' connoted cheap foods with unusual spices and favoured by people whose origins were not British. The term in this context is, however, somewhat unfortunate because it elides national traditions with ethnic minority populations, thereby underestimating the arrival of all manner of foreign cuisine. It also takes for granted a hierarchical relationship between majority and minority ethnic groups and their tastes.

Taste is a term with several meanings. Teil and Hennion identify five 'fairly precise meanings': 'taste as a biological need; as social differentiation of attraction towards things; as a relationship of perception between subject and a product; as the emergence of reflexivity; and, lastly, as the practice of perception'.[1] For present purposes, it is sufficient to distinguish the symbolic and discursive signals of social identity (see Chapter 6) from embodied sensations resulting from the incorporation of foods with specific flavours, odours, pungency and textures. Both depend heavily on collective corroboration and affirmation.

Flavours are the means through which combinations of ingredients in dishes are identified and appreciated. Cuisines can be recognised through dominant flavour combinations, which is the reason why Elizabeth Rozin was able to describe sensory recognition of the provenance of dishes.[2] As she points out, paprika, lard and onions means Hungarian, while fish sauce, lemon and chilli is Vietnamese, and cinnamon, oregano, lemon and tomato is Greek. Different populations inherit repertoires of recipes using different available ingredients (cultivated and wild), sometimes subject to the constraints of religious doctrine, sometimes to the vagaries of dominant classes seeking to display their cultivation, wealth and status, and complicated by the serendipitous experimentation of cooks.

Ahn and colleagues explored global variation in flavour combinations in remarkable depth using a vast historical database of recipes collected from across the globe.[3] They use the idea of 'flavour principles' to explain the distinctiveness of cuisines and hence the varying preferences of different populations. They show that flavour compounds shared by groups of ingredients account for why they are conventionally prepared together and that basic preferences vary by continent and region. People find palatable the flavour combinations to which they are accustomed and therefore appreciating foreign flavour principles may be challenging and require a process of learning.

Spicing up the British palate: a culinary revolution?

Panikos Panayi, in *Spicing up Britain: The Multicultural History of British Food*, examines the spread of the tastes of immigrant groups on British food habits since the middle of the 19th century. He describes the period 1850–1945 and the influence of the culinary habits of Jewish, Irish, Italian, German and Chinese communities, their respective roles in the development of 'the foreign restaurant', and their impact on the majority population both at home and as customers of the catering trade. With the exception of the Irish, the migrants brought distinctive culinary habits with them and through small businesses, shops and restaurants, made ingredients and dishes available to others beyond their own community. However, comparatively small numbers before the Second World War meant a commensurately limited influence.

The second part the book is entitled 'The culinary revolution after 1945'. Many more migrants, from more diverse origins, settling in more parts of Britain had much greater impact. Panayi announces 'the victory of the foreign restaurants', saying that '[perhaps] the most important influence of migrants lies in the innovations they have introduced to the catering trade'.[4] 'The most significant changes occurred from the 1960s when Chinese, Italian and Indian restaurants and takeaways began to proliferate in high streets throughout Britain, US multinationals followed from the 1970s.'[5] Thereupon Britons increasingly encountered restaurants styled by cuisine type. Meanwhile, more mainstream restaurants copied the food served in establishments opened by migrants and US firms.

Panayi maintains on the basis of an extensive study of cookery books published in England since the mid-19th century that most paid little attention to the national associations of their recipes. It was not until the 1950s that cookbooks presenting the cuisines of other nations became commonplace. Only at that point did 'foods develop nationalities'.[6] Increasingly, national culinary traditions acquired symbolic significance, to classify restaurants and takeaways, to identify foodstuffs on supermarket shelves, and to boost the sales of recipe books. 'Gastronationalism' was born.[7] For Panayi, post-war British domestic developments are characterised by three periods – austerity, culinary revolution (mid-1950s to mid-1970s), to arrive at a situation where "multicultural" food is the norm.'[8] Writing in 2008, he sums up the process:

> In the half century since the end of rationing a revolution has taken place in the eating habits of Britons. Led by increased affluence, the impact of immigration and big business, the meat and two veg culture of the 1950s, while not disappearing, sits comfortably alongside curry and rice or pasta with sauce.[9]

There is a good deal of truth to Panayi's account. Minority ethnic groups played a formative and definitive role in the development of multiculturalism in the second half of the 20th century with significant effects on popular tastes. A vast range of new and foreign foods and recipes were introduced to Britain and consumers responded favourably. Supermarkets have aisles full of the ingredients required to prepare 'foreign' dishes or purchase them as ready-made meals. Restaurants came to be classified primarily, although never exclusively, by the affiliation of their menus to particular national cuisines (Thai, Italian, Spanish, and so on). Britain was exposed to the tastes of foreign foods and many people learned to like many of them. The process, still ongoing, accelerated sharply in the 1970s.

People expanded their vocabulary and their range of tastes in response to diversification of available foods and 'foreign' cuisines. Dishes from around the world which were unknown except to a minority of the population in the middle of the 20th century are now widely recognised. John Burnett noted that in a Gallup survey of 1976, 'chow mein and sweet and sour pork were known to seven out of ten, pizza by eight out of ten, and ravioli by nearly as many; chilli con carne was familiar to only four out of ten'.[10] A YouGov poll in 2021, inquiring about recognition and popularity of some of the same dishes, showed that 97 per cent of a nationally random sample recognised pizza, chilli con carne and ravioli.[11] Not only were pizza, chilli con carne and ravioli almost universally recognised, but a majority of respondents had positive opinions about them (72, 67 and 64 per cent, respectively).

Increasing knowledge and appreciation of foreign cuisine arise from their widespread presence in restaurants, takeaway shops and supermarkets, and because they are much discussed by cultural intermediaries who influence what we think we should (and should not) eat. YouGov is one of many websites claiming to identify the most *popular* British dishes; the term 'popular' sometimes implies connection to a British tradition of cuisine and more often to dishes widely available in Britain regardless of pedigree. What shall be considered British is a controversial matter.[12]

Dining out and changing tastes

A prime candidate for the most significant change in habits since the 1950s is the increase in eating out for pleasure. A Food Standards Agency survey of 2014 estimated that one meal in six is eaten away from home, a figure including minor meals like breakfasts and snacks, as well as lunches and dinners. In the TCP study of dining out in 2015, we estimated that the average person ate a main meal out on commercial premises (a pub, restaurant, cafe or similar establishment) on average once every three weeks. A very small proportion (only 5 per cent) never ate out and 21 per cent ate out once a week or more frequently. Comparison with the 1950s is tricky. Average frequency of a meal out seem not very different, but the purposes of those meals are. Evening meals in a cafe or restaurant were rare – about one dinner in 50, or approximately once every two months. Midday meals were more frequent, with about one in 12 on weekdays and Saturdays, but many of these were probably an alternative to a works' canteen, as the rate for men was double that for women. In 1955 only the upper and middle classes ate main meals out in restaurants, and then infrequently. Then the main reason for eating out was inability to return home for meals – because working at too great a distance from home, travelling or being on holiday. For most people in the mid-20th century, meals in factories and workplaces, in schools, and in 'total institutions' like military establishments, prisons and hospitals, were the principal sites for eating away from home. The workplace canteen, where workers purchased subsidised hot food, declined from the 1970s, and the supplying of luncheon vouchers by employers without facilities died alongside. Here lies the origins of today's truncated workers' lunches. Meanwhile, school dinners served as a political football in the period and were intermittently available by locality. When free only for children from poor households they were socially stigmatised, although content seems always to have been scorned by most pupils.

Restaurant meals are a means by which to learn new, and foreign, tastes and to experience the fruits of diversity. Restaurants spread 'foreign' cuisines. A significant, rapid but uneven distribution spread of foreign restaurants has occurred in affluent cities and towns around the world. The number of different cuisines represented in any western city has grown apace. This is a function partly of the growth of eating out in general, although there are major differences between countries; for example, a much greater proportion of Britons eat out regularly in restaurants than do Norwegians or the Dutch.

As the restaurant trade expanded it differentiated its offerings. A walk down the high street where commercial food businesses tout their many types of very visibly differentiated wares reveals the many possibilities. It has become normal for many to feel and express great satisfaction with the opportunities for refreshment, adventure and inquisitiveness. The slogan which Baudrillard took to be the epitome of the postmodern orientation, 'Try everything', resonates in approaches to dining out.[13] The restaurant is the site *par excellence* for expansive experiences with food, offering an opportunity for all but the poorest to experiment with unfamiliar dishes, learn about new combinations and flavours, benefit from the professional skills of chefs, and indulge in novel experiences.

Now a vast number of variously designated commercial outlets serve cooked meals on the premises including restaurants and bistros, burger bars and tapas bars, pizza houses and steak houses, cafes and tearooms, pubs and gastropubs. Some will also supply food to take away, in competition with Indian and Chinese takeaway shops, fish and chip shops, and kebab stalls. Then there are facilities in motorway service stations, railway stations and trains, airports and planes, open at most hours of the day to provide travellers on longer journeys with foods purporting to substitute for normal domestic meals. In addition, outlets with another primary function add on food provision, like the petrol stations, newsagents and chemists which are major suppliers of foods but have no personnel dedicated to food preparation; a lot of British breakfasts, lunches and snacks come straight off the shelf. In one respect equivalent because all provide meals away from home, no single generic term captures them. I will refer to restaurants and takeaways, even while recognising that overlap occurs because many establishments increasingly do both.

When considering taste, both social and sensory, commercial eating establishments are particularly revealing. Restaurant menus name dishes from which diners are required to select items to suit their tastes. Although constraints are many,[14] this must be the setting most closely corresponding to the ideal of free consumer choice in the field of food. A customer, without commitment to its preparation, can opt for a dish in accordance with his or her preference. The TCP survey in 2015 based on respondents' detailed reports of what was eaten at the last main meal out revealed an order of popularity; 10 per cent of main courses were South Asian curries, 9 per cent were burgers, while steak, roast dinners and pasta dishes each accounted for 8 per cent.[15] Fish and chips and pizza were the next favourites with 5 per cent each. Comparing answers to the question 20 years earlier indicated a sharp decline in roast meats, which had comprised 25 per cent of all main courses in 1995, and that burgers and fish and chips had each tripled in popularity. However, curry, steak, pasta and pizza were eaten in much the same proportions in both years. That would suggest considerable continuity in preferences alongside the significant decline in the symbolic roast dinner. The changes in selection of dishes were consistent with measured changes in ingredients of main dishes as salad, bread, pasta, rice, fish, chicken and pork increased, while beef, potatoes and pastry declined. Chicken surpassed beef as the most popular meat.[16] Starters saw a decline in soup, prawn cocktail and vegetable plates, though the last of these remained the most popular. Desserts hardly changed, ice cream is still the most popular, followed by pies, tarts and crumbles.[17]

Food content is determined partly by the type of establishment delivering meals. Restaurants specialising in specific non-British cuisines now almost exclusively sell dishes derived from the relevant culinary tradition, whereas Chinese restaurants in the mid-20th century also sold steak and fish and chips. Aesthetic purification has occurred. Nevertheless, many of the most popular dishes of 2015 appear in several different types of outlet which are relaxed about their attachment to specific cuisine. Curries and steaks, for example, are eaten in fine and casual dining restaurants, hotel restaurants and pubs.

The most commonly frequented outlets in 2015 were casual dining restaurants and pubs. People go to the pub to eat as well as drink. The TCP survey showed that a quarter of last main meals out in 2015 were eaten in a restaurant attached to a pub or the bar food area of a pub or hotel.[18] Formats and quality vary significantly. Gastropubs, a creation of the 1990s, are much vaunted. Some now appear in guides to fine dining, marking a change from 50 years ago when few pubs sold anything other than cold and packaged snacks.[19] Pubs with gastronomic pretensions and also more ordinary places typically offer dishes deriving from several different cuisines. What is generally popular is revealed by the typical bill of fare of the local public house (see Box 4.1). They will include on any day on relatively short menus curry, pasta, pies, fish and chips, meat and two veg, and a vegetarian or vegan dish. Thus some dishes from foreign cuisines have become an integral part of the foodways of the population of

> **Box 4.1: A typical menu of an English pub's 'Classic Main Courses' in 2023**
>
> Duo of Korean Chicken
> Hand-Battered Atlantic Cod
> Beef & Pancetta Lasagne
> Classic Gammon
> Keralan Chickpea Curry (Ve)
> Sea Bass & Seared Scallops
> British Chicken & Ham Hock Pie
> British Slow-Cooked Steak & Ale Pie
> Mushroom & Ale Pie (Ve)
> No Leaf Salad (Ve)
> No Leaf Salad with Chicken
> No Leaf Salad with Halloumi (V)
> No Leaf Salad with Butternut Squash (Ve)
> No Leaf Salad with Salmon
>
> Note: The menu in spring 2023 of my local pub in a peri-urban village in the north of England, part of the Chef & Brewer chain, offers starters (7), steaks and burgers (13, including a vegan sriracha burger), classics (15), sides (7) and desserts (9). The mixture of origins of dishes is considerable. The explicitly British items are pies, with cod and gammon probably similarly familiar. A vegan chickpea curry and a Korean chicken represent Asia and a lasagne implicates Italy. Vegan and vegetarian options are available, and there is an assurance about the source of the fish. Prices ranged from £11.99 to £16.99.

the UK despite not being symbolically identified as British. They are familiar but not naturalised.

Foreign food in women's magazines

Another mediating influence on taste and a barometer of the consequences of diversification is the popular press. 'Women's interest' magazines provide a continuous record of recommendations about what to prepare and eat at home, although their influence may have declined very recently.[20] They reflect the contemporary concerns and popular tastes of their time more faithfully and immediately than cookery books. Their principal instrument of recommendation is the printed recipe. Recipes selected for publication and the terms in which they are discussed indicate both what is appreciated and what is thought to be normal at a particular point in time. Since the 1960s much greater emphasis has been placed on issues of health and convenience.[21] Nevertheless, the magazines have constantly remained conscious of the emotional benefits of doing otherwise. On some occasions it is acceptable and advisable to indulge, to have a treat or to derive comfort from foods irrespective of calorie counts or disciplined diets. Preparation of dishes by hand, or 'from scratch', with the tastes and memories of family in mind and which expresses care and love, justifies not always giving preference to quick and easy recipes.

The magazines have remained undecided about the relative value of novelty and tradition when presenting their recommendations. They seek to keep up with fashions and to introduce unfamiliar ingredients and dishes into discussion of everyday cooking. They also teach and inform about dishes originating from other countries, even though most readers never attempt to prepare the dishes in their own kitchens. (As is often observed by scholars who reconstruct the history of taste and diet from recipe books, they are not records of what people *actually* ate in the past, only indications of possibility.) At the same time, a strong impetus exists to advocate the preparation of dishes meaningful because they accord with tradition, conjure memories of prior experience and previous generations, and express social, usually national, identity. Traditions may be local or foreign, and almost as many recipes are recommended as traditional, or in currently preferred terminology 'authentic', to foreign cuisines as to British. Examination of magazines in the years since 1968 shows that foreign dishes grew steadily more common, although the need to name explicitly the cuisine of origin becomes slightly less important after 1992. This reflects a long-term trend which might be described as the 'routinisation of the exotic'.[22] By 1992 it had become normal to draw on dishes from around the world and by 2016 more than half the recipes originated from non-British cuisines.[23] Thus, increasingly made aware of developments in the commercial restaurant sector, domestic cooks are encouraged to prepare an increasingly eclectic range of dishes drawn from many sources and with disparate origins. Magazines played their part in navigating the challenges of diversification.

Several layers of meaning can be peeled back from recipe columns. First, the way in which recommendations are formulated divulge common understandings of the purposes of food and eating. A vernacular terminology of gratification, interspersed among the technical instructions, discloses both the functional and sensory dimensions of eating; about a quarter of recipes 2016 were proposed because they were filling, nutritious and popular, and about half because of their sensual appeal – as tasty, appetising or delicious.[24] Dishes are expected to satisfy appetites, be good for health, be flavoursome and be culturally appropriate. By implication, many other dishes fail to meet some or all of the four requirements, being condemned as meagre or delicate, without nutritional value, bland and tasteless, boring, or transgressive of culinary convention. It is not incidental that these are often the grounds for denigrating British habits.

Second, in the postmodern fashion the recipe columns navigate carefully around the issue of cultural authority. Acceptance of collective restriction over individual autonomy became rarer in the later 20th century as the process widely referred to as individualisation made it difficult for both states with democratic pretensions and for experts to 'tell people what to do'.[25] Individuals should be free to act in accordance with their preferences and assume personal responsibility for the outcomes. This notion affects many arenas of life, perhaps none more than consumption where personal taste and judgement are deemed paramount. Prominent social theorists observe that people display their identity through the use of goods and services and are judged by others for their tastes irrespective of the degree to which they had effective autonomy in their acquisition.[26] Voluntary choice is presumed and consequently can be condemned as bad taste if mistaken. Magazines accommodate to such a condition by presenting advice as recommendations which authorise the reader to select from the vast range of apparently equally acceptable alternatives in accordance with circumstances and taste. The forbidden is simply omitted or ignored. There is no pretence that any single orthodox way to organise meals at home is correct.

Reception of foreign tastes: four stages of normalisation

The unfamiliar flavours and formats introduced in the 1960s and afterwards were not initially congenial for many. Reactions to foreign foods in Britain passed sequentially through four distinct stages: rejection, naturalisation, improvisation and authentication.[27] Asian food met initially with a considerable degree of hostility and rejection, expressed sometimes in racist terms.[28] Subsequently Indian and Chinese restaurants and takeaway establishments became popular and their number grew rapidly in the 1970s and especially 1980s.[29] In the years between 1965 and 1980, Asian restaurants and takeaways modified dishes to make them particularly palatable to British tastes; the birth of the balti in Birmingham is one example. They also included popular European dishes on their menus. As experience of dining out grew, a space became available for more 'authentic' Asian cuisine, at which point they began to be included in guides to fine dining.

Surveys show a steady increase in the use of foreign and 'ethnic' restaurants by the White British population. Resistance, though much attenuated, did not cease. Some people remain expressly hostile to foreign foods and flavours. The presence of dishes which would never have appeared on tables in the heyday of the urban-industrial working-class diet indicate the widespread incorporation of once foreign dishes into domestic meals. Foreign foods were normalised for the majority population, although non-British minority communities show reluctance to visit restaurants styled as British.[30]

What people claim to 'like' when asked for market research purposes almost certainly does not capture their general practice. The EMP 2012 survey sought to record what people actually eat, showing how items bought in the supermarket get incorporated into dishes and meals. It indicated that dishes eaten in the evening are much more varied than at lunch but in the main are neither exotic nor novel.[31] The most favoured combination is fish and potatoes, of which one third are 'fish and chips', a traditional dish disproportionately appealing to men and the less educated. The combination of prepared or non-carcase meat with potatoes (for example, cottage pie, sausages and mash) is almost as popular as fish with potatoes. Poultry with potatoes (for example, chicken and chips, roast chicken and new potatoes) is the third most common main course. The popularity of poultry and of non-carcase meat reflects both versatility and low price. Carcase meat is more important on both Saturday and Sunday. Roast beef, roast chicken and roast pork, all with potatoes, are among the five most popular dishes. Nevertheless, the cheese sandwich is the third most common option, providing a light weekend evening meal. Roasts are the most common dish at weekends, with beef most popular followed by poultry. Other carbohydrates like pasta and rice, denoting the contemporary influence of foreign-inflected cuisine, appear regularly on weekdays, in 10 per cent of Saturday dinners, but are only half as popular on Sundays.[32]

Variation is significantly associated with age. Younger respondents eat many more Italian-, South Asian- and East Asian-inflected dishes, with 23 per cent of under-40s eating pasta or pizza at an evening meal compared with 10 per cent of the over-60s. On weekdays, older cohorts eat more stews and meals focused around eggs, while younger groups favour stir-frys. At weekends older people prefer fish, while youngsters eat many more burgers and pizza. Nine times more under-40s than over-60s reported having eaten pizza.

Preferences are also associated with education and, to a lesser extent, class. On weekday evenings, less educated respondents eat more roasts and fish and chips, while university graduates have slightly more pasta. At the weekend differences are greater, with graduates eating more pizza, pasta and burgers. Less educated people eat more fish and chips, while the more educated eat fish prepared by methods other than frying. Women consume more dishes focused around eggs on weekday nights, and are more likely to report eating salads, while men eat more pizza during the week and more burgers and curries at weekends.

This is not to deny very many colourful and sometimes eccentric exceptions; flamboyant and idiosyncratic dishes appear occasionally, in marked contrast to regular and routine items. Also, ethnic minorities prepare food routinely in accordance with their own culinary traditions. Nevertheless, while not all dinners consist of meat and two veg, the most popular dishes seem very ordinary and would have been familiar in the 1950s. The pattern of consumption of general population is far from seamlessly and thoroughly multicultural, evidence that practices change slowly.

The uneven dispersion of new flavours

Menus of the 1950s in restaurants in Britain read as a miscellaneous list of dishes, internationally recognisable but without justification in terms of national or regional provenance. Entries to the *GFG* for Manchester in 1951 began with the Rendezvous Restaurant:

> [The Rendezvous Restaurant] specializes in exotic dishes, Chinese and Arabic. Try the Chow Mein or Chicken Pilaff, or ask for the special Chinese menu; if taking coffee, ask for Turkish. Unlicensed and service is slow, which is not unusual with careful cooking. Good Italian food (ravioli, spaghetti) but they shouldn't serve chips with it.[33]

Subsequently, restaurants came to specialise in named cuisines, dishes usually signalled as having origins in a national culinary tradition, more or less authentically reproduced. As Panayi observed, dishes, as represented both in cookery books and on restaurant menus, acquired explicit nationality only in the post-war period. Before then, the culinary origins of the dishes were a matter of very little concern. Thereafter, authenticity became a major dimension of practical and aesthetic differentiation as restaurants signal their dedication to specific national cuisines[34] – Italian, Greek, Mexican, Thai, and so on. These are recognisably 'foreign', arguably the most appropriate term to capture the idea that while people mostly cannot articulate the defining principles of their own 'native' cuisine they nevertheless can identify exceptions and deviations from it.[35] So while unable to pin down what makes a dish British, I am confident that neither moussaka nor Thai green curry is one.

Attempts to define a British cuisine began to surface in the mid-1960s propelled to the fore by the rapid expansion of the numbers of restaurants specialising in named foreign cuisines in the 1960s and 1970s. Raymond Postgate, in an editorial in the *GFG* in 1966, summed up his review of developments as 'a sour catalogue of the continuing inadequacies of British catering'. Most foreign observers considered British restaurant food appalling. He continued by saying '[b]ut the least forgivable inadequacy ... is the absence of any British cuisine at all'.[36] Restaurants faced several difficulties in establishing both local and international reputation. One was the absence of a continuous noble culinary tradition. Britain had had a good reputation for its food in the early modern period, but fell into abeyance after the onset of the nutrition transition in the 18th century. In the 20th century it was difficult to identify qualities that were specifically British. One source of this problem was that no distinctive flavour principles were associated with British food. A second was the long-term decline of regional differentiation, a feature which has greatly enhanced the culinary reputations of France and Italy, for example. Third, a major expansion in the purveying of foreign, ethnic or exotic cuisine exposed the lack of innovation in British cooking.

In the later 1970s, with the identity of British cuisine on the agenda, the *GFG* ran a campaign for Real Food which advocated the superiority of fresh, locally produced, high quality raw materials as the basic prerequisite of good cooking.[37] This became the basis for the style named Modern British Cooking, which Drew Smith in an editorial in 1987 hailed as evidence of '[t]he British revival'. The piece claims that '[o]ur national cooking has reasserted itself' and that '[w]here even a year ago there seemed to be no sign of a national cooking with its own identity, suddenly here it is. For the first time since the end of rationing, British cooks are producing British dishes that bear comparison to the major cuisines'.[38] Smith defined Modern British Cooking in terms of five themes: regionality, market produce, the relishes and spices, the garden and the tradition.

Very soon afterwards another significant development was announced by Jim Ainsworth, the next editor from 1995, who praised 'a new British tradition', distinctive because 'eclectic'. He asserted that contemporary British cuisine was characterised primarily by its flexible appropriation of ideas from other cuisines. In his first editorial he said:

> [T]he restaurant scene has never been so exciting. Many restaurants, as ever, specialise in a particular style of cooking or a national cuisine. ... But just look at what else is happening. Hundreds of dishes, in scores of restaurants, do not fit easily into any single national framework. Tagliolini with ceps and creme fraiche, steamed mussels with curry spices and coriander, roast quail with wild mushrooms and polenta, and lamb steaks

with parsley pesto and Spanish butter-beans. Those are all from just one menu in one restaurant. What a glorious mix.

And this particular brew could only happen here. No other country has quite the same blend of British, French, Italian, Spanish, Indian, Chinese, Thai and other cultures to call on. In that sense, diverse as it all is, it is very British, full of real invention and the sheer exuberance of let's-have-a-go cookery. ... It is British in the sense that Britain is the melting pot. British cooking is no longer defined by just what we grow here, or by traditional recipes and techniques. It is the sum of what we cook here.

British restaurants, and their customers, have been receptive to all this, perhaps, because Britain's food culture is less sharply drawn than some others – a state of affairs seen as something of a handicap until now – and it provides a gap waiting to be filled with whatever ideas can be pinched from elsewhere.[39]

This poses very immediate questions like what might be British about the cuisine since it is explicitly not 'defined by what we grow here, or by traditional recipes and techniques', and what is meant by a new tradition. The metaphor of the melting pot, one often applied to the United States, conjures up a void filled by absorbing and adapting features from other cultures. It appears to acknowledge multiculturalism but posits its transcendence into a transcultural eclecticism which might be considered a creative response to the opportunities afforded by globalisation and contrasted with the more backward-looking and locally focused Modern British Cooking.

By the beginning of the 21st century it had become increasingly difficult to assign menus to specific national cuisines. It was not that gastronationalism had collapsed, but the restaurant trade promoted hybridity, as chefs mixed flavours from different culinary traditions in much the way that a postmodern culture would propose. During the 1990s, British chefs had increasingly incorporated the ingredients, combinations and flavours of exotic cuisines into their menus and upmarket restaurants constructed menus divorced from culinary pedigrees.[40] One example that has stuck with me is Birdcage, London

W1, which the *GFG* awarded 3/10 for its cooking and described its style as 'Fusion-Plus':

> [I]nstead of butter with the bread, you get a dish of pumpkin puree flavoured with green tea and wasabi ... scorpion ('vaguely nutty in taste') appears as both a canapé and, chocolate covered, for dessert ... black-ink hen terrine with white truffles, goat consommé with Irish moss and wakame tartlet, cactus rice knapsacks in a pan-leaf canvas wrap ... starter of pine-smoked reindeer carpaccio with anchovy, wasabi and tomato chutney ... main course of risotto of seaweed, porcini and hemp with coriander marscapone ... [desserts of] tagine-steamed cinnamon and quark jaggery ... gum leaf and wheatgrass brulée.[41]

Hybridity and eclecticism continue to flourish, nowhere more obviously than in tasting menus. Ambitious chefs and aspiring restaurants currently offer a succession of small plates designed to display their skill, talent and inventiveness. Any number of dishes upward from five will be served. Generally, the order follows the starter–main–dessert courses format, with several plates served in succession for each course. There is no choice. The primary guiding principles behind the menu are diversity and quality of ingredients, variety and intensity of flavours and textures, and artful aesthetic appearance. Exquisite, inventive and creative, complementary textures and flavours, a palette for chefs to entertain and impress. It simulates a traditional banquet on a miniature scale; many dishes are available and the diner can try all of them.[42] It appeared as a format in the UK in the mid-2000s and became highly fashionable, encapsulating current principles of excellence in the fine dining sector, although at the time of writing restaurant critics seem to be tiring of it. Expensive, often very expensive, and exclusively commercial, it has no domestic parallel.[43] It embodies professional principles of good taste. It sets certain standards and expectations. Its defining characteristic and main priority is its combination of maximum variety and attention to detail in presentation. Its many small dishes are chosen for contrast; for example, one I encountered had 85 different ingredients in 14 dishes without any of the ingredients appearing twice. Some written menus are indeed nothing but a list of ingredients, with no hint as to how they might be combined (see Box 4.2). It exalts and worships variety. The contrast with the limited and repetitious aspects of post-war menus could not be more stark. The discursive guiding principle is aesthetics. It is important that what is presented on the plate is beautiful; in that regard it learned from *nouvelle cuisine*, inheriting some principles including not only attractive appearance but also contrasts and combinations of flavours and textures. By 2020 the tasting menu was the pinnacle of good taste, although it was more trans- than multi- cultural.

In retrospect, the absence of a sense of national cuisine seems to have been relatively unimportant. It may have mattered in the 17th century but not by the 19th. Whereas the state in France reveres French cuisine, which it is proud of and wishes to boast about to other countries, the British state showed almost no interest in trying to create an image or impression of the distinctiveness of British food. Tourist boards tried fitfully to define a British cuisine at the point it became profitable to accord food a national identity but Britain seems poorly endowed with the material and historical resources to lay claim to an integrated and aesthetically distinctive culinary heritage.

Cultural intermediation and the normalisation of foreign food: the flavours of a revolution?

The habits of the majority White British population were probably more influenced by migrants than many European countries, and perhaps were affected at a slightly earlier point in time when allowing permanent settlement of immigrants from different parts of the Commonwealth before the 1960s. As Panayi shows, ethnic minorities made a very significant contribution to the retail and catering industries, setting up and working in businesses centred on the foods of their countries of origin. New migrants usually have to make immediate adjustments to their consumption and by the second generation have adopted many majority food practices, not because of social assimilation but because the available food in commercial outlets and the host country's institutions make avoidance difficult. The commercial cultural environment steers behaviour, putting otherwise preferred options beyond reach. Ultimately, global trade in commodities is probably a greater determinant than specific

Box 4.2: A tasting menu (Aizle, Edinburgh)

I have entirely arbitrarily selected a menu from a meal I had with friends in the Edinburgh restaurant Aizle in late 2021 as one of many possible examples of how a restaurant is able to prepare and present a meal in a way that would be unrepeatable in the domestic kitchen. It also indicates a form of fragmentation (and not reducing to named dishes on menus), of eclectic arrangement of very specialised and in some cases obscure, ingredients, to construct a novel dining experience. It requires quite a number of customers to make it work, as it needs to use very small amounts of expensive or arcane ingredients in any single serving (so requires the bulk buying power of a commercial outlet).

Aizle
Ingredients list
koji
marmite
sweet potato
rose
beetroot
curds
wild mushrooms
black truffle
venison
pumpkin
day boat fish
artichoke
Scottish beef
salsify
apple
marigold
sorrel
chocolate
whisky

patterns of migration for explaining the introduction of new tastes. Certainly, many popular foreign cuisines are not dependent on a relevant migrant presence.

Migration into the UK, especially from the colonies and the Commonwealth, introduced new tastes as well as supplying many workers to the catering and food supply chains. Britain's 65 million residents in 2021 inhabit a culinary space which affords an almost infinite number of possible combinations of ingredients. They navigate individually among millions of recorded recipes. They have access to supermarkets, restaurants and takeaways which supply dishes and meals which have flavours drawn from most areas of the globe. Globalisation and commodification are powerful forces driving change but insufficient as a full explanation in the absence of identifiable mechanisms for forming new habits. Attention to the processes of cultural intermediation, the increasing communication of advice about how to eat, is crucial. The messages circulated are often discordant and contradictory but patterns based on shared meanings do emerge. Collective preferences can accumulate over time to establish an impression of commonly shared tastes, sometimes even amounting to a tradition, culinary heritage or a national cuisine. Shared understandings arising from education, family experience, eating with others, menus, food journalism and recipes steer individual behaviour and generate *social* patterns.

Learning to incorporate foreign foods is a pivotal, and perhaps *the* major development since the 1950s in what people habitually eat. It is one prop for the thesis of revolutionary change – it affects many levels and aspects of food acquisition and appropriation – and is the most arresting feature among people old enough to have experience prior to 1970. Among a group of TCP interviewees in 2015, those born before 1960 had much more to say about change and pointed to increased variety of ingredients, flavours and menus, to diversity of habits, and to the impact of 'new styles of food'.[44] But if the process of normalisation of foreign cuisines was significant, it was also slow. Already underway for 60 years it is still incomplete. This is partly because much of the innovation in restaurants and food manufacturing factories is hard to transfer into the domestic kitchen. Nothing further distances restaurant provision from domestic practice than the tasting menu. In addition, the process of sensory taste is intertwined with social taste and status. People force themselves to like, or at least to accept, initially unpalatable items – hot, spicy and bitter foods are incorporated as marks of cultivation. For example, middle-class parents seem inordinately pleased when their small children are prepared to eat a wide variety of unusual savoury foodstuffs. The two senses of taste do not operate independently of one another, as will be seen in Chapter 6. Before that, consider domestic practices of food preparation.

5

Meal Preparation

If the restaurant is the site *par excellence* for expansive experiences with food, variety is certainly not spurned in other contexts. Nevertheless, meal content in domestic settings is constrained by time, daily routines, awareness of the preferences of those around the table, cooking skills, the availability of the herbs and spices that differentiate flavourings, as well as imagination. Market research reports estimate now and again how many dishes domestic cooks prepare and press reports emphasise the limited repertoires of the average household. A typical headline message might be the *Daily Mirror* reporting an Ocado survey of 2015 as showing that 'people only cook the same nine meals on a repetitive loop' and that '[o]ne in five people have not changed that menu for over a year'.[1] The exact numbers should be taken with a pinch of salt, but it is unlikely that more than a minority of regular domestic cooks have more than 20 recipes at their command. Enthusiasts who frequently try out new recipes may have many more, but by and large household dinner is a matter of routine and repetition. The same dishes are served very regularly. Weekly household diaries show that dinner plates sport commonly recognisable dishes of mixed provenance but narrow range.[2] Meals are not thereby as monotonous as they once were for large tranches of the working classes. Although not universally applicable – we have already noted the limited fare available to the clients of food banks (see Chapter 3) – home-prepared meals are interspersed with meals bought from supermarkets (and restaurants) which supply a wider range of dishes that may be beyond the competence of many domestic cooks.

Household work and divisions of labour

Meals require preparation. Much paid labour is involved. In 2021 just over four million people, 13 per cent of the employed population, were employed in the food sector – agriculture, food manufacture, distribution, retailing and catering.[3] Imports account for a further massive contribution to Britain's consumption and they too embody vast amounts of paid labour, in growing, preserving and transporting foodstuffs. Paid labour in the formal economy makes a huge input into the production and distribution of the food eaten.

Yet another massive contribution comes from unpaid labour in the domestic and communal sectors. Self-servicing plays a central role in the modern economy. Every household meal involves planning, shopping, cooking and coordination. The repetitive tasks of domestic labour are essential to the way everyday life is organised, to the physical and social reproduction of the whole population. How that labour has been organised and distributed has changed over time and has been a major source of controversy since the 1960s. Two highly contentious issues are intertwined. One is the way in which the domestic labour tasks are distributed between household members, particularly between men and women. This was a major issue in gender politics in the second half of the 20th century. The other concerns the virtues of household provisioning and the proportion of the necessary labour time to undertake in-house and how much to outsource to market provision. This is part of a broad critique of commodification which expresses concern and suspicion over the ever greater intrusion of market forces into private lives.

Juliet Schor contends that we have come to live in a 'work and spend' culture where we enter employment in order to earn the money to buy the goods which, under other socioeconomic arrangements, might be made by us or our friends and acquaintances.[4] Her analysis raises issues about use of time, levels of consumption and the quality of work. Not only do people purchase almost all the food that they eat, they also purchase increasing amounts of equipment to facilitate eating. Kitchens and areas for eating contain goods of many kinds which emanate from the maturation of the system of mass production and consumption in the second half of the 20th century. Most British households possess a refrigerator, a freezer, a microwave, a cooker with timing devices, and probably a dishwasher and a food processor too, not to mention cupboards, pans, utensils, crockery and tables. All require money, mostly sourced as income from employment. A further substantial proportion of income is devoted to refurbishing houses, a part of which involves the regular refitting of kitchens.[5]

Electrical goods and devices are often said to save labour and time. They certainly eliminate hard manual labour but do not remove the need for work per se. Indeed effective technologies may lead to more frequent engagement in tasks, as standards rise and devices require maintenance.[6] Whether overall they save time is also debatable. It seems to me that many key devices like fridge, freezer and microwave are more significant because they make it possible to reorder and reschedule tasks in way increasingly necessary to deal with problems of timing and social coordination in the face of disrupted societal rhythms.[7] This throws light on the appeal of 'convenience' food.

Work is often unwelcome and may be very unfulfilling, especially when subjected to the external control of employers. However, cooking at home, while certainly work, is not necessarily miserable or exploitative; domestic provision, in the form of 'cooking from scratch', has some economic, health and moral virtues lost in processes of market exchange. This chapter explores some of the features of the domestic division of labour and the transfer of activity into and out of the market sphere. In these matters we discover much about what the preparation of meals means to people and how that has relatively slowly changed over the decades since the end of the Second World War.

Gender and cooking: women and men in the kitchen

Food preparation has been a mystery to most men throughout history. Men, with the exception of those in catering occupations, ate food but didn't prepare it. The sociological evidence from British studies of families, households and communities, which is about 75 years young, demonstrated that cooking at home was almost exclusively a role for women. After the 'servant crisis' of the 1920s and 1930s food preparation became a set of tasks which fell to women of all classes to perform. For decades, whether they had the skills, aptitude, temperament or patience, women did almost all the cooking. This was often felt as a burden, although often also viewed simultaneously as an achievement and as an expression of care and love. The pride, love and self-sacrifice associated with providing for a family reinforced attachments to gendered roles.[8] The associated tensions permeated the recipe columns of women's magazines in the mid-century.

These features of the status quo came under increasingly intense scrutiny in the 1960s. In that much misunderstood decade, new social movements emerged to campaign for relief from the social and cultural domination of upper-class White men. The language of the civil rights movement and second wave feminism in particular protested against dependence. In parallel, mainstream politics reshaped citizenship by extending equal social rights. The second of the two world wars produced a political settlement which gradually unrolled systems of social insurance and equality of opportunity which modified the class hierarchies of bourgeois Europe. Labour movements sought restitution for the sacrifice of working-class lives. The women's movement demanded independence and the slogan of second wave feminism, 'the personal is political', inspired some recognition of the unequal gender distribution of labour within family households.

The social world of the 1960s was still envisaged as overwhelmingly populated by heterosexual couples and was organised in their interests. Social policies assumed that matrimony was both the normal and the ideal state, and designed welfare and tax systems to encourage its survival. The male breadwinner wage arrangement was still common, divorce was not yet so prevalent, children were expected to be raised in a nuclear family which was still the basis of household organisation. In addition, the prospects of prosperity raised by the post-war settlement stimulated dreams and aspirations.

The early empirical studies of domestic divisions of labour, inspired by feminist agitation, which were carried out in the 1970s and 1980s, showed that while men might wash dishes after meals and perhaps go shopping for food (usually accompanying their wives) they took little effective part in meal preparation. Very occasionally a man might fry breakfast or singe meat on a barbecue, but in the main they received meals, sometimes gratefully and graciously, sometimes critically and bitterly, but mostly in a taken-for-granted and habituated way. For example, in a study of couple households containing young children in the north of England in the early 1980s,

Charles and Kerr described the orthodox arrangement of family meals.[9] The meal was cooked, by the female partner, and served to all members of the household. A study of mature adults with teenage children still at home conducted in 1990 showed some modification to traditional patterns in a minority of households to accommodate women's careers, with part-time employment replacing the full-time housewife, but little evidence of change since the 1960s.[10] Men had cooked or shared in preparation of the most recent dinner in 16 per cent of households, whereas a woman had been engaged in 84 per cent of last meals. Nevertheless, both ultimate authority and day-to-day responsibility for planning and organising family eating still fell to women; if outcomes were unacceptable blame would be attached to the woman.[11] The template of the ideal family meal survives.

Challenges to such arrangements continue and there is evidence of gradual change. Sullivan demonstrates that the process of levelling up is slow.[12] Most of the research in the later 20th century showed increasing homage being paid to the idea of sharing domestic tasks within couples, but without a great deal of change in behaviour. It was noted that men sometimes carried out domestic tasks popularly stereotyped as feminine, sometimes because there was no alternative, sometimes because they quite liked doing them (ironing and cleaning lavatories not being included in that category), but also increasingly because they were persuaded that in principle they ought to. An ideology of companionate marriage was becoming dominant. This went in association with greater diversity in models of masculinity. According to Neuman and colleagues, at least in Sweden a principal element of the contemporary hegemonic form of masculinity, one which is softer and more family-centred, expects a capacity and readiness to prepare family meals.[13] Not to do so would be a source for dishonour among young men. It seems unlikely that this is yet the case in the UK although younger men are more engaged than their fathers in food preparation.[14]

There is some evidence of greater movement. Male partners in 2015 had prepared the last main meal on 25 per cent of occasions (and shared in 6 per cent more), an increase of 6 per cent (and 3 per cent) on 1995. Women had prepared dinner alone on 64 per cent of occasions, 10 per cent fewer than in 1995. Cooking perhaps has begun to give men some kudos, no longer compromising masculinity. More men express interest in cooking; a majority of men in the TCP in 2015 claimed to be interested or quite interested in cooking. If translated into general practice that would herald a significant cultural as well as a culinary development. Men appear on television cooking programmes and compete on *Masterchef*. Professional middle-class families find it acceptable that their sons should go to catering college and plan a career in the restaurant business. Men are more likely to harbour professional ambitions and to want to show off their competence at home.[15] Kitchens become emblematic of male aspirations, with fine big stoves and streamlined machines, as part of a cycle of endless refurbishment.[16] The reasons why some men never cook may be the same as earlier, but indubitably men cook more than in the 1950s.

Although this marks a readjustment of gender roles, the extent of its institutionalisation warrants some scepticism, as it may be little more than pragmatic adjustment to external pressures. Men do a greater proportion of household cooking because women are spending less time on food preparation than before, rather than because men have heavily increased their involvement. The amount of time spent preparing meals has been declining for several decades. In 1975 in the UK cooking took on average 57 minutes per day, and if we consider only those who did some cooking, the mean was 76. By 2000 the equivalent figures were 41 and 50.[17] It is a lighter burden that is being shared. Ironically, the rise in obesity over the same period implies that despite spending less time both cooking and eating levels of consumption are not reduced.

One reason why cooking time falls is because most people have only one domestically prepared meal each day. In the 1950s a majority of the population had two cooked meals per day, and possibly a cooked breakfast as well, almost all at home.[18] Changing household composition and changes in work patterns including more and longer journeys to work made space for the midday sandwich, the ubiquity of which symbolises the end of the cooked lunch on weekdays. In 2012 more than half of lunches were sandwiches, sometime accompanied by soup or by confectionery.[19] Some sandwiches are made up at home, but many are purchased on the high street, as is much of the soup. As noted earlier, breakfasts too were very simple in 2012, on weekdays a large majority of those who ate breakfast ate cereals and/or toast. With exceptions mainly at weekends, most people eat one home-cooked meal per day, increasingly in the (early) evening. The occasions where cooking might be required are therefore fewer than in the middle of the 20th century, although perhaps not much different from 1995. Paradoxically, greater mass and social media attention to the culinary arts parallels the reduction and simplification of domestic cookery.

Another reason for men's increasing participation is necessity. Many households would be seriously deprived of opportunities to eat meals if men never cooked them. Hungry children and disruptive hours of employment for women mean that men cannot avoid preparing meals.[20] It seems that when men cook they tend to feel virtuous, their marriages are happier and they may quite enjoy the activity, but they will be doing so in many cases because for practical purposes there is no alternative. When alternative arrangements are possible practice reverts to the default position; a common rationale for male avoidance is that because women have shorter hours of employment and get home first it is only sensible that they prepare the evening meal.[21]

Third, controversy about how much has changed is confounded because most research is about nuclear family households containing a heterosexual couple with children. That is of course the most meaningful data for exploring gender inequalities, but they comprise a diminishing proportion of the total population. In 2022 in the UK there were 28.2 million households of which 30 per cent contained only one person (compared to 11 per cent in 1951). With changes in life expectancy and in household and family composition the national distribution of labour in the kitchen must alter. The presence of children is particularly significant as the volume of work is greatest then, but only about 30 per cent of households contain dependent children. As Kaufmann observes when looking at changes over the life cycle, as children leave home, women who never liked cooking (and some who did) find that their willingness to continue to prepare food evaporates.[22] Having recourse to alternatives to the ideal family meal is understandable, as is the fact that a significant proportion of households with children (O'Connell and Brannen suggest about a quarter[23]) never eat together in the evening on weekdays. Many factors compromise the necessary condition of being all in the same place at the same time, including 'parents' combined work schedules, children's extra-curricular commitments, their ages, the size of the family and the degree to which food tastes and preferences are shared and catered for'.[24]

Commodification and the value of convenience

Culinary and nutritional fates nowadays lie in the hands of markets, which we are deceivingly assured maximise economic efficiency. The industrialised system of food manufacturing, coordinated by capital investment and market distribution, provides anything from processed ingredients to complete dishes. You can buy wheat already ground into flour, tomatoes turned into puree or sauce, beef already butchered, pasta dried and peas podded, so when I make meatballs for dinner the effort and skill required has occurred much of the time somewhere other than in my kitchen. Self-provisioning has been in decline over a very long period, despite some much publicised ventures in community gardens and allotments, and cooking follows the same trajectory. This has met with varying degrees of disapproval, often expressed as suspicion of convenience foods.

In mid-20th century home cooking stood for both housewifely virtue and resistance to excessive commodification. Recourse to convenience foods signified dereliction of housewifely duties. The process of commodification was a contentious issue throughout most of the 20th century.[25] At its core is a moral conviction that certain things should not be bought and sold because they are too precious. As part of a widespread idealisation of the family meal – irrespective of the fact that food was no longer to any significant degree based on self-provision, or that pans, crockery and kitchen machinery were almost exclusively mass-produced in factories – a view prevailed that foodstuffs in the final stage of preparation should incorporate the work of a household member.

Home-made stood for the virtues of both motherhood and housewifery. However, it became hard in the 1960s for women (and the cultural intermediaries serving them) to justify being 'only' a housewife. Whether and when mothers should go out to work was highly disputed. An ideological battle raged over the moral and economic dimensions of the role of the full-time housewife. Expectations and justifications altered over time, from being a full-time housewife for ever after marriage, to while there were children at home, to while there were preschool children at home, prior to putting children into nursery, to how few weeks before return to employment. The nub of the domestic labour debate concerned the fairness of arrangements in an era after the male breadwinner wage.

Elaborate and regular daily cooking is avoidable. Available alternatives include eating out, bringing foods from takeaway outlets into the home, and buying a 'ready meal' from a supermarket. The ready meal challenges the norm of daily cooking. The propensity for many meals to be taken in restaurants or to be assembled at home from partly or fully prepared components continues to be treated with suspicion, although not directly condemned. Women's magazines have continued to present cooking from scratch as virtuous, implying that use of convenience foods might be seen as a potential abrogation of caring responsibility, while simultaneously explicitly reassuring hard-pressed readers that in many instances it could be condoned.[26] The suggestion is that compromise is normal, pre-prepared dishes can be acceptable, and the ready meal or the packaged sauce is a tool in the culinary armoury for a great many households. Nevertheless, there remains something mildly disreputable about relying on convenience food. Domestic cooking remains strongly associated with care for household members, the obligation of care impinging primarily on women, especially mothers.[27] Cooking from scratch is much vaunted in some quarters because it has symbolic significance.

Ready meals get a bad press – though there again the press is very often bad. The ready meal captures well the pervasive tension between care and convenience. Some people strongly deprecate their use, although that may be hypocritical given the evidence of the extent of their everyday usage. Ready meals are part of the repertoires of most households. The suitability of convenience products in food delivery and serving has become a very strongly entrenched notion. Acceptability of labour-saving and labour-concealing techniques can be traced in images of household meals in the periodical press. Teresa Davis and colleagues show how the aura of domestic labour has been transformed as images of women in advertisements for food products come to be sited at the table rather than in the kitchen.[28] Sociable consumption at the table rather than domestic work in the kitchen is made to represent a woman's place in the household.

In praise of convenience

What is a convenient product? The public in answering survey questions in 2015 will probably not consider flour and dried pasta as pre-prepared items. One strategy for domestic cooks uneasy about pre-prepared foods is to adapt and build upon or around pre-prepared ingredients. Adding personal touches or cooking fresh vegetables as accompaniments customises industrially manufactured food and imparts some semblance of being home-made. Oddly, contemporary campaigners for cooking from scratch evoke a strange mixture of nostalgia for housewifery and mothers in the kitchen, an obsession with nutrition, and hostility to large food manufacturing corporations. The complaint is less about the simplification of meals and more about the use of pre-prepared foods and dishes like the ready meal.

The ready availability in supermarkets of fully pre-prepared meals, ones which require nothing other than removal of the packaging and the application of heat, is revolutionary for domestic provisioning. At their best they allow people to eat meals of a kind and a quality equivalent to those supplied by the catering trade in their own homes and with minimal effort. Opinion varies on their merits: some bemoan their role in the reduction of cooking from scratch; others are more accepting, but still reflect widespread concern about both the healthiness and the moral rectitude of recourse to convenience products. Their spread is undeniable. Most households make some use of these products. Asked in the TCP survey in 2015 'How often is a cooked, chilled or frozen ready meal served as a main meal in your home?', 11 per cent replied 'every day', 28 per cent said 'several times a week', while 28 per cent of respondents said 'never'. To the companion question, 'How often is a main meal prepared in your home from fresh or basic ingredients?', 54 per cent responded 'every day' and a further 37 per cent 'several times per week'. Should we consider this surprisingly much or surprisingly little?

Ready meals are a means for commercial organisations to add value through extra processing in pursuit of greater profit. They vary significantly in price, but the same dish cooked at home from the same ingredients of equivalent quality would usually be cheaper. Economy favours home cooking as does concern about control over ingredients; there is always suspicion that the manufacturer will use lower quality ingredients, perhaps use more parts of the animal, add water, use fillers by replacing the prime ingredients with cheaper substitutes. Some ready meals approach toxicity. Nevertheless others, often more expensive, contain only ingredients recommended in domestic cookbooks.

To be sure, there are good reasons for avoiding *some* ready meals. They increase the dependence of the population on large corporations (especially manufacturers of meals and supermarkets) and reduce the knowledge and ability of ordinary people to grow and cook food. Ready meals require packaging and some of them use unsavoury additives and chemicals for preservation. The nutritional balance is also problematic with some high in sugar and fat. People have greater trust in raw ingredients than in manufactured foods – particularly apparent when mothers talk about providing for their babies and younger children – although that may be misplaced as it has been suggested that commercially produced baby food is likely to be closer to the recommended levels of energy density, and also perhaps of fat, sugar and salt, than the foods prepared from scratch at home.

The social and emotional significance of cooking from scratch, and the dubious nature of its opposite, is revealed in practices associated with domestic hospitality. There has been an unwritten rule that when entertaining guests the food served should be cooked from scratch. Reticence about offering ready meals to guests reflects the symbolic capacity for home-cooking to mark social relationships of mutual respect and care for others. Hosts have been very reluctant to admit that the meal they are serving has been bought, lock, stock and barrel from a commercial outlet, occasionally pretending to have made themselves items purchased already prepared.[29] However, the prohibition is being relaxed. The template of the dinner party persists, its formal rules more frequently observed by the higher social classes. Almost by mutual consent, it is becoming acceptable to buy one or more courses from a shop or indeed a whole takeaway meal. Some pre-prepared stuff is acceptable so long as it is interwoven with some home-prepared items. Within some social networks collective decisions are made to circumvent the earlier obligation to do it all yourself, endorsing the increasingly common practice of guests bringing one or more courses. Younger people are more likely to increase that proportion having grown up without strong internalised suspicion of the convenience products of the food industry; a Belgian study, for example, found that it is mostly older people who cook primarily from scratch.[30] Other options are acceptable. One professional woman in her late 60s, interviewed for TCP, considering herself a poor cook repays debts for meals received as a guest by taking her hosts to a restaurant. The more relaxed approach to entertaining guests is another strand of the process of informalisation which accepts more alternatives and further entangles commercial and domestic provision.

Overall, while home-cooked meals may be neither technically superior nor better in taste (some ready meals are superb), an entrenched prejudice persists that meals are better if cooked by someone who is in a personal relationship with the diner, although equating personal labour with emotional connection may be diminishing.

Experimenting with convenience

The ready meal is in many contexts an excellent creation. It is one step further along the chain of processing than pre-prepared ingredients. It is now possible to eat to a very varied menu, orthodox or exotic, day by day, by doing nothing more than applying heat to preserved, fully prepared dishes. I know because I spent a fortnight doing exactly that. For two weeks I did no food preparation except applying heat to pre-prepared foodstuffs. I ate items like cheese, tomatoes and fruit in the form that I bought them; I heated ready meals in an oven and steamed frozen vegetables; I warmed baked beans decanted from a can and toasted bread. All labour was not eliminated. I shopped. I washed fruit and salad leaves. I removed packaging. I arranged items on plates. The upshot was that I saved time. It did not appreciably reduce the variety of my diet. I was perhaps required to mobilise some understanding of taste and nutrition, and I read labels to vet ingredients in order to avoid chemical preparations, but did not deploy the skills of cooking. A mix of frozen vegetables and frozen or chilled main dishes, supported by packaged carbohydrates, provided me with a nourishing, nutritious, tasty and very varied diet. I ate curry and rice, fish pie and peas, and moussaka. The result, I declare, was perfectly satisfactory.

Many meals were better aesthetically than I could cook myself and some the equal of all but very fine restaurants. I ate no e-numbers, only free-range meats. I could easily have ensured that I consumed no more salt or fat than usual, and restricted myself to a count of calories in accordance with official guidelines. In fact, ready meals maintain portion control much more effectively than I can as a domestic cook. After the experiment I find it difficult to see why people do not have more frequent recourse to ready meals.

I did have some regrets. It upset my routines, for on days when I work from home preparing dinner is a boundary separating professional toil from leisure. I was deprived of the capacity to exercise my only technical and manual skill. It also meant that some dishes were out of the question – omelettes and scrambled eggs, for example. Others that are available are less good because of loss of flavour or especially texture, including fish and chips, roast potatoes, risotto. Some dishes I can cook better than the factory and other items can be displaced from my domestic setting to places of public restauration. Like many of my compatriots, I eat out often enough to replace the dishes eliminated from my home. Indeed, it is arguable that the main process of substitution occurring with the ready meal is a matter of competition between supermarkets and the restaurant trade. Finally, I felt a little uncomfortable or belittled, anxious that my social reputation and moral rectitude would be endangered if I stopped eating home-made food.

I conclude that the ready meals available in the supermarket provide for most people a much wider range of tastes and ingredients than could be supplied out of even a relatively highly skilled cook's repertoire. The costs, the waste, the uncertainty associated with producing in my own kitchen the flavours of India, several regions of China, Mexico, Thailand and Japan, using exotic spices and so on, are avoided. I also saved a considerable amount of time each day, although during this short experimental period I was rather at a loss as to what to do with the time regained. No doubt I would arrive at a new set of routines which would make an extra 40 minutes per day valuable.

Of course, I had some reservations about this solution to my nutritional and aesthetic requirements. Cost, luckily for me, was not one of those. While the dishes cost more than the raw ingredients would, mass production keeps prices relatively low, there is no waste, one-person sized dishes provide controlled portions, and a single shopping expedition meant that I used less petrol than my normal twice-a-week visits to food outlets. It is not clear, on balance, that I spent any more money than usual. For me, variety, quality and freshness were not compromised and I certainly spent less effort and time in preparing my dinners. It takes less time to scan the labels than to prepare the same food from raw materials.

Of course if I had only a small amount of money to devote to food and had children to feed the story would probably be different. Households in the bottom decile in the year 2019–2020, just before the COVID-19 pandemic, spent £45.60, 18 per cent of total expenditure, on food. To buy only prepared meals under such financial constraints would severely compromise the quality of ingredients and the composed dishes. Reading the list of ingredients in some of the cheaper frozen and chilled packages often fails to inspire confidence. Everyone can eat ready meals nowadays: but in an unequal society some are more pure, more tasty, better sourced and more expensive than others.[31]

Perhaps, then, cooking from scratch is overrated. Some very fresh foodstuffs and some freshly cooked dishes are superior in flavour, texture and aroma. Yet, freezing at the point of harvesting preserves the flavour in some vegetables better than any supermarket can match with raw versions on the open shelf. Only a small number of dishes seem necessarily inferior as a result of having been subjected to cook-chill or freezing techniques. Airline omelettes, defrosted light white bread and oven-baked fish and chips are among the candidates. As Freidberg (2009) demonstrates so well, freshness itself is a highly contestable concept.[32] Preservation techniques, maximisation of shelf-life, facilities for cold storage, the process of ripening in transit, and so on, all destabilise common-sense understandings of what it means for an item to be fresh, rendering the association of freshness with quality hazardous.

Ready meals are a triumph of the modern organisation of the food manufacturing industry and a welcome corollary of effective processes for preserving foods and reducing domestic drudgery. Like snack foods, about which even greater suspicion is expressed, ready meals can be horrid and unhealthy, but many are not and they provide good food which is easy to deploy at home or at work to satisfy hunger. They also increase flexibility, making it easier to coordinate family meals because they do not require a period of cooking immediately before eating. In the light of these positive things, the standard explanation for the ascent of the ready meal, that it was caused by the entry of married women into employment in the post-war period, seems shallow.

Learn eating not cooking?

Campaigns to cement cooking classes into the school curriculum, for boys as well as girls, recur at regular intervals. One reaction might be to say that the instructions in cookbooks are now so detailed and precise that anyone who can read should be able to cook elaborate dishes. However, that would be a mistake since a great deal of tacit knowledge is required to follow a recipe. Cookery is a highly skilled craft activity and cooking badly is unrewarding hard labour. However, it does not follow that the subject is worth teaching in school.[33] There may be better things to learn than how to cook, and many better things to do than cooking. While contestants in cookery shows on television may be having great fun while entertaining millions of viewers, a yawning gap distances theatrical performances from the logic of everyday subsistence.

Perhaps we should reflect upon how much cooking matters. Almost certainly learning to cook is not a major contribution to progress, harmony and sustainability in the modern world. It may on occasions be fun – as Jay Rayner puts it, you probably should cook *sometimes*.[34] But the inspiration for that is probably less likely to come from compulsory cooking classes in school, and more from an appreciation of the taste of food and the pleasures of its consumption.

Wendy Leynse examined how French children come to learn an attachment to local produce and cuisine in a context. Based on examples of excursions for children and families – a school trip and food festivals – a naïve reporting of observations articulates 'how people come to understand, internalize and identify with a place (or places)'.[35] One example is a four-day field trip for 10-year-old school children living in a town in the Loire, in which they visit various historical monuments, landscapes and farms. A form of integrated pedagogy which includes science, agriculture, ecology, geography and food, the children are taken to talk to farmers, to pick strawberries and to smell wild mint in the hedgerows. These activities they record in the log of the trip, reporting appreciatively on experiences of tasting. This tells something about French understanding of both France and food, a condition possible because food already has a central place in national culture. This is one of many opportunities to reinforce the sense that food matters. Leynse describes mechanisms and processes which constitute the loose but tangible sense of belonging to a region; in this case a result of exposure to and identification with food products which are said to be, and treated as if they were, defining properties of a locale. France is conceptualised as a patchwork of local food areas, of which residents want to have knowledge and experience, to celebrate and derive meaning and pleasure from variation in produce and cuisine, and they start with their own. In the context of learning identities are created, rather routinely, sometimes by virtue of networks of others wanting you to learn, but in an integrated way across a range of practices.

France teaches taste rather than cooking. People can do without knowing how to cook; but it would help if they knew how to eat. Would it not be better to teach how to taste or how to eat rather than how to cook as has, for example, been tried, if with mixed results, in Italy through school dinners?[36] Liking to eat and liking to cook don't necessarily coincide. By analogy, I like drinking beer, and even believe I can discriminate between beers quite well, but I have never brewed any, nor had any inclination to do so – partly because of my experience of home-brewed beer which has rarely been as appealing in taste as the commercially manufactured stuff. Cooking was necessary for most of history, although only for some people: men and children have mostly been exempted, while the vast majority of adult women have been recruited for millennia. The wonder of the contemporary food supply system is that meals can be supplied to all with minimal domestic labour. Not only is a raw diet possible but labour need involve nothing much more than arranging already prepared foods on a plate. Why fret about limited cooking skills? Focusing on learning to eat rather than to cook might be better preparation for eating out and for selecting among pre-prepared supermarket dishes. It could encourage better political citizenship by passing on an understanding of the environmental consequences of the current food system. Of course, greater dependence upon commodities increases the centrality of the capitalist food industry, although it is less a matter of reduction of dependence on markets as movement between different markets. Perhaps, then, it is better to resist the urge to cook more often and determine to teach children more about the taste of food than about how to follow a recipe.[37]

Nevertheless, it might be conceded that cooking offers some satisfactions. It may relieve anxiety by giving better control over the quality and quantity of ingredients used and thereby enhance health status. It is an exercise of skill which generates the rewards associated with creating or making things. It promises bespoke meals, offering flexibility in meeting personal tastes. Also, few cooks would wish to forego gratitude and congratulation on having served a pleasant meal. Over time such provision expresses care, love and intimacy, generating binding ties and interdependence which justify the idealised family meal. Finally and not least, greater appreciation of food comes from engagement with preparing it and understanding its fabrication. As to whether these merits will continue to outweigh its annoying and burdensome features remains to be seen.

Labour and care revisited: residual virtues of cooking

A gendered division of labour persists although it is changing – slowly. The ideology of sharing tasks altered much faster. Cooking has acquired some status as a creative aesthetic activity. Many men have learned to cook, not entirely as a result of the normative commitment but because often they have little option. Nevertheless, cooking is one of the few glamorous and probably the least tedious of the regularly recurring and mundane household tasks.[38]

How the ideal of the family meal will stand up to the unremitting pressure of alternative commercial arrangements is debatable. While the household mode of provision is still predominant, the catering sector seduces consumers with small pleasant interludes and supermarkets parade meals for two. In the long run, justifications of behaviour adapt to actual practical changes. Flexible adaptation to evolving external circumstances is frequently disruptive; as O'Connell and Brannen say, at the personal level 'the complexities of family life' underpin 'the dynamic nature of eating arrangements'.[39] Whether pragmatic shifts in behaviour will remove the overarching responsibility of women for ensuring that families are fed is questionable, for so long as men generally have greater power, resources and opportunities, deficits in the exercise of domestic responsibility are unlikely to be laid at their door.

But why bother with inconvenience? Cooking was once a central matter of housewifely duties, but the obligation has lessened. Household composition, family relations and family ideology have moved on since the 1960s. Greater autonomy and more options mean that people can be more flexible in their ways of provisioning themselves and their households. Cooking is not all drudgery; it is a practice from which many obtain the satisfactions of exercising practical skills, expressing care for others, and even contesting the ever greater encroachment of processes of commodification in everyday life. Nevertheless it may be better to foster an appreciation of eating rather than cooking.

6

Eating with Style

The foodie syndrome

According to Ann Barr and Paul Levy, authors of *The Official Foodie Handbook* (*OFH*), the terms foodies and foodism were first coined by *Harpers & Queen* in August 1982.[1] That is over 40 years ago. They define a foodie as some who is 'very very very interested in food'.[2] The portrait painted is of a person who requires food to meet exacting quality standards, on the subject of which they will engage in obsessive discussion, to the point of boring most listeners to death on topics like fungi, offal and olive oil. They helpfully pose some indicative questions to their readers who might want to check whether they fall into the category (see Box 6.1).

OFH is serious humour. It simultaneously lampoons an affectation and compiles practical advice about what to buy and where to buy it. While foodies are presented as obsessive and slightly foolish, it recognises that some readers will be seeking to acquire knowledge to enhance their own pleasure in eating. To that end the authors alight upon symbolically significant aspects of an emergent, specialised, minority approach to eating.[3] They cover various dimensions of the activity – shopping, what to cook at home, fashionable kitchen equipment, which restaurants to visit and cuisines to sample, where across the world the best foods are to be found, and which celebrated names one should recognise in case they are introduced into conversation.

The questions in the quiz point to the importance of discernment, observation of technical standards, advanced and arcane knowledge about ingredients, techniques and personalities, aesthetic judgements, requirements of highest quality of and commitment to the practice

---

Box 6.1: Are you a Foodie?

Foodie tests of taste

1. What do you feel at the thought of missing a meal?
   A Relieved   B Hungry   C Incredulous
2. Do you taste your companion's food when dining out?
   A Never   B If you live with him or her   C Always
7. What is the most important invention since the wheel?
   A Atomic power   B The microchip   C The food processor
8. What do think of tomato ketchup?
   A Nice   B Nasty   C What is tomato ketchup?
10. What really matters?
    A Wealth   B Health   C That the fish is not overcooked

The correct answer is, of course, C in all instances.

Source: Barr and Levy (1984: 8)

---

of eating well. In the later 20th century this mindset was brought to many forms of recreation. In the 1960s, there was much discussion of the leisure society, in recognition that there was more time for many people to pursue activities beyond work and the reproduction of their labour power. Communally arranged and commercially provided opportunities multiplied. Do-it-yourself, gardening, motoring, physical exercise, and so on, which cross the divides between work and leisure and between market and non-market provision, garnered attention. In all such fields some participants became enthusiasts, devoting exceptional levels of time, effort, material resources and mental space to whatever activity they found personally meaningful and absorbing. Foodies were an example of such an orientation whose focus was the many dimensions of the practice of eating.

Barr and Levy's 'discovery' was prescient, previewing a set of social and cultural tendencies destined to increase in significance. Although imprecisely employed, the term foodie subsequently entered everyday vocabulary. Academics argue over its definition; the most authoritative scholarly study was satisfied with the depiction of an 'individual who is passionate about the pursuit of good food, with a longstanding passion for eating and learning about food':[4] Barr and Levy observed that a person with such a passionate and committed interest in food was previously referred to as a gourmet, who was 'typically a rich male amateur to whom food was a passion'.[5] As Mennell noted, such persons were not very prominent in Britain, unlike in France where gastronomy flourished. Barr and Levy averred, however, that the typical foodie was 'an aspiring professional couple to whom food is a fashion'.[6] Julie Parsons advocates using instead the term 'epicurean' to label one of five prevalent orientations to eating that she found among 75 autobiographical narratives collected around 2010.[7] The other orientations – which are readily recognisable as current and common rationales (she calls them 'foodways') – focus on family relations, maternal concern, health, and body management considerations. She defines the 'epicurean' orientation as taking 'particular sensual pleasure in "good" food and drink' and 'a connoisseur of good food; a person with a discerning palate'.[8]

OFH was a literary intervention, a humorous work based primarily on personal observation and anecdote. The figure of the foodie was a composite fictional character. However, there are good grounds for agreeing that the orientation did take hold in the later 20th century. Josie Johnston and Shyon Baumann, Canadian sociologists, confirmed its existence in the United States when they analysed the characteristics of self-professed food enthusiasts.[9] They showed how print media specialising in food had by the early 21st century begun to endorse and legitimise an aesthetic orientation towards eating. They interviewed self-professed foodies who present themselves as accomplished adjudicators of the quality of food and the experience of dining. These arbiters of fine foods and good taste celebrate a wide range of styles and types of cuisine, the simple and rustic as well as the refined and innovative. Foodies especially value 'authenticity' and 'exoticism'. They perceive themselves to be open to an omnivorous and equal engagement with diverse food cultures. Haute cuisine is thus toppled from its exclusive pedestal.

Something very similar happened in Britain where the term is now in common use. Almost every one of our interviewees in the TCP study in 2015 recognised the term. About a quarter used it as a term of abuse or disparagement, while another quarter happily applied it to themselves with a positive, if sometimes self-deprecating, glow. Those self-identifying as foodies were mostly not the fastidious and pernickety nerds lampooned by Barr and Levy. The self-identifiers were mostly women who exhibited an enthusiastic, inquiring orientation, open to a variety of new experiences and fully appreciating many aspects of eating.

It seems unlikely that foodie sensibilities could have spread beyond a tiny minority without the expansion of dining out. The experience of eating out and the increasing publicity given to restaurants were powerful influences on changing perceptions of good food and best practice. Central conceptions, discussions of standards, evaluation of ingredients and dishes were publicised in an increasing literature on upmarket restaurants, in guides designed to help consumers in their understanding and their decision-making and by restaurant critics in the newspapers after the 1990s. For initial experience of authentic and exotic dishes is unlikely to occur in a domestic setting. The tendency to prepare a wider range of foreign dishes at home was a lagged adaptation to exposure to restaurant and takeaway meals beginning in the 1960s. Clarissa Dickson Wright sees Delia Smith's three-volume recipe book accompanying a BBC television series (1998–2001) as a landmark for the introduction of dishes from a wide range of cuisines (not just French and Indian which had been apparent in the mid-20th century) into normal parts of a British household repertoire. The groundwork for that process of normalisation was laid by exposure to commercially provided foreign food eaten away from home.[10]

Dining out: a case study in changing tastes

Commercial opportunities to dine out grew considerably after the middle of the 20th century. Every city in England now contains a multitude of restaurants, of many different types, serving cuisines from across the world, at different levels of quality and a wide range of prices – the larger the city the more the alternatives. The dishes and menus available are not fundamentally different from other western countries, although the relative distribution of restaurants of different types and styles would place the UK midway between North America and continental western Europe in terms of variety, formality and frequency of dining out. Commercial innovation is routine, though overestimated in the breathless excitement about novelty that typifies promotional culture. Market research would suggest that key developments affecting dining out in the last two decades include concentration of ownership, more provision for informal minor meals, expansion of 'fast casual dining', cafe culture, greater concern for healthy eating, and more retail outlets selling sandwiches, tapas, sushi and other small items.[11] The reception of diversification was the focus of the TCP research which revealed two overarching trends: familiarisation and diversification.[12]

Familiarisation

Familiarisation[13] refers to a process whereby dining out, in restaurants and at other people's homes, becomes an unexceptional form of activity ever more taken for granted as a normal part of everyday life. In 1995 dining out was held to be special, something out of the ordinary. For older respondents this was entirely understandable – the great expansion in dining out for recreation had occurred during their middle age. As a 69-year-old man in Preston recalled, "Oh yeah, it was a luxury to eat out." That aura of luxury had evaporated by 2015. Almost everyone sometimes eats on commercial premises; only 6 per cent of respondents never did so in the 12 months to May 2015. The mean frequency of eating a main meal in a restaurant is about once every ten days, but had increased very little if at all since 1995. The most powerful factors underlying the propensity to eat out frequently are: being younger (aged especially under-35), having no children at home, having experience of service class (that is, professional and managerial) occupations, and having a high household income. Identifying as White British and living in London also predict greater involvement. Sex and education are not statistically significant.

Asked to respond to statements about their behaviour, aspirations and feelings about dining out in restaurants, respondents indicate that the activity is seen in 2015 as less special and more ordinary than in 1995. Children are more acceptable in restaurants, people feel less 'on show', they express less aversion to formality overall (although this remains an attraction for a minority), and they are less distressed by eating alone. Also while, as in 1995, people are remarkably satisfied with the experience in all its facets, satisfaction with the food, the atmosphere and the service fell significantly.

Among sources of diminished enjoyment are three different processes which contribute to familiarisation – casualisation, simplification and regularisation. Various aspects of meals out have become less exceptional as people have gained in familiarity through more restaurant visits. The proportion of meals deemed to be special occasions fell, from 29 per cent to 22 per cent. Fewer meals are eaten on Saturdays and more mid-week, and they happen earlier in the evening, suggesting that they function as a substitute for household dinners. Casualisation is indicated by a concomitant increase of 7 per cent in the proportion of last meals out which are described as 'Quick and Convenient' (26 per cent in 2015). Respondents are less likely to dress up. They make the decision to eat out without reference to others more often. Repeat visits to the same restaurant increase. Simplification is indicated by meals being of very significantly shorter duration and involving fewer courses. For example, meals lasting an hour or less increased from 20 to 35 per cent and meals with three or more courses reduced from 33 to 22 per cent. Regularisation is a function of increased accessibility, availability of a wider range of formats and more types of restaurant, so that people readily find places with which they feel comfortable. The rapid expansion of the 'casual dining restaurant' in the 21st century, in which 30 per cent of respondents took their last main meal out, accommodates just such requirements. Thus dining out has become a simpler and more casual affair as the activity has grown more familiar to each new cohort in the study. However, the tendency towards normalisation is offset by another trend, towards greater diversity, which works in the opposite direction.

Diversification

Greater availability and awareness of more types of food, more varied cuisine on offer, more publicity and discussion of food, aestheticisation and, overall, an increase in diversity are aspects of growing interest in food. Table 6.1 indicates that people are increasingly inquisitive about food and prepared to adopt culinary innovations. More people say that they get excited about going to a new place, hinting at greater adventurousness and appreciation of novelty. Six per cent fewer people assent to the proposition 'I am suspicious of foods that I do not know'. More people talk often about eating out, learn about food from restaurants and acquire knowledge from eating out abroad. This interest extends to more positive

Table 6.1: The growth of interest in food, 1995–2015

	Strongly agree	Slightly agree	Neither	Slightly disagree	Strongly disagree
I get excited about going out to eat in a new place					
1995	13	28	18	23	16
2015	31	37	13	9	6
I often talk with others about eating out					
1995	15	36	14	20	14
2015	20	39	19	13	8
I have learned about foods through eating out					
1995	15	36	14	20	14
2015	21	42	14	13	11
I eat things now that I learned about on foreign holidays					
1995	14	21	12	20	31
2015	19	33	19	12	16
I am interested in using recipes in the media and press					
1995	18	34	11	15	14
2015	17	33	13	13	17
A vegetarian meal would never be my first choice					
1995	42	14	10	16	17
2015	28	14	12	20	26
I am suspicious of foods that I don't know					
1995	21	26	11	20	22
2015	16	25	15	23	21
When I eat out I like to choose things that I don't eat at home					
1995	41	33	8	10	6
2015	36	40	12	9	3
I am interested in everyday cooking					
1995	16	39	13	19	11
2015	30	39	11	13	6
I am interested in cooking for special occasions					
1995	28	35	8	14	12
2015	35	35	8	11	6

Note: Responses to some questions in the TCP survey of 1,100 adults in three cities in England in 2015 and 1,001 adults in the same cities in 1995.

Source: TCP, see Warde et al (2020b)

evaluation and greater tolerance for vegetarian meals. However, it is epitomised by positive references to unfamiliar foods and attendance at restaurants selling foreign cuisines.

Penny, a single woman in her early 30s and living in London, told us of her quests for new gustatory experiences, which she thinks she has attained: "I'd say I'm pretty happy with my palate, but I know what I like and like I said, I'm always looking for new things to try." She views adventurousness and the extension of the breadth of her knowledge and her repertoire very positively. Discussing holidays, she said:

> 'I think when you're in a new country, if you want to learn about the culture and the history, food is such a big part. ... I think it's always important to have a nice range, just to broaden your horizons and taste buds. You might try something that you've never heard of before and it might be one of your favourite things. It might be a taste explosion and you didn't realise how good something can be.'

Penny's orientation is just one example of broader engagement with and welcoming of ethnic cuisine. In 1995, 48 per cent of respondents had never in the last 12 months eaten in an ethnic restaurant,[14] a proportion which fell to only 22 per cent by 2015.

What sort of restaurant was attended on the last occasion is a good measure of preference (see Figure 6.1). Traditional British remains by far the most popular (41 per cent of all meals), with Italian and 'Other ethnic' (including Spanish, Mexican, Middle Eastern and Greek) the next most popular styles each registering 13 per cent.[15] Across this wide range of restaurant provision the most popular dishes for a main course were Indian curry, burgers, roast meat, pasta and steak, which between them account for 43 per cent of the total.

Omnivorousness

To the extent that styles of cuisine are socially marked in a hierarchical fashion, discovering who goes where marks social differentiation and inequality. Cultural preferences express self and social identity, which when recognised and rewarded by others, contribute to the

Figure 6.1: Percentage of respondents visiting restaurants with different cuisine styles within the last year and on the last occasion, 2015

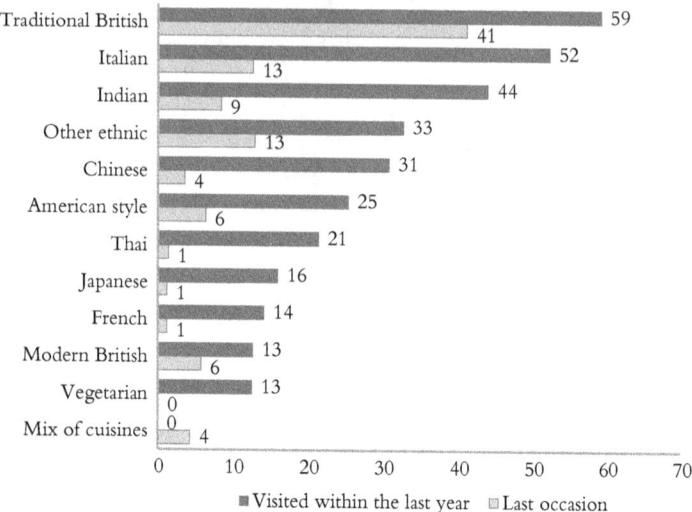

Note: Excludes those who never ate out in the last year.
Source: TCP; see Warde et al (2020b)

formation and perpetuation of social hierarchy. Good taste is marked by a preference for and participation in elevated and 'consecrated' activities. In the mid-20th century the eating activities regarded as high status, by means of which performances could signal the good taste of their bearers, centred on formal manners and French cuisine.

In our study we set out to systematically identify hierarchies of taste. Styles of cuisine have symbolic significance. The most common designations of styles of cooking identify national culinary traditions and these appeal to different sections of the population. The survey asked about experience of 11 cuisine styles, revealing three 'blocs of taste' which reflect symbolic meanings of cuisine styles in contemporary Britain.[16] The first component contains rarer and more arcane foreign cuisines like Thai, Japanese and vegetarian, relatively recent additions to the UK repertoire (see Table 6.2). The second group, where the style with the strongest presence is Traditional British, includes the most popular styles like Chinese and American. These are well known, well established, and in their locally adapted forms supply relatively unchallenging food. Most

Table 6.2: The hierarchical ranking of cuisines served in restaurants in England, 2015

Blocs of taste	Cuisine styles
Exclusive	French, modern British
Uncommon	Thai, Japanese, other ethnic, vegetarian Indian
Popular	Italian, Chinese, American Traditional British

Source: TCP, from Warde (2018, p 7, figure 2), reproduced with permission from University of California Press

respondents have eaten in restaurants serving one of more of these cuisines. The third component bears just two items, Modern British and French. These are relatively expensive, often delivered in formal settings and, according to the gastronomic evaluation of British food guides, carry greatest prestige. Price and quality vary both within and between cuisine styles.

Combinations of style allow intricate signalling of cultural taste and reflect different orientations towards dining out. Some respondents combine experience of styles from each bloc and by thus transcending hierarchical cultural boundaries might be deemed culturally omnivorous.

In recent decades people of high socioeconomic status have tended to display knowledge, liking and participation of a wide variety of cultural activities and genres. The 'cultural omnivore' thesis contends that this is the foremost contemporary way to exhibit distinction.[17] The basic contention is that while in the mid-20th century distinction was expressed through mastery of High Culture (of opera, classical music, modern literature, and so on), a sole focus on such forms of legitimate culture came to be seen as narrow and snobbish, and that to display cultural competence requires the incorporation of elements of popular culture. The most profitable disposition of cultural capital now requires command of forms on both sides of the boundary between High and Popular cultures. As in other fields boundary crossing is apparent in dining out.[18] Some respondents had been customers in most styles of restaurant; Penny, for example, had eaten out in all except two during the previous year. The combination of high volume and boundary transgression defines the culinary omnivores who eat in exclusive, uncommon and popular restaurants and in addition are heavy users of most forms of takeaway provision. Their food behaviour is distinctive both in restaurants and at home. Table 6.3 contrasts omnivores with those who had only eaten in places serving popular cuisines.

Table 6.3 shows the extremes of culinary orientation and practice on the part of the adherents of two distinct and opposed styles of eating. It implies a strong relationship between what happens in the market place and what happens in the household. It also reveals great enthusiasm on the part of one section of the population (about 9 per cent of the sample) who eat out very frequently, avoid very brief restaurant meals, source their food distinctively, cook for others and are interested in cooking for themselves. The other section of the population (28 per cent) is more likely to dine out because of a special occasion, avoids entirely restaurants serving uncommon or exclusive cuisines, is less interested and overall less involved in food, its preparation or its evaluation. Ironically, they enjoy eating out more than do the omnivores.

The practice of dining out: three principles

From the testimonies of interviewees we can extract some dominant principles governing the practice of eating out in 2015. All honour and seek to obey three principles: variety, comfort and knowledgeability. Pursuit of variety is the first priority. Appreciated by a substantial majority of the population, it is for some an imperative. Enthusiastic omnivores cherish breadth of experience and are prolific in accessing cuisine styles, types of restaurant and other channels of food supply, including takeaway outlets and specialist food shops.[19] However, they are not exceptional in valuing diversity. Most other people do too, propelled by the imperative to be adventurous when deciding where to go and what to eat. A greater proportion of the population are now excited about going to new places, choose to eat things that they would not at home and like to talk about food that they have eaten out. The appeal of this orientation towards food – a preference for diversity and novelty over the traditional and established – is also confirmed when children (or perhaps their parents) are complimented if they eat a wide range of foods and, conversely, by the apologetic tone of those

Table 6.3: Comparison of distinctive features of omnivorous and restricted behaviour, 2015 (percentage reporting behaviour)

	Restricted	Omnivore
Frequency of eating out		
Several times a week	3	23
Once a week	9	30
Frequency of eating at a friends		
Once a fortnight	5	22
Once a month	13	34
Frequency of eating at a relative's		
Once a month	17	28
Once every three months	19	22
Never	23	9
Attitudes: Agree		
Choose things I don't eat at home	68	92
Complain if meal unsatisfactory	71	84
Get excited about going to eat at a new place	52	87
Often talk with others about eating out	47	78
Last occasion		
Reason for last meal out		
Special occasion	28	14
Just a social occasion	43	57
Meal duration		
Less than an hour	7	1
2–3 hours	49	59
Eaten similar dish before …		
… while eating out	84	82
… at home	71	67
How receives recommendations		
From friends	62	88
From colleagues	22	60
Taken there by someone else	23	61
Domestic activities		
Hosting		

(continued)

Table 6.3: Comparison of distinctive features of omnivorous and restricted behaviour, 2015 (percentage reporting behaviour) (continued)

	Restricted	Omnivore
Hosts guests at home	64	92
Hosts family (of those that host)	84	74
Hosts friends (of those that host)	64	94
Frequency of grocery shopping		
Several times a week	32	45
Once a week	49	32
Frequency of online grocery shopping		
Once a week	2	13
Never	78	49
Visits independent food stores		
Yes	23	61
Very interested in …		
… reading recipes	14	28
… using recipes	12	30
… everyday cooking	26	39
… special occasion cooking	26	63
Dietary practices		
Food behaviours		
Limit meat consumption	17	36
Eat three meals a day	46	66
Five a day of fruit and vegetables	42	69
Use up leftovers	58	84
Dietary requirements (last year)		
Vegetarian	5	10
Vegan	0	5
Pescatarian	1	7
Gluten-free	2	8
Lactose-free	1	9

Note: All 2015 respondents. Total observations (n=841) as analysis excludes respondents that where data are missing (n=21), or are 'inactive' (n=66), or have 'other' types of taste (n=173).

Source: Extracted from Warde et al (2020b, pp 192–193, table 10.2 and p 194, table 10.3), reproduced with permission from Manchester University Press

who perceive themselves as limited in the breadth of their tastes. For everyone there are limits, but the limits lie at different coordinates. Omnivores are characterised by cultivating diversity and variety.

A second principle involves being able to exercise a sufficient degree of control to permit feeling comfortable and at ease when eating out. This is underpinned by the general societal tendency towards informalisation,[20] and is facilitated through both normalisation and the greater availability of informal venues. Two-thirds (66 per cent) of respondents in 2015 say that they 'feel comfortable in any type of restaurant'. A similar proportion deny feeling 'on show' when eating out. People achieve control of the social aspects of the occasion by being sufficiently attuned to the conventions of the venues they visit. Few people report embarrassment. A general feature of middle-class cultural capital, competence in public, is demonstrated by feeling comfortable in a range of places where different implicit rules of behaviour and conventions obtain. To be able to match behaviour to different occasions and settings facilitates participation and is associated with the third principle of cultivating a suitable level of informed appreciation of dining out.

Not everyone needs the same amount or type of knowledge in order to be able to get by as a customer in restaurants or in conversations about food. Horizons of experience and the characteristics of companions affect what it is necessary to know or be able to say. Interviewees differ in their awareness of the panoply of restaurant experiences, their ability to describe their experiences, and their capacity to ground judgements about what they like or dislike. Such differences are generally consistent with levels of interest and exposure to the field. Nevertheless all share understandings of what it means to eat out and what, for instance, main meals might be. Even the least articulate and least engaged describes and passes judgement on food quality, atmosphere, menus and value for money. They rarely exhibit embarrassment or anxiety when asked their opinions. Even when admitting to having less mastery than others over the range and intricacies of food culture they are neither apologetic nor ashamed. Some are proud to announce a positive preference for traditional food. Knowledge, genuine or pretended, helps people to feel in control and thereby to exhibit competence. So while connoisseurship comes in different degrees the form of the activity has common features.

Making most profitable use of the affordances of these three principles is predicated upon class pedigree, having high income and higher education – all forms of privilege concentrated within the professional-executive class. However, the principles are shared more or less universally and serve to define for everyone good practice, practical understanding and competence. Cohort, class, ethnicity and location are important sources of differentiation, but almost everyone is subject to and influenced by similar imperatives to experience variety, feel comfortable and display adequate practical knowledge. The honour claimed for proficiency in these activities is neither contested nor rejected by other classes. Hence, those who might seek to derive advantage from their mode of participation are unlikely to meet with disparagement or censure. In 2015 distinction is expressed by obtaining greater varieties of food, attending more varied social occasions and having greater knowledge of the field – that is to say by engaging more intensively. Cultivation or exploitation of these possibilities may, *in extremis*, result in pretentiousness, a criticism levelled at 'foodies', for example. However, when pretentiousness is avoided, the boundaries between cultivation and vulgarity blur, making differences of social position easier to manage interpersonally. The omnivorous orientation does not jar with those who do not or cannot practice it.

Culture and style

The appeal of variety and greater flexibility in respect of new foods, procedures, timings and venues became apparent in the 1970s.[21] The normalisation of dining out and expectations of greater variety encourage shifts in orientation towards eating. Practical understandings associated with dining out echo the temper of other contemporary cultural practices. Aestheticisation, an omnivorous orientation, the drawing of cultural boundaries, the complex interweaving of local and global influences on taste, commercial promotion, and market segmentation are common features of many cultural practices and are not specific to eating out. These features of the cultural landscape are underpinned by social processes of globalisation, commodification and cultural intermediation. Globalisation – the acceleration in the circulation of ideas, products, people, messages, associated with international trade, migration and information technology – expands the scale and scope of options.[22] Few can remain unaware of ingredients, dishes and cuisines which connote far-away places. Pressures on a commercial catering industry to exploit opportunities for further commodification involve the ceaseless devising of means to sell more experiences, novel foods and formats but without abandoning established, well-selling favourite items. The process is more augmentation than substitution. The accompanying intensified communication results in a profusion of resources for the aesthetic judgement of food.

Growing post-war affluence and the expansion of mass consumption were bases for the intensification of cultural communication. Marketed goods and services became more than ever bases of meaningful experience, tools for expression of personal identity, and vehicles for the organisation of sociability and the conduct of everyday life. Britain acquired a consumer culture. Consumer culture emphasises style. Individuals donned 'lifestyles'. Increasingly, consumption came to be seen as a means by which individuals and groups express their identities through symbolic displays of taste. It facilitated new expressions of belonging, notably in youth sub-cultures. It prizes symbolic as well as material rewards. A key emergent figure was 'the expressive individual' whose activities, possessions, projects and judgements were directed towards symbolic communication of identity, summarily designated as a lifestyle.

By contrast, in the 1950s eating and cookery were treated in primarily utilitarian terms, necessary and beneficial but of little symbolic significance. They were domestic matters, matters of household economics and not much exposed to public discussion or scrutiny. That changed gradually as cultural intermediation on behalf of commercial organisations looking to sell new products devised marketing techniques to give eating meaning, glamour and exposure. Mundane activities were redefined as avenues for aesthetic creativity and appreciation. It was as if food consumption was redefined from being a battery of mundane, necessary and unremarkable chores into a worthy and valuable form of recreation. Consumer culture re-presents needs and necessities as play and fun. Eating is presented as not so much a matter of social reproduction as sociable recreation.[23]

Scholars agree that in recent decades aestheticisation has affected many aspects of the selection and circulation of commodities. Promotion of products on the basis of aesthetic merit accelerated in the 1970s.[24] Additional activities were subjected to aesthetic criteria. An aesthetic disposition was applied to mundane and ordinary activities like home-making, self-adornment, hobbies and pastimes, and also to the products of many manual and creative occupations. Crafts were elevated to the status of art. Eating and cooking were among the practices caught up in the waves of aestheticisation. Learning about, knowing about and talking about style and taste became commonplace. Stephen Shapin, emphasising the centrality of inter-subjective agreement in matters of taste, claims that actually people do very little except discuss tastes.[25] The effects on food consumption is profound, for aesthetic judgement can be applied to many aspects of eating, including categories of foodstuffs, quality of ingredients, technical cooking skill, presentation of dishes and table settings. Marketing, advertising and commercial journalism seeking to influence purchasing decisions promoted competing products on the basis of their aesthetic qualities. The glimmerings of a new informed appreciation of food and its wider expression in print and visual media that laid the foundation for unprecedented interest in food can be traced back to the 1970s.[26] The substantial increase in mass media outputs – in the press and on television – devoted to cooking and eating from the 1990s reinforced the tendency to construct culinary culture in terms of art.

Besides the commercial and aesthetic impulses that consumer culture generates, two other developments – deindustrialisation and the emergence of substantial body of professional cultural intermediaries – brought art to the dinner table. Manufacturing declined as much industrial production was moved out of the UK to cheaper sites across the world, resulting in higher levels of employment in the service sector. Highly qualified workers recruited to deliver public and cultural services were major contributors to the creation of a new cultural hegemony. Employees in the cultural services were strategically placed to reform and redefine the cultural value of commercial goods. Their numbers grew rapidly. A section of the population rich in cultural capital – they increasingly held higher education qualifications even though often receiving only modest incomes – they challenged prevailing definitions of good taste in cultural matters. Variously called the creative class, the cultural fraction of the professional-managerial class, and the new middle class, they created a cultural world and a picture of good taste in their own image.[27] This new middle class substituted their own predilections and orientations for bourgeois dispositions towards formal manners, menus in French and white table cloths which were condemned as signs of snobbishness and a stuffy establishment culture. This involved engagement with cultural forms and practices previously snubbed, and in the process recalibrated cultural value by extending the range of honourable and worthy activities.

One function of cultural intermediation was to solve dilemmas of style arising in the absence of a cultural orthodoxy. As Zygmunt Bauman observed, consumer choice may cause anxiety for individuals obliged to construct a self-identity with marketed commodities because the possibility of making embarrassing mistakes is ever-present. He argued that the market also allays anxiety because '[s]ocial approval of free choices (i.e. freedom from uncertainty) is another service it offers to its consumers', as adverts, endorsements and tests are invoked by intermediaries to reassure them that their choices are well made.[28] Most such advice was not, except perhaps in relation to health, in the form of commandments. Everyone to her own taste, but woe betide if that taste is bad. The ethos of food promotion was one of tolerant pluralism. That mood was espoused by strategic members of the generation born around the end of the war and coming of age in the 1960s. Part of the birth of the new middle class, they mobilised for the extension of individual and civil liberties, for which the 1960s are remembered, and supported cultural pluralism and multicultural sympathy. They were also attached to the value of compassion enshrined in universal welfare state provision, from which they themselves were later to benefit substantially as both producers and consumers. That mix of libertarian and collectivist dispositions, which is now the object of fury among conservative reactionaries waging culture wars, laid the ground for multiculturalism to flourish in fields like food where foreign culinary traditions became celebrated.

Class and culture: deciphering distinction

In the second half of the 20th century, as mass consumption accelerated, the cultural bases of social divisions received increasing attention. Culture and taste were recognised as a key independent contributors to inequality, hierarchy and domination. As Pierre

Bourdieu argued, social distinction is conveyed through the cultural accoutrements that social classes adopt to signify their own position and to judge the position of others. He depicts taste as 'the source of the system of distinctive features which cannot fail to be perceived as a systematic expression of a particular class of conditions of existence, i.e., as a distinctive lifestyle, by anyone who possesses the practical knowledge of the relationships between distinctive signs and positions in the distributions'.[29] In other words, the distinctive features of different lifestyles allow a competent observer to estimate the social class position of others. People come to be positioned by others in a hierarchical social order by virtue of the preferences and judgments displayed through their pattern of consumption. Reputation, a matter of concern for most people, is linked to taste. This is a reason why the concept of cultural capital became popular in the early 21st century when researchers were exceptionally interested in how tastes, expressed through consumption behaviour, not only communicated a sense of personal identity but also conferred social advantage and preferment through their recognition by others as legitimate or creditworthy.[30] Cultural capital matters because prospective employers, friends and companions, but also strangers, make positive or negative evaluations on the basis of one's expressions of taste.

Culinary omnivorousness became the primary expression of cultural capital in the field of food towards the end of the 20th century. Culinary omnivores are disproportionately of high socioeconomic status. The social factors predisposing survey respondents in 2015 to greatest breadth of culinary experience are identifying as White British, belonging to the professional and managerial class, having the highest level of income and holding a degree level qualification.[31] An omnivorous disposition confirms position in the social hierarchy.

By definition the orientation would not convey distinction if everyone was a culinary omnivore. Many are not, as another glance at Table 6.3 affirms. The experience of the 'restricted' category is clearly much narrower than the omnivores. The difference is significant and not an accident of the data or the sample. One factor is the lack of the financial resources to engage with food in the same way as the more privileged professional-executive class. Another is the adoption of other priorities and an alternative set of systematic preferences, as is the case for some ethnic minority populations who consume the food typical of their cultures of origin. Other groups apparently remain attached to the urban-industrial working-class diet. So, while there is a hegemonic understanding that variety is good, not everyone welcomes greater diversity. An exploratory approach may feel uncomfortable. Misadventure might cause embarrassment and mistakes be riven with the possibility of visceral disgust. Some people prefer familiar places and familiar foods. Wanting to feel relaxed and at ease, they adopt strategies to avoid places and foods about which they are apprehensive – one reason for the overwhelmingly positive experiences of dining out reported. They choose dishes with which they are already acquainted, containing ingredients that they recognise and like, and they make repeat visits to places that they have previously enjoyed. Asked about their attitudes in 2015, 12 per cent preferred to eat the same things in a restaurant that they ate at home and 41 per cent claimed to be 'suspicious of foods that I don't know'. Some people prefer familiar and plain dishes cooked at home; 51 per cent (6 per cent more than in 1995) agreed that meals prepared at home are superior in quality. Those adopting the restrictive pattern might be seen to value comfort over variety but this does not constitute resistance to the hegemonic formula. There is no oppositional culture of eating.

Many scholars after 1980 took the view that class differences were declining. Yet since the mid-1970s inequalities of wealth have grown rapidly. Social mobility has stalled. Menial and poorly paid employment is rife. There is a reluctance to talk about such matters in terms of class, partly because the labour movement has found it politically expedient to avoid using the term. In a very engaging book, Pen Vogler shows that over a long period of time, manners, material artefacts, recipes, patterns of consumption and tastes associated with eating have reflected class differences.[32] She charts the foibles, idioms and injustices of class in British foodways, pointing to the many domains where class appears on the landscape, in the names of meals and their timing, norms of polite behaviour, fashions and fads, fish knives and table cloths. She sees class persisting most obviously in the priorities of those with high cultural capital who value the 'fresh, local, home-made, healthy, organic' in contrast to 'the food of mass consumption: ultra-processed, industrial, packaged, unhealthy, fast food, sliced bread'.[33] It might be concluded that the once glaring differences between classes have become more subtle and nuanced, requiring more sensitive antennae to detect. The rich and privileged are now prone to emphasise their own ordinariness and would be embarrassed if accused of asserting their superiority on the grounds of class or by vulgarly displaying their opulence.[34] Contemporary elites try to present themselves as ordinary folk who just happen to have worked hard or been lucky. Yet structural differences in the life chances of people born into different classes remain. This is partly concealed by the stratum of cultural intermediaries who associate openness and tolerance with equality of status, masking their own role in maintaining inequality by legitimising the types of cultural capital to which they have greatest access. Cultural omnivorousness actually symbolises a socially superior position and has similar effects to the more immediately apparent class differences of the past. Now, however, no systematically organised opposition challenges such expressive forms of symbolic domination.[35]

The upper and upper middle classes always enjoyed more variety when eating than did the poor. So too now. Differences in content became less stark in the two decades immediately following the end of the Second World War, although differences in quality remained extensive. With more alternative ways to sample diverse foods, access to variety stretches further down the social scale. The promotion of style masks and disguises social class division. The dominant understanding of good food revolves around the contrast between mass and niche consumption, with a larger and diverse middle class well positioned to exploit their cultural and material privileges to both promote and enjoy the benefits of higher quality and distinctive products.

The new middle class generated a widely accepted understanding of what it means to eat well. It vehemently rejects the urban-industrial working-class diet and its more recent developments. The new middle-class orientation is widely diffused and largely embraced by others in the higher social classes. The divisions within the dominant class symbolised by the culture wars, which pit a reactionary populism against liberal tolerance, have had little impact on culinary matters. So, despite some meaningful differences between those who possess primarily economic capital and those whose principal asset is cultural capital (see Chapter 3, in the section 'What people buy and eat'), no major rift exists in the field of food. For good reason, other social divisions and sources of discrimination – gender, ethnicity, sexuality and the effects of colonialism – now attract greater scholarly attention.

7

Anxious Pleasures: Eating and Happiness

The pleasures of a good meal?

Eating is not an optional activity. However, the contexts for eating are managed in multiple ways to meet physical, emotional, cultural and social objectives. Many events are primarily functional, a means to basic physical reproduction, episodes to quell hunger which are of no great significance. Mostly, however, additional gratification is expected. Even simple and meagre refreshments may be very pleasurable under the right circumstances. Tea and biscuits played an important symbolic role in Britain throughout the 20th century. Meals offer greater potential for enjoyment, delivering strong doses of happiness, repeatedly.[1] Success depends upon the fit that an event achieves between the site and its atmosphere, the people present, and the qualities of food provided. The setting, the company and the menu, when well-integrated, make for a good meal. Success is never guaranteed, but acting routinely in accordance with the norms and conventions of one's social circle mostly prevents disappointment.

There is no systematic collection of evidence to answer the question of the proportion of events which are gratifying. National accounting rarely addresses the question of whether people are happy or content, although a little more attention is now being paid to general measures of happiness and wellbeing. By international standards Britain is moderately happy – 19th in a table of 137 countries in 2023, just behind the Czech Republic and just ahead of Lithuania.[2] It is mostly assumed that people enjoy eating, which is likely since it offers several different types of enjoyment. Eating a meal may be sensually pleasing, functionally satisfactory, normatively meaningful and socially convivial. Some meals meet all these criteria, albeit with different degrees of intensity. Elaborate and celebratory meals typically are expected to:

- deliver visceral bodily pleasure;
- be good value in the light of the resources of time, money and effort expended;
- be culturally legible, meaningful and acceptable in its arrangements; and
- provide congenial companionship at a sociable occasion.

Ordinary meals may meet the same criteria although not to the same degree. These general criteria were as relevant in 1950 as now, although it is an open question if, and if so when, their relative importance shifted. Any answer would need to distinguish between regular household meals and other more special occasions.

Eating out is particularly good at providing enjoyment. We know from our survey evidence in 1995 and 2015 that people when eating out in restaurants enjoy their meals very much. Almost no one says that they dislike any aspect of the occasion which most 'like a lot' and most others 'like a little'. Company and conversation are the most appreciated features but the food is liked by 93 per cent and the service by 85 per cent in 2015 (see Table 7.1).

Were it not so reliably enjoyable people would be reluctant to pay to participate, yet almost everyone dines out sometimes. Not every meal is perfect of course. Some are disappointing and occasionally evince complaints. Most people, however, are reluctant to complain.[3] For even when some aspects of the experience is very poor, other sources of gratification compensate. I cannot forget the interview where a woman reported a "bar-type" lunch where the food was "so salty I couldn't eat it", "some had finished their meal before the others were served" and a faulty jukebox had played for 15 minutes. Yet she concluded that "we quite enjoyed the meal on the whole".[4]

As Table 7.1 also shows, eating at someone else's home is even more enjoyable than eating in a restaurant. Domestic hospitality is little studied and little reported, probably because ostensibly a gift and no money changes hands. In 2015, about two-thirds of respondents

Table 7.1: Enjoyment of last occasion dining out at commercial establishment (left) and someone else's home (right) (percentage)

		Commercial		Someone's home	
Food		1995	2015	1995	2015
	Liked a lot	81	72	87	87
	Liked a little	13	21	10	10
	Neither liked nor disliked	3	4	2	3
	Disliked a little	2	2	0	0
	Disliked a lot	1	1	0	0
Company		1995	2015	1995	2015
	Liked a lot	91	86	94	94
	Liked a little	6	9	5	6
	Neither liked nor disliked	3	5	1	1
	Disliked a little	0	0	0	0
	Disliked a lot	0	0	100	100
Décor		1995	2015	1995	2015
	Liked a lot	57	48	91	93
	Liked a little	24	29	6	4
	Neither liked nor disliked	15	20	2	2
	Disliked a little	2	2	1	0
	Disliked a lot	1	1	0	0
Service		1995	2015	1995	2015
	Liked a lot	65	57	84	78
	Liked a little	22	28	9	9
	Neither liked nor disliked	6	10	7	12
	Disliked a little	4	3	0	0
	Disliked a lot	2	2	0	0
Conversation		1995	2015	1995	2015
	Liked a lot	82	79	88	89
	Liked a little	14	15	9	8
	Neither liked nor disliked	4	6	2	3
	Disliked a little	0	1	0	0
	Disliked a lot	0	0	0	0

(continued)

Table 7.1: Enjoyment of last occasion dining out at commercial establishment (left) and someone else's home (right) (percentage) (continued)

		Commercial		Someone's home	
Value for money		1995	2015	1995	2015
	Liked a lot	69	56	–	–
	Liked a little	18	28	–	–
	Neither liked nor disliked	6	11	–	–
	Disliked a little	5	4	–	–
	Disliked a lot	2	1	–	–
Overall		1995	2015	1995	2015
	Liked a lot	82	77	92	94
	Liked a little	14	18	6	5
	Neither liked nor disliked	3	5	1	0
	Disliked a little	2	1	1	0
	Disliked a lot	0	0	0	0

Note: Respondents between ages 16 and 65. Responses to questions about the experience of the last occasion dining out.
Source: TCP, see Warde et al (2020b)

had invited people home for a meal in the last year.[5] There is a general tendency for reciprocal exchange, such that most invitations are returned, but overall more people are guests than host. It differs from an economic transaction, even though it requires work by one party to deliver a service, because it involves eating the same meal together, creating shared memories of enjoyable social events and fostering a sense of mutual attachment. It is a significant form of social interaction which envisages conviviality and commensality in anticipation of enduring warm social relationships. Its several forms, though they lack precise definition, run on a continuum from formal to less formal dinner parties, through buffets and barbeques, to events where the guests each bring some food to put on the table. The formal dinner party appears to have become proportionately less common since the middle of the 20th century when it was an exclusive institutional arrangement of the upper echelons of the middle class.

By the 1990s events of domestic hospitality had become typically rather informal, a tendency which has persisted. The outcome is an affirmation of the positive role of the gift in a communal mode of provision in cementing local social relations. While sharing food is the *raison d'être* for each individual event it is not usually the main attraction. The food served is, though, an interesting indicator of the penetration of the influence of cultural intermediation and the culinary revolution into contemporary practice.

When inviting guests, especially for friends, hostesses and hosts almost always prepare something that is a little more special than they would put on the table for dinner for household members. Albeit constrained by culinary skills, financial resources and their own and their guests' taste, they seek to please their visitors. Most aim to serve food similar, but of a higher quality, to that of a normal family meal.[6] This often means dishes at which the cook is especially proficient, tempered by reflection on guests' preferences, and is rarely adventurous or experimental. The foods recorded in our study were many and various and included tagine, tofu, fish pie, Chinese takeaway, biltong, beef Wellington and vegan curry. However, the most frequent main courses were curries, roast dinners and pasta, which accounted for 44 per cent of all occasions. Chicken dishes, grilled or baked fish, barbecued meat and casseroles comprised a further 21 per cent of centre-pieces. If hosts are mostly cooking slightly elaborated versions of their normal family meals, then the list reflects the state of the practice of domestic cookery in 2015. Mainstream repertoires have incorporated curries and pasta dishes which would not have featured in the 1950s and which have gradually become normalised. Also some of the meals now offered by more adventurous hosts would have been entirely unknown to almost everyone. Nevertheless, many dishes could easily have appeared at the table throughout the period. The menus seem to indicate the delayed and protracted effects of culinary development since the 1960s.

Although there is no reliable evidence about change over time, there probably was rather less domestic entertaining of friends in the 1950s, it being a practice of the established middle classes and largely alien to the working class. The working class entertained kin at home, as is currently the case; there are currently no class differences in the likelihood of being a guest in the home of kin.[7] However, to invite friends home for a meal was rare.[8]

We don't have equivalent information about the pleasures of eating at home. The ideal family meal is imagined to deliver considerable gratification. Of respondents in 2015, 18 per cent disagreed with the statement 'meals prepared at home are superior in quality', and only 10 per cent agreed with the statement 'I like to eat out because I don't like the meals I have to eat at home', which together offer a fairly strong and positive endorsement of domestic meals. Nevertheless, run-of-the-mill dinners at home are not expected routinely to deliver the intense pleasure or convivial sociability of the better restaurant experiences. A meal eaten alone will not deliver social enjoyment; a bowl of leftovers will not generate contemplative rewards; the daily bowl of porridge for breakfast is unexciting; most domestic cooks have a limited repertoire of dishes that they prepare; the company is largely predictable, drawn from a given small range; and conversation is likely to be mundane and practical. Nevertheless, for many people the repetition of social routines and the consumption of familiar foods is viewed very positively. Household meals, as a champion of the family meal would assert, serve to strengthen familial bonds, give emotional comfort, reinforce identities and provide food that members prefer. That is not to deny that family meals are often socially disappointing; not all family members like them or like them in the same way, and the standard of preparation may be problematic. Not everyone recalls their childhood meals positively.[9] Whatever, with respect to forms of enjoyment, dinners at home serve different ends and purposes to those eaten out.

Most accounts assume that eating should be enjoyable and that by and large it is. It is probable that pleasure and satisfaction – eating enough tasty food – is neither more nor less common in 2020 than in 1955. Magazines in the mid-20th century emphasised that food should be tasty, hearty and satisfying and likely it was. Subsequently a smaller proportion of income was needed for food and the spread of convenience foods made food easier and quicker to prepare. A diverse and pluralistic culinary culture perhaps made it harder to feel confidence in what to serve and eat. In the 1950s, the narrower range of foods and greater homogeneity in definitions of good meals lowered the stakes associated with style. As regards sociability, the ideal version of the family meal occurred more frequently and was a little more leisurely in the 1950s; hurried meals, eaten alone or with only some household members, often eating different foods, compromises the rewards of commensality. Yet still eating is often very pleasing, although it certainly has the potential to be more enjoyable on many more occasions.

Eating arouses many positive emotions for it can be highly engaging and enormous fun. Events necessarily vary in the degree of enjoyment to be obtained, with some predictably more pleasurable than others. The more eating is regarded as recreation, as a source of novelty and adventure, or as a source of new knowledge and experience, the more gratification it will deliver. Yet even if it is most common to reach just a moderate level of satisfaction that might be seen as an achievement. To be able to be indifferent to what we eat is reassuring. The minority who are unable to source or prepare enough food for themselves hold a mirror to the rest who can achieve the pleasure and satisfaction of satiation.

Perhaps the pleasures of food explain the prevalence of its misuses, as is arguably also the case with narcotics and alcohol. Given a generally reliable source of enjoyment and pleasure, one may be tempted to eat more, more often and more harmful foods than is advisable from a purely functional and physiological point of view. Clearly people can moderate the quantity of food that they eat or change its composition without eliminating enjoyment, but it is important to recognise that many aspects of the practice of eating, including appetite, are powerfully embodied habits.[10] Most people do not want to abandon pleasurable habits, although those habits are for many also a source of anxiety. Eating can be stressful and distressing. In general more ink is spilled in considering its downsides. Anxieties reduce pleasure, not least because of the increased and detailed attention paid to the relationship between the production and consumption of food and the health of the people and the planet.

Troubles and anxieties

In *Anxious Appetites*, Peter Jackson analysed contemporary food worries. He defines anxiety as 'a physically embodied state involving mental and emotional distress, combined with a more diffuse sense of uneasiness about impending events'.[11] Comparative survey evidence shows widespread concern about many food issues across the Organisation for Economic Co-operation and Development countries. There are significant variations by country but the overall impression is that a great many people express concern about food safety, food quality and the trustworthiness of the organisations and institutions responsible for the supply and governance of the system. The same conclusion, that worries are very widespread, was drawn from our study of six European countries in 2003.[12]

Jackson sees the prevalence of anxieties as an effect of 'a variety of (public and private) institutions vying to control our level of anxiety'.[13] Thus issues come and go. Which is not to say that the problems are imaginary, but that their relative prominence is a function of media exposure, the overall effect of which is to make the current period an age of anxieties. Jackson insists that anxiety should be analysed as a social and collective fact. Preferring to examine episodic events as collective in terms of 'their lifestyle, social context and political geographies',[14] he looks at the specific grounding of health concerns and moral outrage about issues like convenience foods, organisation of family meals, parental unease, technological change and 'food scares'. Implicitly his attention is focused on publicity around food safety and their construction as food 'scares'. These are episodes which attract, for a time, great publicity and cry out for some kind of political or managed remedy. While some problems have been alleviated, the story is not one of triumphant progress. It might be seen more as indication of the need for eternal vigilance, as similar issues emerge and as some solutions lead to other types of problem. Because food is a natural substance exposed to pathogens it always has a potential to threaten human health, but attempts to neutralise the pathogens through industrial processing frequently creates additional risks and hazards.

In longer-term perspective we can detect a historical sequence of major concerns in industrial Britain, from absolute shortages of food, through nutritional quality and the prevention of illness, to ethical disquiet about production and consumption. Dominant concerns emerged in a sequence shifting from food security, through safety and health, to social justice in the form of questions of environmental sustainability and the social distribution of distress.

This is not a perfect sequence. Issues of social justice were present in periods when simply obtaining enough food was a chronic problem for sections of the population. The sources of malnutrition were also associated with the chemical composition of the foods that were available. Fraud and mislabelling and unhygienic practices are a permanent problem which requires policing to avoid predatory economic behaviour by commercial enterprises – as for instance in the horsemeat scandal in 2013 when horse was substituted for beef in various products including burgers. The chemical composition of manufactured food remains exceptionally important – as with the role of ultra-processed foods (UPFs) in causing obesity and diabetes – even while natural justice is identified as a critical problem. Currently issues of security have risen up the agenda once again in the context of the COVID-19 pandemic and war in Ukraine.

However, the population may be less discontented than some critics suggest. Probably there is greater awareness of potential harm than before because publicity disrupts senses of contentment. The British public do not trust most aspects of the system, and least of all the politicians who are responsible for making, implementing and policing food policy.[15] Whether Britons trust food more or less than before is an open question. In a study carried out in 2003, Britons were the most convinced of the six European nations that food quality had improved over the previous 20 years. However, public discourses and political arrangements do not map directly onto personal predicaments. People find their own remedies and own practical solutions in the belief that they can exercise personal control over the quality of the food they eat.

Dealing with anxiety

Habit

The most common response to feelings of unease is simply to ignore for practical purposes the dangers and threats and to continue eating in an accustomed and habitual manner. Food is about the body and the mind, and most eating is habitual and does not entail much deliberation. Habit conceals and suppresses conscious concern and is usually reassuring. People may worry when their attention is drawn to the threats posed by the food system but pay no attention in the normal course of everyday life. For they mostly eat without thinking – a situation neatly captured in the notion of 'mindless eating' proposed by Wansick.[16] Habit is the default mode.

While much behaviour is habitual and automatic, and much reflection is shallow and inconsequential, people do stop to deliberate sometimes. Episodes of reflection are most common and consequential when making corrections to overcome impediments to routines. The most immediate is when a routine performance goes wrong and a diagnosis of error is required. A menu felt to lack aesthetic or nutritional balance, a meal taken so late that it hinders digestion and sleep, or a dish with a displeasing mix of flavours give pause for thought – experiences from which something might be learned. Second, sometimes the circumstances surrounding previously congenial routines disappear, as when resources are depleted, the commercial environment changes, or other members of a social circle adopt new convictions. Instances include receiving a medical diagnosis, for which part of the cure is a change in diet, and migration, when new surroundings disrupt previous habits and impel modification. A third important ground for deliberation is being called upon to give a justification of past conduct. Although challenges are comparatively rare, habits like eating unseasonal fresh food or animal flesh, or discarding as waste edible food, are open to ethical objections and may require explicit justification. These are circumstances encouraging re-evaluation of past performances and consideration of future possibilities.

Attempting to take control

People occasionally deliberate about their diets and try to change their habits, often recently by following a dietary regime with prescriptive nutritional rules. Following prescribed diets, carefully measured and monitored, can give confidence and reassurance. Avoiding some foods, or increasing the intake of others, are solutions to potentially harmful effects of eating the wrong food. People sometimes deliberate about their diets, particularly when faced with an identifiable disruption. To know that what one ingests affects health and vitality is not at all new. How one eats is one basis for maintaining good health according to a great many different world traditions of medicine. Physical and mental wellbeing are generally affected by the foods we eat. People are probably better informed, more self-aware and more concerned to monitor their diet (through self-diagnosis and self-medication) for the prevention of illness and debility than in the past. Often their problem will have been pointed out by media, and the imagined solution will draw upon expert advice. In recent decades that fundamental insight has been expressed in a way that treats food as almost exclusively a medical matter, which some refer to as 'healthism'.[17]

We are constantly cajoled to monitor and to regulate our diets. Magazines tell us how to count calories and how many we are permitted. Advertising hoardings recommend 'lite' versions of popular foods. Government nutrition guidelines describe what it means to 'eat five a day', although perhaps it should be nine. Celebrities pronounce on the quality of school dinners. Nutritionist discourse warns about the evils of excess salt, fat and sugar – and panel discussions in the mass media dispute which of these is the real culprit. An epidemic of obesity threatens to infect all, to damage our bodies and compromise our social reputations. We are encouraged to calculate our energy ratio (the pedometer was uncommon as a medical instrument in the 1970s but *de rigueur* by 2020) and to take more exercise to offset excessive food intake; the concept of the metabolic rate is currently more widely recognised than might be expected. This is all part of a tendency to pay more attention to healthy eating and medical intervention in the recommendation of what to eat.

The transcendent goal of good health is unproblematic for no one wants to be poisoned, diseased or ill. However, the obsessive, intrusive and narrow pursuit of health tends to obscure or reduce other benevolent aspects of food consumption and may also be misplaced or misleading. Until the 1970s weight was not a medical problem and nor was it measured precisely. Body Mass Index (BMI) won the competition to establish a metric to assess corpulence at a point where excessive weight came to be seen as a predisposing cause of various medical conditions.[18] Despite recognition of its many faults, BMI was adopted throughout the world because of its convenience in clinical contexts. An essentially arbitrary classification of normal weight, overweight and obese, BMI came to be commonly accepted as objective and scientific, with deviation from the normal treated as indication of disease.

The Department of Health, the National Health Service and DEFRA are major sources of public advice and public health recommendations. There is a steady outpouring of generic advice from official channels. They concentrate on volume of food eaten, recommend a 'balanced diet' and tend not to condemn particular foods or promote others. Official advice is sensitive to the fact that food manufacturers protest when the state suggests that people should stop eating food that they find profitable to sell. Official recommendations are accused, often unfairly, of being confusing because constantly revised. Changes of instructions reduce public confidence. Complementary and alternative medicine introduces further complexity into a field of scientific or allopathic medicine by drawing on other forms of knowledge and diagnosis. To add further to the complicated picture, competing proprietary diets are commercially sold with strict instructions about what to eat, in what quantities, how often and at what intervals. These sometimes also require specific patent foodstuffs. People trying to eat healthily find competing prescriptions. One response is to follow assiduously a prescribed diet, sometimes permanently, sometimes intermittently.

Diets can be characterised by the particular items eliminated. One area where medicine validates the exclusion of some foodstuffs from an individual's diet is that of allergies and intolerances. These are much more commonly declared than in the past and are always associated with specific foodstuffs. Regulations first introduced in 2014 and revised in 2021 require by law that products for sale shall indicate the presence of any of 14 food allergens, namely celery, cereals containing gluten, crustaceans, eggs, fish, lupin, milk, molluscs, mustard, peanuts, sesame, soybeans, sulphur dioxide and sulphites, and tree nuts. In FYS in 2018, 24 per cent of respondents reported 'clinically diagnosed' food allergies and 44 per cent intolerances. Sufferers avoid specific ingredients as part of a personal strategy for health because of a fear of adverse physical reactions with effects ranging from food poisoning through to bodily discomfort. The 2015 TCP survey registered similar proportions with about 40 per cent of people saying that they had been on a special diet during the previous 12 months: for 9 per cent this was a vegetarian diet, 2 per cent vegan, 3 per cent gluten-free, 2 per cent due to lactose intolerance and 13 per cent for weight loss. The reasons behind aversions and avoidance motives must be heterogeneous and the consequences diverse, although the scale of such concerns is remarkable given the minimal degree of such concerns 50 years earlier.

Health is only one of many widely accepted justifications for avoiding specific foods. If some people eat everything, others deny themselves particular foods. Restriction occurs increasingly for reasons of health but also for political, religious and ethical reasons. Individuals avoid foodstuffs because they dislike the taste, texture or aroma of the item, and also often because of associations with previous bad experiences or memories of their consumption. Such dislikes may be purely idiosyncratic aversions, but the absence of commonly available items may reflect underlying principles. Sometimes it is clearly a matter of religious or ethical principle, some categories of food being taboo, such as pork for Muslims or meat for vegetarians. Other times, avoidance is a matter of social prestige, as with aversions to items considered inferior, like many types of offal or the dishes served in fast food restaurants. Much can be learned from avoidances.[19]

Greater individual discretion and a wider range of available products does not necessarily increase the variety of foods consumed because, paradoxically, people can afford to have more dislikes and avoidances than before. Possibly, systematic avoidances are a tacit reaction against omnivorousness, an indication that people are more comfortable when they have rules to follow and justifications for their observance. To the extent that eating is a distinguishing element of lifestyles, with practices seen as expressions of self-identity, electing to follow a collectively recognised pattern may be strategic. Such associated routines are likely to be shared by friends and acquaintances, and by others not known personally but in similar social positions, items renounced signalling social belonging and solidarity.

People declare allegiance to many different diets. Patel suggests that the dietary regimens most discussed in 2022 in the UK were: the ketogenic diet, recommending high fat and very low carbohydrate composition; 'gut health', based on the role of probiotics; veganism, avoiding all animal products; DASH (Dietary Approaches to Stop Hypertension) which emphasises potassium, calcium and magnesium alongside two and a half hours of exercise per week; the Mediterranean diet, with no explicit prohibitions but requiring high levels of vegetables and pulses; and the flexitarian, a flexible but primarily vegetarian regime.[20] Other currently popular types involve intermittent fasting. Most, besides promising to enhance health, also promise to reduce weight.

Many people are aware of these diets but do not pursue them rigidly, improvising and selecting the recommendations that suit them. Some of the emergent nutrition strategies seem eccentric, at least to me. In 2004, a woman in her late 40s described the method that she and her partner adopt:

> We eat in a kind of cycle in that, as you can see we're both pretty podgy, but what we do is, on January 3rd, and we've been doing this of the past few years, we start the Atkins Diet and we really stick to it. ... And we get nice and slim for the summer and then come October we are, for three months pig out on whatever we want and we get really fat and then on January 3rd we start over again. And it's not yo-yo dieting, it's a cycle of dieting: it works for us ... we are pretty good, we don't eat the carbs, we don't eat the bread and the potatoes so much, although we love them and the pasta, and then we just start to pig out for a few months over the miserable bit of the winter.[21]

Not all dietary regimens are directed towards weight loss, but most are. Increasing publicity is given not only to potential hazards but also to ways of perfecting and displaying the body. Appearance is as important as its optimal physical functioning. A heightened degree of reflexivity with respect to control of the body accompanied the emergence of diet as a statement of identity and lifestyle. To be on a diet is a project of control over a wayward body, a hope that exercising self-discipline at the table will restore a lithe torso, self-respect and public admiration. However, long-term success in purposeful body-discipline of this kind for its own sake is rare.

People became fearful of food after being told by medical authorities that some combinations are harmful to health. Incontrovertibly, excess weight, imagined or real, has grown as a source of anxiety. It is almost a hundred years since being stout, well-padded or plump was positively regarded, a judgement typical where food is in short supply and only the well-off are adequately fed. Concern grew with eating disorders from the 1980s, when anorexia and bulimia became widely acknowledged and discussed medical conditions popularly associated with the pressures, especially on young women, to achieve a thin body. Simultaneously the obesity crisis began to have a major impact in shaping eating habits and strategies for change.

Obesity: a collective and an individual anxiety

It is estimated that the average human calorific need is no more than 2,500 calories per day.[22] Current government guidance is only 2,000. The average consumption in western countries is higher, with differences between men and women, ethnic groups and social classes. The paradox of the obesity problem is that while almost everyone wants to avoid becoming overweight, collectively we grow bigger. To be overweight is perhaps less a threat to good health than a moral and social hazard incurring a penalty because viewed as a symptom of being out-of-control, gluttonous or lazy. Consequently, dieting for the purpose of weight loss became for a time a form of moral crusade, turning into a medical matter justifying intervention for health purposes from the 1980s when it began to be seen as a worldwide epidemic.[23] Obesity is a primary source of anxiety about eating habits for both individuals and the state.

Some people probably do eat too much. Britain is not in the same league as the United States where, as Marion Nestle says, American industry produces and sells almost twice as many calories as are regularly recommended as sufficient for good health.[24] True, many of these calories are transferred to rubbish bins without ever having passed through a human body; waste is less bad for individuals than for the environment! The feeling of satiation is malleable. Casual observation of navigation around breakfast buffet tables in hotels implies that the quantities of food to which people are accustomed vary enormously. However, appetite is not easy to change.

Average BMI began to rise in the 1960s and accelerated significantly in the 1980s which became the pretext for announcing that it has reached critical or epidemic proportions. The reasons are controversial. Common sense tends to accept the energy balance thesis, that eating too much and exercising too little, alongside succumbing to the temptations of an obesogenic environment which parades abundant supplies of diverse and appealing foods, leads to weight gain. This accords with a contemporary ideological view that individuals can and should exercise self-discipline when selecting food in order to ward off unwelcome consequences for personal appearance and health. However, it is no long generally accepted by expert researchers.

Scientists of various ilks trying to cut through the noise and clutter of dietary advice offered to individuals have focused on the question of why obesity should have taken off on such a large scale, across many countries, at a specific point in time. The conjecture is that something in the global environment must have changed. One popular but insufficient explanation in terms of the social environment is that food became more abundant, households more affluent and work less effortful. Those changes did occur in Britain, but the corollary that people could and therefore voluntarily ate more rich food, stored as fat, does not follow. An explanation getting increasing support since 2010 is that the increased proportion of UPFs in diets in rich and middle-income countries underpins the trends. 'Only eat food' is a much repeated slogan based on the idea that the spread on a global scale of industrially manufactured products using a combination of highly processed ingredients best accounts for the timing of a trend which is strong and widespread.[25]

The argument is that the 1970s was a watershed in the development of food systems. Markets became flooded by a reliable supply of cheap, highly palatable products which were energy dense and very moreish. Some categories of heavily advertised and basically similar products were sold in larger quantities across the world. Key components of the UPF products whose sales increased were ingredients like sweeteners, fats, sodium and cosmetic additives, the techniques of processing which have spurred some to question whether they should be called food at all. They contain a lot of sugar and fat, but it is maintained that what matters is how sugars and fats are processed and combined with artificial flavourings, colourings and stabilisers. For some parts of the world (although not Britain) these foods arrived at the beginning of the nutrition transition. Britain with its urban-industrial working-class diet had already made that transition, without any associated crisis of obesity. However, the innovations in food chemistry and new manufacturing processes altered the nutritional and physiological properties of the central foodstuffs in the diet of the 1950s.

The mass production and global trading of non-perishable processed foods dates back to the mid-19th century. However, as Phillip Baker and colleagues note, UPFs became significant from the 1950s and, in some cases, including the UK, became the main source of dietary energy. They quote research studies to the effect that 'the greater contribution of UPFs to total energy intake results in poorer dietary quality, and also higher risks of all-cause mortality, obesity, cardio-metabolic diseases, cancer, gastrointestinal disorders, asthma, frailty and depression'.[26] UPFs and beverages include baked goods, breakfast cereals, confectionery, sweet biscuits, savoury snacks, instant noodles, dairy products and alternatives, processed meats and seafood, sauces and ready meals, carbonated soft drinks, juice drinks, flavoured mineral waters, sports and energy drinks. In other words, a wide range of products that are in common use.[27] Obesity is just one of several adverse medical consequences of having a high proportion of UPFs in the diet.

The extensive consumption of UPFs is consistent with the timing of the onset of the increase in overweight and obesity and with knowledge about the physiological mechanisms and metabolic origins of weight gain. The nature and extent of the processing to which many contemporary products are subjected is somewhat alarming, and well and arrestingly described by Chris van Tulleken. 'Usually the aim of UPF is to replace the ingredients of a traditional and much-loved food with cheaper alternatives and additives that extend shelf-life, facilitate centralised distribution and, it turns out, drive excess consumption.'[28] Descriptions of the invention of techniques for manufacturing UPFs are disturbing: 'traditional ingredients are often replaced with cheap, sometimes entirely synthetic, alternatives. These are generally molecules that are that are extracted from crops grown for animal food ... [which] ... are refined and modified until they can be used to make practically anything'. For van Tulleken, a central feature of UPFs is that they have addictive properties designed into them, encouraging both larger quantities to be consumed at a sitting and an inclination to repeatedly return to them when the opportunity arises or when cued by advertisements. They form habits.

To change eating habits is not a matter of reasoning correctly. Thoughtfulness and good intentions are not sufficient preconditions for a successful escape. Eating has an emotional and habitual dimension which is a function of national and local institutional arrangements. In explaining how institutions affect behaviour – institutions being shared norms and understandings which underpin or surround habituated responses to repeated situations – the notion of an obesogenic environment is a useful concept. Social settings contain a myriad of cultural messages and cues which nudge people in the direction of eating more of specific types of food. Public space is full of signs enticing passers-by to buy and eat. Most cues are ignored altogether, some are registered and maybe stored in memory, and on rare occasions they prompt action. The most common signs point to foods which are not regarded as good for health. Corporate spending on advertising is very great on breakfast cereals, confectionery, fast food, branded and packaged processed foods, but negligible for cabbage, tomatoes or oily fish.[29] The supermarket, and thereafter the domestic refrigerator, offer similar temptations. People encounter continuous encouragement to eat because exposed to an environmental infrastructure biased towards increasing consumption.

A resolution to the obesity crisis requires a social environment conducive to healthy and enjoyable eating. It requires recognition that when individuals embark on projects to change their practice they are more likely to succeed if they have explicit social support than if they rely purely upon willpower or just good intentions. Weight-loss diets are mostly unsuccessful in the long term, although they have more chance of being effective if they are pursued in association with others, in classes or clinics, where personal endeavours receive social support.[30] Giving oneself 'a good talking to' doesn't work. Cooperation mitigates the associated sacrifices, indignities and difficulties because the onus of breaking habits is not borne entirely by the individual. A favourable context, a sympathetic family, peer approval or a collective programme make individual change more likely. The same is true of those who would abandon meat eating.

Vegetarianism

If foodies prioritise aesthetic considerations, others, including vegetarians and vegans, hold ethics paramount. The exclusion of meat from diets has characterised some social groups for millennia.[31] Vegetarianism, despite all its current variants, is neither a recent fad nor a fashion. Justifications for abstinence from meat alter in emphasis from time to time and place to place but rationales share similar elements. Sympathy for vegetarianism has grown in the last half century.

Visions of being able to eat meat regularly and in large amounts have recurred over the centuries among the lower classes in Europe.

Donna Gabaccia showed that one major reason for Italian migration to the United States in the early 20th century was the reports from earlier migrants that it was possible for working-class people to eat like the proprietors and professionals back home.[32] Britons also have valued butcher's meat highly. George Orwell's inter-war portrayal of the vegetarian as a sandal-wearing eccentric conveys the strength of popular disgust and distrust of what was then a jarringly unorthodox dietary regime. More meat was purchased during the 1950s than ever since, according to official statistics. The growth was part of the post-war democratisation process, a reaction to and reward for the shortages induced by rationing during the war, complemented by increasingly availability of meat from global and imperial origins. Some people self-identify strongly as meat eaters. A 29-year-old clerk and mother in 2004 said "We both like meat. I think every meal we have meat in some form", a comment associated with a declaration (shared by 23 per cent of the UK population at the time) that a vegetarian restaurant was their least favourite type. However, it was followed up by the statement that "if friends were going, we'd go along". People who do not relish eating in vegetarian restaurants don't mind if other people do. This typifies increasing tolerance of unconventional behaviour in the second half of the 20th century. Twenty years later, vegetarianism seems less worthy of comment. It is some measure of pluralism – of allowing people to act in accordance with their own taste, the collapse of a dominant consensus, and a function of the shift from rules to indicative conventions – that vegetarianism and other specialised diets have become widely accepted and acceptable.

Joseph Boyle notes that embarking upon specialised dietary regimes like vegetarianism involves both a shift in behaviour and a conscious adoption of a new identity, that of having become a vegetarian.[33] Vegetarian observance has many different 'levels', with some who claim to be vegetarian including white meat in their diet, others fish, and most eggs. Novices rarely adopt the more extreme and taxing versions, like veganism or fruitarianism, although some will progress to these later. To become a recruit, and to participate in a specialised previously unfamiliar mode of activity, is to join in a collective movement with its own rules, motivations and justifications. Thereafter a 'career' becomes a possibility. Joining a movement may inspire a desire for improvement or refinement of personal performances, which may well involve reflection on present performances and purposeful greater immersion.

Personal transformation in eating habits is usually a matter of shifting allegiance between already established alternative types of practice. Changed eating habits must always be a process of modification for it is impossible to engage in eating completely afresh. Children have well established eating patterns long before they have any capacity to conceptualise, countenance or practice significant alternatives. Even a process of radical conversion is more appropriately considered one of selection among optional modes of eating. Becoming vegetarian is an interesting case because it does not require additional economic resources. It is usually considered a voluntary personal decision; in interviews vegetarians frequently talk about the process retrospectively in terms of a considered personal project for which they have reasons and rationale.[34] However, it is organised and coordinated by the apparatus of a long established social movement keen to attract adherents.

As an experiment I ate a vegetarian diet for two weeks. It proved to be very little problem regarding taste, variety, preparation skills or health. The required knowledge was easily available; I didn't need to be highly motivated to work out how such a diet would be possible practically. The principles are well articulated in many places and there was no need to experiment in cooking as the 2010s saw a rush to publish cookery books for vegetarian and vegan diets. Also, infrastructural facilities are in place, with vegetarian and vegan dishes on restaurant and cafe menus. I was more or less following advice and rules from a well-established movement. I would anticipate little difficulty in maintaining adherence if it was deemed necessary, although there are some foods I would miss.

The viability of vegetarianism is partly a matter of infrastructure; the facilities and atmosphere are more conducive in the UK than in France, for example.[35] It also proves attractive to a particular group within the population. Young people, especially young women, were the most likely converts in the later 20th century but in the 21st century the community is broader. However, the proportion of vegetarians in the British population seems to have remained constant. Many convert, but most converts lapse. Defection is frequent.

Political and ethical anxieties: eating for the planet

Sustainable consumption is an objective for social movements and governments worldwide. Some individuals would like to change their own behaviour, and they may go to considerable lengths to discover and follow means to cast aside old habits and acquire new ones. Many more people would like to change the behaviour of others, so that the collective burden of socially damaging activity is reduced, minimised or eliminated. For the food system is one of the three major sources of greenhouse gas emissions (the other two being transport and indoor temperature control).

When Schumacher famously equated the small and the beautiful he married ethical and aesthetic vision.[36] His call occurred at the dawn of the modern environmental movement when it was possible to think that drawing attention to a looming global catastrophe caused by excessive exploitation of natural resources would be sufficient to induce a transformation in political and economic arrangements. Not so. Obstacles are many. Not least are petrol station forecourts. Besides their primary function in dispensing polluting fossil fuels, their sprawl and ugliness epitomise two features of the British retail environment since the 1970s, an apparent tendency for each shop to sell everything and for a majority to sell some food and drink. The typical garage stocks a wide category of food items that might be sold to passers-by, whatever their purpose, age, stage or schedule. Those items tend to be the lowest common denominator quality, products which, but for a premium added because acquired conveniently while doing something else, would otherwise be cheap. A classic case of matter out of place, they inspire the utterance that 'less is more', much repeated by campaigners who now realise that people are mostly unwilling to give up things that they like and to which they have grown accustomed.

Sacrifices associated with abstinence or denial have little popular appeal in consumer culture. Eat less, eat less meat, eat no meat have all received support as recipes for dealing with the problems of excess in the food system, but they are injunctions to which many people take exception. Ethically inspired commands grate with the ideology of the sovereign consumer, even when self-interested behaviour promises clear personal benefits.

Solutions to the environmental crisis require most people throughout the world to develop different habits. It is difficult not to conclude that Britons eat too much food, of poor quality, and throw too much away. They don't have to do any of these things, but they need political assistance to remedy their defects. Individuals earnestly trying to behave better rarely solve crises of the magnitude of that associated with climate change or obesity. In this exercise aesthetic considerations might fruitfully be harnessed to ethical purpose. Aesthetically grounded messages promising greater pleasure might have more impact. Indeed, environmental campaigns have now recognised that it is possible to exploit the penchant for novelty and style which is so great a part of contemporary markets. For ultimately the world's populations, particularly majorities in the richest countries, must eat differently in order to remediate the environment. They must comply or be compelled to alter what food is produced and consumed in order to avoid a tragedy of the global commons.

The 'EAT-Lancet Commission on healthy diets from sustainable food systems' is an important and instructive document.[37] It proposes 'global scientific targets based on best evidence available for healthy diets and sustainable food production'.[38] It identifies a 'universal healthy reference diet' which could match best possible estimates of the nutritional needs of a global population of ten billion people in 2050 consistent with the environmental carrying capacity of the earth. It concludes that the food system needs to generate approximately 2,500 calories per person per day, with an appropriate balance of foodstuffs delivering sufficient protein, carbohydrate and fat to satisfy nutritional guidelines. The outline of the reference diet is shown in Figure 7.1.

Among the major implications for a typical western citizen are requirements to restrict total calorie intake and reduce protein from farmed animals, with legumes and nuts as replacements. The example of a compliant diet includes: 15 grams of beef, lamb or pork per person per day, which equates to four medium meatballs per week; and 29 grams of chicken per day, or three small chicken thighs per week. By the same logic, each person might have in addition one and a half eggs per week and a medium sized white fish fillet. Items are mutually exchangeable according to taste, but clearly that would not allow anything like the current levels of meat and fish consumption in

Figure 7.1: EAT-Lancet Commission reference diet for a sustainable planet

	Macronutrient intake (possible range), g/day	Caloric intake, kcal/day
Whole grains*		
Rice, wheat, corn, and other†	232 (total gains 0–60% of energy)	811
Tubers or starchy vegetables		
Potatoes and cassava	50 (0–100)	39
Vegetables		
All vegetables	300 (200–600)	–
Dark green vegetables	100	23
Red and orange vegetables	100	30
Other vegetables	100	25
Fruits		
All fruit	200 (100–300)	126
Dairy foods		
Whole milk or derivative equivalents (eg, cheese)	250 (0–500)	153
Protein sources‡		
Beef and lamb	7 (0–14)	15
Pork	7 (0–14)	15
Chicken and other poultry	29 (0–58)	62
Eggs	13 (0–25)	19
Fish§	28 (0–100)	40
Legumes		
Dry beans, lentils, and peas*	50 (0–100)	172
Soy foods	25 (0–50)	112
Peanuts	25 (0–75)	142
Tree nuts	25	149
Added fats		
Palm oil	6.8 (0–6.8)	60
Unsaturated oils¶	40 (20–80)	354
Dairy fats (included in milk)	0	0
Lard or tallow||	5 (0–5)	36
Added sugars		
All sweeteners	31 (0–31)	120

For an individual, an optimal energy intake to maintain a healthy weight will depend on body size and level of physical activity. Processing of foods such as partial hydrogenation of oils, refining of grains, and addition of salt and preservatives can substantially affect health but is not addressed in this table.
*Wheat, rice, dry beans, and lentils are dry, raw. †Mix and amount of grains can vary to maintain isocaloric intake. ‡Beef and lamb are exchangeable with pork and vice versa. Chicken and other poultry is exchangeable with eggs, fish, or plant protein sources. Legumes, peanuts, tree nuts, seeds, and soy are interchangeable. §Seafood consist of fish and shellfish (eg, mussels and shrimps) and originate from both capture and from farming. Although seafood is a highly diverse group that contains both animals and plants, the focus of this report is solely on animals. ¶Unsaturated oils are 20% each of olive, soybean, rapeseed, sunflower, and peanut oil. \|\|Some lard or tallow are optional in instances when pigs or cattle are consumed.

Table 1: Healthy reference diet, with possible ranges, for an intake of 2500 kcal/day

Source: Willett et al (2019)

Britain. Approximately four times as many calories of protein would have to come from dry beans, lentils and nuts. Other ingredients of the diet would require less adaptation – grains, fruit and vegetables and dairy products are less strange, although quantities are diminished overall. The outcome would be not a vegetarian diet but certainly one much more heavily dependent on plants.

The rationale for the diet's components is derived from environmental limits. Achieving sustainability requires reduction of agricultural greenhouse gas emissions, less use of agricultural land for grains to feed animals, reduction of water use, diminishing the effects of excessive application of nitrogen and phosphorus fertilisers, and avoiding of biodiversity loss by converting natural habitats to agricultural land.[39] With the aim of ensuring that everyone on the planet is adequately nourished, it recognises that environmental constraints make this a zero-sum game; only a limited number of calories can safely be made available for consumption globally and if some individuals, groups or countries take more than their share then others will be deprived and malnourished. The report sees the problem as one of collective management of the production of food on an international platform, not of individual choice. No blame is attached to individuals. There are many different ways to meet the nutritional standard, recognising variability in production possibilities and cultural taste across the world. Nevertheless, the degree and rate of change in habits and practices that would be required in the UK is staggering. The report thus makes for instructive contrast with the scale of actual change over the last 70 years.

In the interest of science, and as an omnivorous resident of the UK for almost my entire life, I conducted an experiment – implementing the reference diet. I found it seriously challenging to apply the guidelines to deliver a menu for a fortnight comprising my usual culturally familiar foods. It took several planning sessions to match weights of products, ensure which foods belong to which categories, to calculate equivalents, and to transpose ingredients into dishes and courses. The process required re-education, serious behaviour change, a lot of deliberation, time and acceptance of novelty of a not altogether welcome kind. The report rightly refrained from offering gastronomic direction. It has no pretention to be a cookery book, though were the reference diet to become common or mandatory a plethora of cookbooks and recipes would emerge to offer guidance.

In the end, I devised two weekly meal plans. The first steers close to my currently preferred style of eating. The difficulties were not inconsiderable. A second week aimed to adopt a menu better suited to the logic of the scheme, using international recipes, easily available and affordable ingredients, with less attachment to my established tastes using cheap and accessible foods available in an average British supermarket. My endeavours persuaded me that while these menus did provide enough nutritious food, it was at some considerable loss of my customary culinary practice. I suspect that many others would have a similar experience and be reluctant to commit unilaterally to such a diet. Several associated questions arise. Will the ethical injunction be persuasive and would personal sacrifice be forthcoming if it were to solve the problem of world food shortages? How would the necessary transformation be implemented among entire populations? To what degree can eating habits be changed quickly and permanently?

More pleasure, more anxiety

Peter Jackson dwells momentarily on the possibility that anxieties and their moralisation might be a 'necessary or normal part of the human condition'.[40] Maybe. However, it seems more appropriate to focus on the dynamic dialectic of pleasure and anxiety in concrete historical conjunctures. *Prima facie* the population of Britain, on aggregate, probably experiences both greater pleasure *and* greater anxiety than in the 1950s. A full balance sheet would be very hard to draw up. It seems unlikely that intensity of bodily and sensory gratification has changed. Satisfaction may be little different, although to the extent that food is cheaper and absorbs less of the household budget than in the post-war years, it may cost less. Likewise there is no reason to think that social gratifications have altered in quality, although since more people eat alone in 2020 than in 1960 the opportunities for experiencing the benefits of commensality are reduced. Aesthetic experience, however, is almost certainly enhanced.

Ironically, what *not* to eat is currently the primary focus of attention. Avoidance and reduction frame current approaches to achieving a balance between health, sustainability and enjoyment. Elimination or even reduction in the consumption of currently popular foods, the ostensible target of many interventions, will be extremely difficult without due consideration of ways to preserve and enhance the pleasures associated with eating. Modern Britain has never put much emphasis on enjoyment. Eating is more appreciated elsewhere for its gastronomic interest and its role in sociability. Nevertheless, in the period since the 1950s Britain has experienced more flexibility, allowing for pluralism in practice. In the process eating has become more fun and more gratifying. Long may that last.

8

An Unfinished Revolution?

Directions of change

The story of eating habits in Britain since the Second World War is a complex mix of new and old products, modification to practices, evolving norms embedded in social structural shifts and long-running cultural processes. One impression is that eating is subject to permanent turbulence. Products emerge and disappear, dishes go in and out of fashion, ways of doing things are abandoned only to be revived in episodes of nostalgia. Nevertheless, since the middle of the 20th century some significantly reconfigured culinary regularities and norms have emerged. While none impacts upon everyone and some are expressly resisted, several important trends have gradually established new regularities in aggregate behaviour regarding acquiring food, cooking and meal arrangements, and norms and taste.

Supermarkets came to dominate distribution. They are the conduit for the ready availability of the increased diversity of ingredients in British kitchens. They facilitate the importing of food and ideas from around the world and increase the prevalence of mass manufactured foods. Supermarkets and commercial catering establishments, core institutions in the ongoing process of commodification, form a powerful nexus with mutually supportive effects on innovation, knowledge and preferences. They have been vehicles for the introduction and distribution of novel products and new tastes, including the UPFs which fuel obesity. Food selection developed in a cultural context where health and nutrition became central; food is advertised as medicine and consumer purchasing behaviour is compliant in response. Nutrition has been a professional discourse associated with health promotion for over a century, but its messages seeped into lay discussion in a climate of self-help health care and body management in the later 20th century. Fostered by state promotion of healthy eating, new forms of anxiety about ingredients, their combinations and their processing emerged.

Behind the commercial retailers lies a complex and evolving supply chain. Over the period Commonwealth preference gave way to heavy dependence on European supply after joining the Common Market. Imports, though, were sourced globally throughout by multinational corporations vested in international trade. The supply chain proved robust and reliable even during the COVID-19 pandemic, although food security and sufficiency in the light of war in Ukraine and exit from the EU single market began to make it seem precarious. The production and distribution systems over the period came to provide cheap, counter-seasonal and increasingly diverse foodstuffs that expanded options for the everyday eating of all social classes.

The amount of time devoted to domestic cookery declined steadily, a trend widely welcomed. It was accompanied by general acceptance of pre-prepared foods; convenience became normalised and justified. Among the implications were the decline of the cooked breakfast and the contraction of lunch from a cooked meal to 'soup and sandwiches'. These events became less formal. Informalisation was also apparent at main meals, in the scheduling of eating events, in etiquette and in manners more generally. Eating occasions became more casual and more simple, both at home and in restaurants. The increase in the rate of eating alone probably encouraged such tendencies. As a consequence, some aspects of social anxiety, uncertainty and fear of embarrassment were allayed. Meals became more relaxed and probably gave greater pleasure as social occasions.

The criteria of good taste became more widely discussed and were revised. Cultural intermediaries increased in number in the field of food and attention paid to food in mass and social media burgeoned. Since the 1980s much greater consideration has been given to the aesthetic aspects of food, signified by many more television programmes, restaurant reviews in newspapers, the publication of gourmet food magazines and improvements in food photography. The publicity accorded to food made its qualities and its significance for personal identity highly visible. The expansion of eating out for pleasure has been pivotal to the transformation of taste, and in the consolidation of the judgements promulgated by the new middle class.

The increase in eating out has had a profound influence on culinary practice. That it absorbs a much greater proportion of expenditure on food indicates its significance. It impacts all types of meal, although commercially purchased breakfasts and most lunches are more functional than expressive. Dining out, especially dining out for pleasure and recreation, has had symbolic and culinary effects. Culinary horizons were extended by increased awareness and experience of foreign cuisines and dishes. Restaurant culture played a major role in the spread of gastronomic sensibilities, expanding tastes, nurturing foodies and providing a channel for distinction. A section of the middle class with high cultural capital came to exhibit style and knowledge through the embrace of omnivorousness and variety. In the process of paying homage to variety a hegemonic understanding emerged, despite its implementation being uncongenial to a substantial proportion of the population who prefer familiar or traditional foods and value customary repetition.

There is no doubt that these developments constitute momentous changes and that the landscape of the 2020s is very different from that of the 1950s. However, they are not necessarily evidence of rapid transformation. The key trends took off at different points after the 1960s and most have now been in train for several decades. They have gradually influenced larger numbers in the population, with older cohorts adapting to new circumstances. However, the overall effect was not to make behaviour more homogeneous. Rather the opposite. Diversification led to fragmentation and a 'pick and mix' approach to culinary order. More options and alternatives have emerged with few concerted efforts made to control or steer behaviour towards a common culinary practice. There has been, however, acquiescence to a widespread cultural orientation which values variety and concentrates attention upon aesthetic and ethical dimensions of eating.

At the point of post-war reconstruction tastes were socially fairly uniform such that there was, *de facto*, a national diet, although it was not described as such. Neither was it celebrated, the patterns of consumption being subsequently condemned as monotonous and plain. Viewed as typical of working-class habits, it was increasingly contested by sections of the middle class. For the middle classes, wartime austerity was a temporary imposition or restriction rather than a welcome source of national identity. When, subsequently, culinary practices diversified, attempts to identify or create collective symbolic meaning in British eating practices were unsuccessful. Never since industrialisation had it been possible to tell a good story about British cuisine or culinary culture. The British urban-industrial working-class diet was neither wholesome nor stylish. While the state made successful attempts to improve nutritional adequacy, it made no progress in promoting or enhancing culinary style. The system of mass production and distribution for an urban industrial working class from the mid-19th century was not fertile ground. Britain's staple foods supported a cheap and efficient dietary regime but did not generate a distinctive sensory taste profile.[1] Regional specialities and seasonal products were few, reduced due to industrialisation and mass distribution. The paucity and very belated registration of protected geographical indication (PGI) and protected designated origin (PDO) food products is one indication. No unifying style was discovered or created to symbolise Britishness.

There are a number of reasons why, despite being a country rich in financial and cultural resources, Britain cannot lay claim to a distinctive cuisine. Identifying a national culinary tradition was a matter of very little importance before the 1960s – and by then it was too late. Britain mostly avoided the gastro-nationalist tendencies of the later 20th century, its ethno-national identity perhaps invested in practices other than food. Attempts were made to compile and construct 'a tradition' in the later 20th century as writers of restaurant guides and cookery books sought to give symbolic national meaning to the menus of restaurants and households. However, the practices, ingredients, techniques and flavour combinations proposed failed to define a tradition relevant to the late 20th century. It would anyway have gone against the grain in a period when the authority of tradition was seriously challenged by mass consumption and postmodern cultural tendencies. Consequently multiculturalism and eclecticism arrived earlier than elsewhere. The drive towards developing Modern British Cuisine in the 1970s lost momentum. In the professional kitchen style and taste were demonstrated by experimental dishes and eclectic combinations, which cannot be transferred into domestic settings and therefore inhibit the diffusion of a national tradition or style.

Britain's undistinguished cuisine also has deeper roots. From the enclosures of the 18th century onwards, patterns of landownership penalised small-scale, specialist and localised production. A small land mass serving a large population meant that land for peasant farming, crofting and even cultivation of allotments was in short supply. Hunting, fishing and foraging was severely restricted for the common people. Britain also apparently lost what Jane Grigson considered a noble tradition of vegetable cookery.[2] Additionally, little seems to have been learned about the culinary arts from the Empire, partly because White settlers in the colonies retained the meal patterns and formats and combination of main ingredients similar to those in the UK, and partly from racist assumptions precluding learning from colonial subjects.

The new middle-class understanding

The shaping of taste in the period after 1970 reflected the dispositions of a new middle class. In the field of eating out a hegemonic understanding of the desirability of experiencing maximum variety, incarnated as the omnivorous orientation, diffused through the population. Everyone agrees, whether able to act accordingly or not, that when dining out the goal should be to pursue varied experiences, in comfortable circumstances, paying attention to meals and contexts.[3] Freedoms exist when diners select individually from a menu and from their exercise of some (usually joint) discretion over the venue, although dining out actually surrenders many aspects of control to the restaurateur.

Domestic provisioning is different in that the degrees of freedom are apparently much greater. The dominant preoccupations and procedures of the middle classes are well described by Kate Gibson in *Feeding the Middle Classes*. Her dissection of dispositions towards taste, shopping and the preparation of food exposes the paradoxes and ironies of middle-class practices. Based on interviews with a (small) sample of adults with university degrees in 2016 she remarks that '[p]articipants' food narratives appeared to focus on individual preference, strategic decision-making, and self-surveillance. However … preferred practices and preferences are remarkably similar across the sample. This suggests a shared classed knowledge around food which operates around critical selection, valuing making an effort, and self-control'.[4] She notes the reassurance derived from the belief that exercising individual control over their own shopping and food preparation will ensure the avoidance of the bad habits of others (with whom they associate the working-class urban-industrial diet). Thorough absorption of the ideology of consumer choice allows them to see themselves as self-disciplined actors dedicated to the avoidance of 'bad' food.

The framing and the tone of discussion about eating since the 1970s was suffused with the concerns of sections of the middle classes endowed with high cultural capital. Cultural omnivores and 'the worried well' nurtured the dominant approaches to engagement with food. Both orientations were fed by the ever larger phalanx of cultural intermediaries whose influence spread in the later 20th century with the expansion of the culture industries. They used the institutions and opportunities afforded by consumer culture to redefine standards of taste and normalise procedures for the expression of individual agency and self-identity. An impression exists that distinction based directly on income and class diminished, without entirely disappearing, during the years of rising living standards and the expansion of the welfare state. However, culinary matters were indelibly embossed with the largely uncontested cultural preoccupations of the new middle class which had supplanted both the high culture of the older established upper middle class and the popular culture of the working class. Thereafter, during the austerity of the 2010s, rapidly growing inequality and the waning of the cultural influence of the new middle class began to dispel the impression as class groupings richer in economic than cultural capital began to exert greater influence over definitions of good taste.

What has not changed?

Institutional arrangements are a basis for stability over time. They exist by virtue of shared norms and behavioural regularities which in modern societies are neither frozen nor rigid. They are subject to cultural forces and trends and to economic development. They adjust to economic tendencies, political interventions and sociocultural trends. But adjustment is often slow and contrary. Many crucial features of British eating habits have seen little change in the period since the 1950s. Some are primarily the outcome of normative and moral commitments, others a result of the practical routines which underpin everyday eating. Domestic provision remains predominant. Family meals are still the backbone of the system of food consumption. Family provision is a moral matter, ideologically heavily bolstered, as evidenced by most respondents to the 2015 TCP survey not wanting to eat out more often and very much appreciating dinner at home. The pattern of three meals a day, hierarchically ranked for their importance, persists throughout, although the names given to them vary by class and region. A general commitment to functional eating also persists, at least partly because no alternative positive image of British cuisine is available. Eating patterns continue to symbolise status, reflect social hierarchy and confer cultural capital. Most practices are still differentiated by class, although in a more nuanced and less overt manner than a century ago. Similarly, a gendered division of labour still leaves the majority of food related tasks to women despite the normative justification being now very weak. The rules and expectations associated with domestic hospitality and its support of conviviality also remain the same, as does the preference for eating in company.

Food continues to be regarded as both pleasure and medicine. Hedonism and bodily discipline vie for precedence in circumstances where subsistence is almost guaranteed. Probably greater emphasis is now placed upon *both* pleasure and health. Finally, it remains the case, as Grignon contended, that eating patterns are determined primarily by forms of employment and remuneration and household structure.[5] Household meals are organised around employment schedules, as is functional eating out in commercial settings, which still constitutes a significant proportion of all events taken away from home. These very significant institutional continuities are both cause and effect of the attachment of individuals to their own *personal* habits and routines. Recognised as hard to change, habits explain the slow rate of change in eating patterns.

Is Britain any better off? An audit

The case for improvement

Industrial Britain had a poor reputation for its food and its diet, and is still mostly compared unfavourably with other culinary traditions like France, Japan, Italy and most other Mediterranean countries. However, if starting from a weak position, improvement was detectable. In 1977, Gault and Millau in a restaurant guide to London observed that '[t]he tragedy, with English cuisine, for a very long time, was not only that it was fundamentally bad, but that the English were persuaded that it was very good'.[6] However, interestingly, their opinion had clearly changed by the mid-1990s:[7]

> [T]he city has become a high place of gastronomy. It had a reputation earlier only for foreign restaurants, Indian and Chinese principally. In the last few years everything has changed with the arrival of talented young chefs, imposing little by little a new and seductive cuisine which has been called 'modern British' ('nouvelle cuisine anglaise'). Those who believe that British cuisine is limited to boiled meat flanked by over cooked vegetables ought to take a trip to Bibendum ... or Alastair Little's.[8]

Restaurants improved relative to international standards. Informalisation and aestheticisation enhanced, respectively, the convivial and the presentational aspects of the modern restaurant. The availability of cheaper restaurant meals of fair quality means that most people get to eat out, though some more than others, and almost everyone seems very happy with their experiences in restaurants.

Perhaps eating improved significantly overall towards the end of the 20th century. Interestingly, therefore, when asked in 2003 about whether conditions regarding prices, quality, farming methods, health and safety had improved or deteriorated in the last 20 years, the British public was more positive about the previous two decades than other Europeans.[9] Some major obstacles to enjoyment had been removed in the last quarter of the 20th century. Supply became better controlled and regulated, and hygiene standards were raised. A wider range of foods and tastes were available to more people and to a larger proportion of the population. Plentiful and varied foodstuffs, and copious advice about their use, made a difference. Food remained cheap – if sometimes dangerously so – throughout.

More informal eating reduced the domestic oppression and misery associated with the formal bourgeois family meal, as a result probably giving greater intrinsic pleasure. Commensal eating activities contribute to good health and a sense of wellbeing and most people are able participate to a reasonable degree. Few have to eat alone all the time. The domestic division of labour became less skewed; slow but steady reduction in gender inequalities benefits women. Pragmatic acceptance of convenience food allows relief from arduous and time-consuming tasks and permits greater flexibility in management of meals. More enjoyment seems to be derived from cooking.

Food became more appealing, more attractive in both flavour and appearance. Innovation and global trade increased range of tastes and generated new ideas. People pay more attention to, and exercise greater reflection about, their diet and their preferences; they now take photographs of their dinner, talk a lot about food and watch TV programmes on the topic. Attentiveness also permits consideration of matters of ethics, aesthetics and nutrition. There are more opportunities to question habits, employ judgement and review alternatives. The ideology of the sovereign consumer boosted the sense of agency conducive to imagining that individual reflection and choice could be effective in controlling outcomes.

Most observers probably would not deny that these are positive benefits, although critics might point out that some are mixed blessings, not available to all equally, sometimes offset by counter-trends, sometimes meeting with resistance. Some trends have stalled and further improvement is far from guaranteed. Indeed, some of the social conditions sustaining a climate of improvement and providing an environment for eating better in the later 20th century were depleted in the 21st.

The case against improvement

Changes in everyday eating were never universally praised. Members of the public found many features unsatisfactory and there are outstanding causes for dismay. Concerns about food provenance arose, with repeated intermittent scandals over hygiene and fraud receiving wide media coverage. Newspapers regularly bemoan the individualisation of eating habits. Profound disagreements about the most appropriate diet provoke fierce argument. The commercial strategies and advertising ploys of the major corporations arouse justifiable suspicion. The lobby against the inadequacies of the industrialisation of the food supply is particularly vociferous. The new middle-class indictment of mass-manufactured and over-processed food circulates widely expressing a comprehensive critique of the system of production and consumption. Social and consumer movements have mobilised in parallel, publicising and instituting alternatives to the dominant mode of supply.

Palpable disquiet arises from the view that much of what is eaten is injurious to health. Obesity is a pressing problem that portends general decline in the health of the population and earlier age of death for subsequent generations. Despite the complexity of the phenomenon, eating too much of the wrong types of food is a contributory factor. Critics identify many problematic aspects of the system of production and manufacture which emerged in the era of cheap, mass-manufactured food. One pillar of the hegemonic understanding urges extreme caution about the hazardous properties of food. The commercial catering and hospitality industry is also indicted by those who champion domestic cooking from scratch. Takeaway outlets, sandwich shops, cafes and restaurants are ubiquitous, visible and enticing elements of an obesogenic urban environment constantly touting for customers. The critical voices leading public discussion consider that the conditions for eating a nutritious diet are not yet satisfied.

The food system bears the imprint of social inequalities of many kinds and is subject to criticism on the grounds of its injustice. Not everyone benefits from the positive features as a result of economic inequality and the distribution of cultural capital. It is not just the indigent poor who suffer as many other groups fail to derive sufficient benefit. The pace of change in the division of household responsibilities is much too slow for women. The residents of areas classified as food deserts have inadequate access to high quality fresh produce. Among the most disadvantaged are members of ethnic minority communities who experience multiple deprivation and have poorer than average health and opportunity. Perhaps the greatest injustice is heaped upon the next generation because of laggardly political responses to the effects of climate change on future food supply. Current arrangements are unsustainable; the entangled institutional settlement which aligns the economics of farming, methods of technologically advanced crop and animal husbandry, manufacturing techniques, global market pricing and profit maximisation perpetuates eating habits which compromise planetary integrity. The level of waste is just one depressing symptom of the ramifications of western eating habits for global and environmental justice.

Anxiety remains palpable. Ironically, those who take most interest in eating and who eat out most often appear to derive least pleasure from it and are the most troubled. The new middle class is foremost among the beneficiaries of improvements and yet harshest in its evaluation of the system. Through its roles in cultural intermediation it orchestrates opinion on problematic and controversial issues like food processing, prices, Brexit and environmental hazards. With no direct self-interest in the management of the agro-food system it does not have to be reserved in pointing out the deficiencies of current arrangements and explaining to the public why anxiety is warranted. It is inclined to comment on the ineffectiveness of government policy and failures of regulation. By contrast, those with a big financial stake or sunk costs in present arrangements have different reservations. Organisations at a different point in the food chain with contrasting interests to defend find fault with each other – the farming lobby, for example, routinely criticise retailers and policy makers – and also with consumers and their champions. They find the campaigning new middle class very irritating. Meanwhile, the general public perhaps has different bones to pick with the evolved state of the food system. Some people feel that too much attention is paid to eating. Food has succumbed to the logic of consumer culture and its cycles of innovation, advertising, promotion and affirmations of style, which can seem perverse. As one interviewee in 2015 declared, 'I think we are lucky to be able to eat at all and the idea of incredibly elaborate preparations being made passes me by. Food is not a recreation for me, it's a pleasure but it's a necessity'.[10]

Concluding the audit

Clearly, eating in Britain could be better, very much better. Eating could be more pleasurable, more sociable, more sustainable and more healthy. More people could regularly have better experiences of eating. Descriptions of fine dining in earlier periods were founded upon massive inequalities, the exploitation of servant labour, class and patriarchal domination, colonial exploitation, all symbolised by the luxurious foods served at banquets that only the rich could afford. Nostalgia for the centuries of selfish, inconsiderate and mindless behaviour of the dominant classes is misplaced.

Unequal access to food of the highest quality is a feature of many institutional settings. The powerful and those of higher rank have almost always been better fed: officers in the army, managers in factories, aristocrats on their estates, heads of households, and dons in their Oxbridge colleges received rations of higher quality than that served to their colleagues and dependents of lower social standing. High Table in college symbolises social hierarchy by having some eat their dinner on a raised up platform which materially displays their superior status. Social prestige coincides with better victuals. European aristocracies ate sumptuously while the peasantry were restricted to repetitive diets based primarily on grain porridge and cabbage, occasionally leavened by meat, fish or garden vegetables, depending on local conditions. I occasionally wonder whether I would have liked to eat in Britain in some previous era. I have not found a golden age to which I would want to return. I conclude that it would depend very much on my position in society. If I were a clergyman, a knight or a large landowner, I might have eaten well. If a landless labourer, coal miner or night soil operative, probably not. As a professor I might have eaten relatively well throughout the last three centuries, although if I were committed to gastronomy it would have been advisable to emigrate.

A substantial proportion of the food consumed in Britain is of mediocre quality and those with low incomes are most at risk of poor and inadequate food. The grossly unequal distribution of income and wealth constantly shows its effects. Those who can afford to should perhaps feel an obligation to pay more for their food – to preserve supply, encourage producers, maintain quality, raise standards and nurture specialities. To some extent food enthusiasm may be helping, although redistribution of income and wealth would be a more effective measure than relying on the recreational proclivities of a group of cultural omnivores. Nevertheless, many aspects of eating in Britain improved steadily in the second half of the 20th century, with positive tendencies originating in the 1970s benefiting from a period of higher standards of living and the aestheticisation of lifestyles. Eating in the UK is relaxed. Dominant standards are not enforced to an extent that unconvinced sections of the population find very troublesome. Arguably Britons share knowledge about what to eat, what not to eat, how to eat and what price must be paid, and use that intelligence to pursue and consolidate different types of practice. In these senses eating in Britain is a weakly regulated and weakly coordinated activity. There are multiple options, no compulsion and few prohibitions. The alternative standards and opportunities for compromise permit very varied personal solutions.

Climate change, social change and new habits

Much of the growing literature on behaviour change recognises that to change permanently the way people do things requires the redesign of infrastructures, both social and material.[11] People need reconditioned habits. This is nowhere more apparent than in respect of sustainability. The shadow of climate change darkens everything. Commitment to sustainable production and consumption remains weak and the policies and instruments put in place are limited in their effectiveness. It is delusional to imagine that the solution lies in the hands of individual consumers acting through markets. The improvements of the late 20th century were not generally ones that individuals achieved for themselves by dint of their own independent efforts. Systems of provision, regulation, communication and orchestration of meal occasions are beyond individual control. The forming of new habits and routines is difficult. In the absence of ideological conformity or undisputed authority institutional change is always hard to achieve.

Any solution to the threat of environmental catastrophe posed by climate change requires habits to be altered much more and much faster than has occurred since the 1950s. Discussion about how to change behaviour increased at the beginning of the 21st century, a result partly of neoliberal political projects of 'responsibilisation', the shifting of responsibilities for certain social problems onto the shoulders of individual citizens. Policy then typically sees the problem of change as a matter for individual choice, whether rational or expressive, and the making of decisions in circumstances where they exercise substantial control over their own personal fates and destinies. However, encouraging individuals to behave more responsibly is rarely successful. That is acknowledged by EAT's systems-based approach to the problems of climate change which concludes that only by agreement among governments and firms involved in the production of food can the dangers be eliminated.[12] Regulation is essential and without radical reform or reconstruction of institutions and infrastructure it is unlikely that the crisis caused by greenhouse gas emissions from agriculture, or indeed the obesity epidemic, will end soon enough.

Nevertheless, the question remains of how easily or willingly populations will accept and adopt new consumption practices. The difficulty of persuading, cajoling, incentivising or directing people to change should not be underestimated. In the face of climate change most people know what they could do, and mostly want to be good, but they actually do something else in the face of barriers to changing patterns of behaviour in everyday life. Current arrangements for consumption provide levels of satisfaction, comfort and ease which people are reluctant to jeopardise. Other matters and concerns take precedence over consuming virtuously. Individuals often sense that personal sacrifice will have negligible effect. Cynicism about politics and a sense of political powerlessness compound a general inclination towards continuing to conduct household business and everyday life in the usual manner. As the so-called value–action gap, identified in studies of individual non-compliance with policy, implies, even with general goodwill and widespread acceptance of the necessity for change many people will find themselves incapable of implementing radical change. How individuals behave depends upon their social context and the collective understanding and observance of suitable norms. A cultural change is required, but, as the failures of the many organisations who have sought to solve their difficulties by promising managed 'culture change' show, it almost always takes a long time and, besides, rarely goes to plan.

Those advocating radical change in household behaviour divide pretty equally between those who accord primary responsibility for change to voluntary individual action and those like myself who are unconvinced that individuals can or will behave better as a result of information, encouragement and alternative visions of everyday life and that therefore other strategies are required. This will necessitate that organisations and bodies with the executive power – corporations and the state – alter collective conditions for daily life act to promote and support material and institutional transformation. Both the problems of obesity and the environment require very radical action to which the timidity of governments and the vested interests of capitalist corporations are major obstacles. Sustained, large-scale, organised public pressure must be brought to bear on companies, parties and governments in order to keep the securing of a sustainable future high on the political agenda. An articulate new middle class and the mobilisation of protest movements probably offer the best hope of transforming public and political consciousness.

Eating and sociocultural change

The overall trajectory of eating habits in Britain was subject to powerful cultural processes. If it is proper to refer to a 'revolution' having taken place in the 1960s then it had matured by the 1990s. By then, most visible in commercial dining out, a common British diet has been all but dismantled and removed, replaced by the eclectic drawing on many culinary traditions in the name of variety, a virtue thoroughly established by the end of the 20th century. A varied diet means many different things. It is apparent in fads, health food diets, aversions, and so on. It is called upon in the instruction to eat a balanced and varied diet. It is the preeminent rule governing use of restaurants for the purpose of signalling status where cultural expression of social superiority, expressed through consumption behaviour, took the form of culinary omnivorousness.

Cultural processes generate general understandings, affecting not just food but many other practices. They are not necessarily consistent with one another and they face resistance. They are long-running, arise from regularities and habits of behaviours, and evolve slowly. They appear as cultural cues in an environment which steers habits. Prominent among those processes most relevant to change since the 1950s, discussed throughout the book, are diversification, commodification, aestheticisation, individualisation, stylisation and informalisation. These processes have operated in a social context profoundly shaped by the effects of deindustrialisation on occupational and industrial structure, with the growth of the culture industries providing new occupations and new services, including the expansion of higher education. They are mediated and supplemented by demographic change, corporate reorganisation, the recalibration of temporal rhythms and welfare provision, all of which themselves have cultural aspects and consequences. These processes are fundamental to the reformulation of practices and habits and an essential part of any explanation of change.

Cultural change is slow. The significant differences between classes evident throughout modern British history were modified during the 20th century due to state welfare policies, exploitation of an international supply chain facilitated by Empire, and the political consequences of war.[13] The differences between classes, while remaining large, diminished during the Second World War, which proved to be a watershed, with the 1940s engendering, paradoxically, a major improvement in national health and nutrition. Policy was informed by medical knowledge and advice, social surveys documenting hunger and malnutrition, and the pressure increasingly exerted by a better organised working-class movement. Subsequently, other problems in food supply and consumption were to emerge – in part because of the unforeseen consequences of the mid-20th century diet. The balance between pleasure and anxiety oscillated. After 2010 the blight of poverty and the plight of the poorest returned with a vengeance as a consequence of the imposition of years of austerity.

Throughout the period of writing this book I have regularly pondered whether the changes that occurred in the period since the 1950s deserve to be called a revolution. They certainly amount to more than turbulence. I am not inclined to quarrel with Panayi or Burnett in their characterisation of a revolution in the catering trades and the practice of dining out. An understanding of eating out as a recreational activity had many effects, most importantly normalising multicultural cuisines whose tastes and flavours were widely diffused, a precipitating factor for many other developments. It created space for foreign cuisines and greater aesthetic appreciation of food and the incorporation of eating into lifestyle and identity expression. However, what the population learned from eating out was not so obviously or immediately translated into new forms of domestic practice. The infiltration of recipes from foreign cuisines in the women's magazines and the adoption of pizza, pasta and curry as household staple dishes is significant. It is an effect both of the developments in sensory taste that originated in the takeaway and modest restaurant provision in the years after 1960 and of the willingness of supermarkets to stock the types of vegetables, spices and sauces that make it possible to cook East Asian, South Asian and Mediterranean cuisines at home. However, foreign foods seeped into domestic practice at only a moderate pace. Not everyone uses them, and hardly anyone does so all the time.

Overall, the picture is uneven and begs the question 'whose revolution?'. For those courting the omnivorous orientation, new horizons and opportunities appeared as welcome alternatives to meat and two veg. They were the inheritors and beneficiaries of some fundamental developments. They are the most likely to think that a great deal has changed, despite remaining among the most critical and least satisfied sections of the population. The class of employed professionals who were primarily responsible for the cultivation of culinary distinction also nurture the strongest critical positions about mass and cheap food. For us, there was much discontinuity but not enough change. For others, it would be difficult to see developments as revolutionary, especially for the fraction of the working class who by and large have been unable to afford to dine out frequently; I'm reminded of focus groups in 2003 comprised of the low-paid and the unskilled working class, who said 'I never go; though I would love to go out for meals' and 'We haven't got the money for restaurants. I haven't been to one for years'.[14] For another section of the youthful and more affluent working class the period witnessed more a change in the form and content of industrial mass-produced foods as American and corporate influence extended; fast food and UPFs are as much a continuation as a departure from the urban-industrial diet. Hence, I am not inclined to say that I have lived through a culinary revolution. Given the rate of change it feels more like molecular transformation. It was not a transition of the depth and moment of the one that initially produced the urban-industrial diet. Nor did it approach the level of change that would be implied by the adoption of the reference diet of the EAT-Lancet report which would be a real revolution. Such a transition would require a complete transformation of habits for most people but, if previous history is any guide, that would take ages, which is exactly what the planet cannot afford.

Notes

Chapter 1
1. Wintle, 2006: 64.
2. Otter, 2012: 812.
3. Otter, 2012: 813.
4. Offer, 1989: 333, quoted by Otter, 2012: 817.
5. Otter, 2012: 813.
6. Otter, 2012: 815.
7. Panayi, 2008: 112.
8. Panayi, 2008: 106.
9. Panayi, 2008: 110.
10. See, for recent expositions, Parsons, 2015; Vogler, 2020; Purkiss, 2022; Gibson, 2024.
11. Burnett, 1989: 181.
12. Frame food was a recently introduced patent food for infants/invalids (Burnett, 1989: 211).
13. Burnett, 1989: 211.
14. Burnett, 1989: 192–215.
15. Spencer, 2004; Dickson Wright, 2012.
16. Mennell, 1985: 119–121.
17. Zweiniger-Bargielowska, 2000: 112.
18. Vogler, 2020: 325.
19. Zweiniger-Bargielowska, 2000: 44.
20. Dorling, 2014; Piketty, 2014.
21. Zweiniger-Bargielowska, 2000: 87.
22. The report was also employed extensively as evidence by Burnett (1989) in his interpretation of post-war domestic practices.
23. Otter, 2020.
24. Mennell, 1985.
25. Burnett's (2004: 288–319) final chapter was entitled 'A revolution at table, 1970–2000'.
26. Evans and Tilley (2017) in a study of the continuing impact of class on British politics distinguish usefully between old, new and

junior middle classes. The old middle class consists of managers, the self-employed with employees and self-employed professional working in occupations like business ownership, CEOs, barristers and farmers. The new middle class includes employed professionals and intermediate non-manual groups, employed as architects, teachers, university lecturers, nurses, social workers, occupational therapists and dieticians. The junior middle class is equivalent to routine white-collar occupations in other class taxonomies.

[27] Oesch (2006) distinguishes 'socio-cultural specialists' among the new middle class who exert cultural capital influentially in fields like food and eating.

[28] Warde et al, 2020b. See also Chapter 6.

[29] Gibson, 2024: 103.

[30] Warde, 2013.

[31] Warde, 2016.

[32] Runciman, 2015.

[33] Dorling, 2020.

Chapter 2

[1] Douglas, 1975.

[2] Warren, 1958. See Chapter 1, pp 9–10, for details of the study.

[3] Warren, 1958: 69.

[4] For the EMP study see Yates and Warde (2015, 2017) and Warde and Yates (2017). In the study, 2,784 panel members of a supermarket loyalty card scheme completed an online survey in exchange for card points during September 2012. Respondents reported on their eating activities over two 24-hour periods, one for the weekday prior to filling in the questionnaire and the other for one day during the previous weekend. Each was asked to detail up to three 'main meals' for each day, plus up to four 'additional meals or snacks'. They described the food in their own words and then answered questions about when, for how long, with whom and where it was eaten, as well as its origin and manner of preparation. Data was collected in a time-diary format. Socioeconomic and demographic characteristics were obtained. The response rate was 45 per cent and the achieved sample size was 2,784. A total of 17,582 eating events were recorded. As self-selecting members of a consumer panel the sample is not statistically representative of the general population. Older, more affluent, better educated respondents and respondents without children are somewhat over-represented. Nevertheless, the findings might be considered valid for middle Britain today.

5. The level of detail in self-reports is variable.
6. Incidentally, they also reported more fish and chips, slightly fewer 'other fish' based meals, fewer pies and pastries, and fewer vegetable or salad-based dishes.
7. See also the Mass Observation inquiry about Sundays in 1937 (Southerton, 2020: 126–135).
8. Yates and Warde, 2015.
9. Yates and Warde, 2015.
10. Warren, 1958: 65–66.
11. Warren, 1958: 119.
12. Warren distinguishes between high tea and tea. See also Vogler (2020) on the naming of meals.
13. See Vogler, 2020: 8.
14. Yates and Warde, 2015.
15. O'Connor, 2013 [2006].
16. The first full edition of Mrs. Beeton's much reprinted work was published in 1861 (Beeton, 1861).
17. Otter, 2012.
18. Warren, 1958: 18.
19. Warren, 1958: 19.
20. Warren, 1958: 23.
21. In addition, one-tenth reported eating both cereal and fruit, and one-twentieth cereal and toast. See Yates and Warde, 2015.
22. If one consults Google, as I did on 28 June 2022, by asking what is the 'typical English breakfast' or 'a normal UK breakfast', sites will primarily tender the answer 'a Full English Breakfast'. This is neither typical nor normal in the general understanding of the terms. Some web sites are more accurate in distinguishing between typical and traditional. The full English (usually English rather than British, or Scottish, Welsh or Irish) is at best an invented tradition, as O'Connor demonstrates. Perhaps the most revealing and informative site asked the question 'what do *only* Brits eat for breakfast?', coming up with the answers 'full English, sausage roll, British pancakes, crumpets, egg soldiers, bubble and squeak, tea and biscuits, beans on toast, baked bean omelette, bacon butty'.
23. Warde et al, 2020b: 72.
24. This is very clearly demonstrated for Italy, see Pirani et al (2022), but the same is likely true of the UK.
25. Brannen et al, 2013.
26. Rotenberg, 1981; Vogler, 2020.
27. Southerton, 2020: 125–145.

[28] Southerton (2020: 144) compares interviewee testimony in Bristol in 2000 with the Mass Observation Day in the Life studies of 1937 first collected to mark the Coronation of King George VI.
[29] Brannen et al, 2013; Southerton, 2009.
[30] Southerton et al, 2012.
[31] In 2012 for the evening meal, 22 per cent of respondents ate a dessert, nearly all of the simpler variety. A few per cent ate additional courses of cheese, of sandwiches or of soup, varying substantially by season and day of the week. Only 1 per cent of meals in 2012 involved three or more courses. Potatoes were eaten in around a third of meals, the same proportion ate at least one other vegetable, and around half ate bread – although rarely as a sandwich. Yates and Warde, 2015.
[32] On Sundays, 19 per cent lasted more than 30 minutes, of which 46 per cent were roast dinners. Warde and Yates, 2017: 107.
[33] Herpin (1988) deconstructed the component elements which might offer (differing) indications of the waning of the meal. He identified five elements: disimplantation, as meals no longer occurred at regular times; de-synchronisation, meals being less and less coordinated between individuals and family members; de-localisation, with meals being eaten neither in kitchen nor dining room, but in other rooms or out of the house entirely, in restaurants, in parks and while traveling; de-concentration, with less eating occurring at the 'principal meals', with principal meals being simplified; and de-ritualisation, as people no longer observed a difference between special occasions and the ordinary daily round.
[34] Warde and Yates, 2017: 15.
[35] Warde and Yates, 2017.
[36] Warren, 1958, *passim*.
[37] Approximately 45 per cent of adults had early morning tea, 92 per cent breakfast, circa 55 per cent mid-morning break with food items accompanying a beverage in half the cases (biscuits, cake, sandwiches, bread and butter), 98 per cent had a midday meal, around 55 per cent took a mid-afternoon break (tea being the predominant beverage, with food in half the cases, where cake, scones and pastries came into their own), just over 90 per cent ate a principal evening meal (either high tea/tea [67 per cent] or dinner), and about 80 per cent had late supper (comprising more or less equally: biscuits and bread and butter or toast; sandwiches; cooked foods).
[38] Warde and Yates, 2017.
[39] See Yates and Warde, 2017.
[40] The ten most common snack food items in 2012 listed in order of importance are fruit (709 mentions, over both days), biscuits (502),

chocolate (344), crisps (334), cake (186), bread (with 56 instances of toast, 38 of sandwich and 19 of bread, 113 altogether), cheese (92), ices/ice-creams (83), nuts (81) and cereal (50). Warde and Yates, 2017: 24.

[41] Murcott, 1997.
[42] Murcott, 2019: 38.
[43] Southerton, 2003.
[44] Darmon and Warde, 2019.
[45] Brannen et al, 2013.
[46] Marshall and Pettinger, 2009.
[47] Warde and Martens, 2000; Marshall and Pettinger, 2009; FSA, 2014.
[48] Burnett, 2004; Warde et al, 2020b.
[49] Warde and Martens, 2000: 34; Warde et al, 2020b: 23.
[50] Warde et al, 2020b: 31–34.
[51] See Warde and Martens, 2000; Julier, 2013; Warde et al, 2020a.
[52] The TCP examined change over the period 1995 to 2015. Lydia Martens and I carried out a study of eating out in three cities in England in 1995. The study was repeated by Jessica Paddock, Jennifer Whillans and myself in 2015. The focus was main meals, on the assumption that more important meals would best reveal the symbolic meaning of the practice of dining out. The re-study used an almost identical survey to the first and some additional qualitative interviews. Three instruments provide the data. A survey of a thousand people conducted in April 1995 in Preston, Bristol and London examined, *inter alia*, the frequency of eating out at different types of restaurants, motivations and attitudes towards dining out in commercial establishments and in the homes of others, and social and demographic information about respondents. A repeat survey in the same three cities in Spring 2015 asked many identical questions. Follow-up, in-depth, semi-structured interviews were conducted with respondents to the second survey across the three cities to explore understandings and experiences of eating out and the integration of routines of eating out and eating at home. For further information, see Warde et al, 2020b.
[53] Fischler, 2011: 539.
[54] Yates and Warde, 2017.
[55] Halsey and Webb (2000: 77) and ONS (2022). Put another way, in 1961 one person in 25 lived alone, but one person in eight in 2019.
[56] Southerton et al, 2012: 21.
[57] Lawrence, 2019.
[58] Most vividly expressed by Bourdieu, 1984 [1979].

59 Warde et al, 2020b: 81.
60 Warde et al, 2020b.
61 Wouters, 2008.

Chapter 3
1. DEFRA, 2017: 14.
2. ONS, 2020.
3. ONS (2023) ONS, Retail Prices Index: Long run series: 1947 to 2023. https://www.ons.gov.uk/economy/inflationandpriceindices/timeseries/cdko/mm23
4. The rapid inflation in food prices in the 2020s, which were said to have increased by 18 per cent in the year to February 2023, is a sharp but probably temporary increase due to exceptional circumstances. It is probable that prices will return to the relative levels of the last century in the medium term. In the long-term global climate changes might be expected to bring an end to the stability of real prices.
5. Dorling, 2014; Piketty, 2014; Savage, 2021.
6. DEFRA, 2019, chart 1.6.
7. See Chapter 2, p 32.
8. Spending on food and non-alcoholic drinks in the bottom decile is just more than half that of those in decile 10, while overall spending for the bottom decile is less than one-third of that of decile 10, meaning that those at the lower end of the income distribution are spending proportionately more on food than those at the top. ONS (2020).
9. Atkinson, 2021.
10. Atkinson, 2021: 904.
11. Atkinson, 2021: 903.
12. Atkinson, 2021: 904.
13. Atkinson, 2021: 904.
14. Atkinson, 2021: 904.
15. Thompson, 1971.
16. Sen, 1983.
17. Garthwaite, 2016.
18. *Food Banks in the UK*, House of Commons Library Research Briefing, 14 July 2021, p 17. It is also noted that 'The Independent Food Aid Network estimates that there are at least another 3,000 independent food aid providers working beyond the food bank model across the UK including social supermarkets, soup kitchens, community food projects and school holiday meal providers' (Garthwaite, 2016: 29).
19. Standing, 2011.

20 Garthwaite, 2016: 49.
21 Garthwaite, 2016: 48.
22 Zweiniger-Bargielowska, 2000 (also mentioned in Chapter 1).
23 Lang, 2019: 106.
24 Lang, 2019: 100.
25 Lang, 2019: 83.
26 Mintz, 2008; see also Mintz, 1985.
27 Warde, 2009: 227. Appadurai (1990, 1996) postulates that globalisation involves flows of people, money, goods, ideas and commands.
28 Appadurai, 1990: 306.
29 See Wilk (2006) for a stimulating account of those processes in Belize since the 16th century.
30 See Harvey et al (2002) for an account of the transformation of the tomato in the 20th century the identity of which lies more in its name than its material substance.
31 See Lane, 2014; Leschziner, 2015.
32 DEFRA, 2019: The five were Tesco, Sainsbury, Asda, Morrisons and Aldi.
33 Harvey, 2002.
34 Diversity does however have costs as well as benefits, when markets tend to extend the breadth rather than the depth of available ingredients. Wilson (2019: 49) filled a typed page with the varieties of apple beginning with the letter 'c' to emphasise the effective loss of types once available in Britain each with distinct tastes and properties.
35 ONS, 2019. It also records 650 farmers' markets.
36 Metcalfe and Warde, 2002: 191–196.
37 Elder-Vass, 2015: 456.
38 See, for example, Kneafsey et al, 2008.
39 Incredible Edible was one of several community gardening organisations in the town during the 2010s. See Farrier et al, 2019.
40 Warde et al, 2020b: 383.
41 Warde et al, 2020b: 380.
42 Warde et al, 2020b: 384. It should be noted that most others (18 per cent) reported 'liking' the commercial event.
43 WRAP, 2013.
44 Evans, 2014.
45 Lane, 1991.

Chapter 4

1 Teil and Hennion, 2004: 20.
2 Rozin, 1992: xiv. Of flavour principles she says, 'we will find within each culinary tradition the pervasive use of certain combinations of

seasoning ingredients. Every culture tends to combine a small number or flavouring ingredients so frequently and so consistently that they become definitive of that particular cuisine'.
3. Ahn et al, 2011.
4. Panayi, 2008: 215.
5. Panayi, 2008: 154.
6. Panayi, 2008: 36.
7. See Moehring (2008) who describes a similar process in Germany.
8. Panayi, 2008: 216.
9. Panayi, 2008: 209.
10. Burnett, 1989: 312.
11. https://yougov.co.uk/ratings/food/popularity/dishes/all
12. The most popular ten 'British' items in the fourth quarter of 2021, according to the poll, were: fish and chips, chips, roast chicken, English breakfast, mashed potatoes, soup, roast beef, bangers and mash, beans on toast, and pigs in blankets (https://yougov.co.uk/ratings/food/popularity/dishes/all). Note the heterogeneity of the items, that they are all savoury, and bear in mind who might have paid for the information or be primarily interested in it. (In this case it would appear that it is the food manufacturing industry as most of the items, and the rather strange list of only Italian and Mexican [not Indian or Chinese] foreign dishes are ones that might be found on a supermarket shelf or in mid-market restaurants.)
13. Baudrillard, 1998 [1970].
14. Warde and Martens (1998: 144) point out that 'the availability of resources, systemic inequalities of power in decision-making, shared cultural and aesthetic judgement, and "situational entailment", all constrain individual choice'.
15. Warde et al, 2020b: 131.
16. Warde et al, 2020b: 129.
17. Warde et al, 2020b: 129–132.
18. Warde et al, 2020b: 42, figure 3.1.
19. Lane, 2018.
20. Their circulation has fallen very significantly, and their coverage of food has reduced as some of their functions have been usurped by websites (see Warde and Hirth, 2022).
21. Cooking nutritious and healthy dishes, and saving time and effort have become much more prominent injunctions over the last 50 years.
22. Warde, 1997: 61.
23. Few dishes are explicitly identified as 'British' but, by implication, for those 'unmarked', it is taken for granted that they are not of foreign origin (on the marked and unmarked, see Zerubavel, 2018).

24 By comparison, in 1968 the proportions were 12 per cent and 46 per cent (see Warde and Hirth, 2022: table 1).
25 Sulkunen, 2009.
26 Bauman, 1988; Giddens, 1991.
27 See Warde, 2000.
28 Hardyment, 1995: 129–131.
29 Burnett, 2004.
30 Warde et al, 2020b: 214.
31 The most popular main dishes at evening meals during the week are, in rank order: fish with potatoes (for example, fish and chips, fish and new potatoes); non-carcase meat and potatoes (for example, cottage pie, sausages and mash); poultry with potatoes (for example, chicken and chips, roast chicken and new potatoes); pasta accompanied by non-carcase meat (for example, spaghetti bolognaise, lasagne); and poultry and rice (for example, chicken stir-fry). The equivalent line up for dinners at the weekend is: beef and potatoes (for example, roast beef dinner); poultry with potatoes (for example, roast chicken dinner, chicken and chips); cheese and bread (for example, cheese sandwich, cheese on toast); fish with potatoes (for example, fish and chips, fish and new potatoes); and pork with potatoes (for example, roast dinner, chops and new potatoes).
32 Yates and Warde, 2015.
33 *GFG*, 1951: 88.
34 By cuisine should be understood not just cooking or flavour principle, but all that the composition of meals entails for a social collectivity – tools, recipes, condiments, typical ingredients and the organisation of eating This would be the orthodox understanding in the contemporary literature on gastronomy (see, for instance, Gault, 2000).
35 Ashley et al, 2004: 76ff.
36 *GFG*, 1966: 15.
37 The campaign took some cues from the very successful Campaign for Real Ale (CAMRA).
38 *GFG*, 1987: 8.
39 *GFG*, 1995: 21.
40 See Warde, 2009.
41 *GFG*, 2001: 55.
42 It also echoes the much less elevated *table d'hôte* format – you eat that which the cook or chef has prepared for you, no choice.
43 On the rationale and practices of fine dining restaurants see Lane (2014) and Leschziner (2015).
44 Warde et al, 2020b: 246–247.

Chapter 5

1. *Daily Mirror* (2015).
2. Another *Daily Mirror* column from January 2021 (Daily Mirror, 2021) under the headline 'More than half of Brits eat just six different meals on a loop, study finds', gave a rank ordering of the 'Top 30 meals Brits cook on rotation': 1. Spaghetti Bolognese; 2. Pizza; 3. Pasta with a sauce; 4. Roast dinner; 5. Fish and chips; 6. Curry; 7. Jacket potato; 8. Stir fry; 9. Sausage and mash; 10. Shepherd's pie; 11. Lasagne; 12. Soup; etc. The rank order seems not implausible and is perhaps a fair approximation to the contents of mundane domestic cooking.
3. DEFRA, 2019.
4. Schor, 1992.
5. See Hand et al, 2007.
6. Cowan (1983) makes a strong case that modern domestic goods make 'More Work for Mother'.
7. See Warde, 1999 and Chapter 2, this volume.
8. This was especially well articulated in Marjorie DeVault's (1991) study of women in Canada.
9. Charles and Kerr, 1988.
10. Warde and Hetherington, 1994.
11. That is to say, if a husband refused to do a domestic task, the ideology of housewifery compelled his wife to make a respectable shot at it to protect the household's status in the neighbourhood or social network.
12. Sullivan, 2000.
13. Neuman et al, 2017.
14. Warde et al, 2020b: 87–88.
15. Julier, 2013; Parsons, 2015.
16. Hand et al, 2007.
17. Cheng et al, 2007.
18. Warren, 1958.
19. Yates and Warde, 2015.
20. Metcalfe et al, 2009.
21. O'Connell and Brannen, 2016: 42.
22. Kaufmann, 2010.
23. O'Connell and Brannen, 2016: 60–79.
24. O'Connell and Brannen, 2016: 78.
25. Abercrombie, 2020.
26. Warde, 1997: 131–133; Warde and Hirth, 2022.
27. Parsons, 2015; O'Connell and Brannen, 2016.
28. Davis et al, 2016.
29. Mellor et al, 2010.

30 Daniels et al, 2015.
31 The median British household spent £101.70 on food (41 per cent of which was on catering services). The richest decile spent £147.60 on food, 50 per cent of which was on catering. The highest decile spent over four times as much as the lowest on food – though rich households do contain more people – and that was 10 per cent of total expenditure. ONS, *Family Spending*, 2019–2020.
32 Freidberg, 2009.
33 See Short (2006) for a revisionist account of ordinary everyday cooking, how many factors other than skill determine its worth, and how it could be more sensibly taught.
34 Rayner, 2016.
35 Leynse, 2006: 131.
36 Oncini, 2021.
37 Paddock and Warde, 2015.
38 Of a long list of domestic tasks presented to adults in family households in 1990, only shopping for clothes and nursing children were less likely never to be enjoyable. See Warde and Hetherington, 1994: 768.
39 O'Connell and Brannen, 2016: 79.

Chapter 6
1 Barr and Levy, 1984: 7.
2 Barr and Levy, 1984: 6.
3 The four sections of the book are entitled 'The foodie at home', 'The foodie eats out', 'The global foodie' and 'A foodie's who's who'.
4 Cairns et al, 2010: 591.
5 Barr and Levy, 1984: 7.
6 Barr and Levy, 1984: 7.
7 Parsons, 2015.
8 Parsons, 2015: 135.
9 Johnston and Baumann, 2010.
10 Among the precipitating factors we should consider not only the forces identified by Panayi – migration, globalisation and affluence – but also the growing number of students living away from home, greater access via car ownership, tourism, cultural intermediaries and the burgeoning service sector which emerged to serve a more affluent population.
11 For example, Allegra, 2009; Mintel, 2017.
12 See Chapter 2, n 52, for a description of the study and the methods employed. The central part of this chapter originated in the Annual Distinguished Lecture at SOAS Food Studies Centre in 2019 and was

published as 'Changing tastes: the evolution of dining out in England', *Gastronomica: The Journal of Critical Food Studies*, 18(4): 1–12, Winter, 2018. I am grateful to the Food Studies Centre for the invitation to deliver the lecture, to *Gastronomica* for permission to reprint parts of the article and to Jess Paddock and Jen Whillans who worked on the joint project.

13 Other aspects of the process of normalisation are discussed in Paddock et al, 2017.
14 Warde and Martens, 2000: 83.
15 'Traditional British' is a heterogeneous and possibly residual category, denoting ambience as well as cooking style. The most frequently consumed dishes were roast meat, steak, fish and chips, chicken and burgers. Over half of all meals described were obtained in either a pub or a casual dining restaurant. In such places menus include items originating from several different culinary traditions but if requiring an overall typification of their cuisine would probably be seen as 'Traditional British'.
16 Principal Component Analysis was used to group together respondents' preferences generating Factor 1, the *uncommon*: Vegetarian, Thai, Japanese, Other ethnic and Indian; Factor 2, the *popular*: Traditional British, American, Italian and Chinese; and Factor 3, the *exclusive*: Modern British and French.
17 Peterson and Kern, 1996; Lizardo and Skiles, 2016.
18 Johnston and Baumann, 2010; Warde et al, 2019.
19 Only in their patronage of takeaway fish and chip shops are they beneath average in obtaining meals from any of the sources of food about which the survey inquired.
20 Wouters, 2008.
21 Burnett, 2004.
22 Appadurai, 1990.
23 There is, of course, much to be said for turning drudgery into pleasure and unwelcome labour into rewarding work.
24 Wernick, 1981; Haug, 1986.
25 Shapin, 2011: 176.
26 See Driver, 1983.
27 Atkinson, 2017; Reckwitz, 2017 [2012] and 2020 [2017].
28 Bauman, 1988: 64.
29 Bourdieu, 1984 [1979]: 175.
30 Sallaz and Zavisca, 2007; Santoro and Solaroli, 2016.
31 Warde et al, 2020b: 173. Being in middle age groups, living in London or Bristol and not having dependent children are also significant.
32 Vogler, 2020.

[33] Vogler, 2020: 414.
[34] Friedman and Reeves, 2020.
[35] Resentment is not necessarily eliminated, however. In 2003, 49 per cent of respondents to a survey of cultural taste in the UK disagreed with the statement 'The old snobbery once associated with cultural taste has now all but disappeared' (Warde et al, 2007b).

Chapter 7

[1] Eating is a so-called traditional pleasure, one that gives pleasure and satisfaction repeatedly. Modern consumption, by contrast, operates by perpetually changing wants, as possessions lose their charm and require replacement by novel alternatives. (Eating also has modern features.) (See Campbell, 1987: 58ff; Scitovsky, 1976.)
[2] United Nations, 2023.
[3] Warde, 2015; Warde and Martens, 2000: 175–184; Warde et al, 2020b: 125–128.
[4] Warde and Martens, 2000: 180–181.
[5] Seven per cent of respondents entertained guests several times a week and a further 13 per cent did so weekly, the median frequency being once every six weeks. Fifty-six per cent had invited a family member, 56 per cent a friend and 10 per cent a colleague during the previous year.
[6] See further Warde et al, 2020b: 97.
[7] Warde et al, 2020b: 39.
[8] My own memory suggests that the lower middle class sometimes invited friends to buffet tea on Sundays!
[9] Meah and Watson, 2011.
[10] Warde, 2016: 100–121.
[11] Jackson, 2015: 39.
[12] Kjaernes et al, 2007.
[13] Jackson, 2015: 51.
[14] Jackson, 2015: 48.
[15] See Kjaernes et al (2007: 39) on which actors, in the case of food scandal, could be trusted to tell the truth.
[16] Wansick, 2006.
[17] For example, Guthman (2011: 191): 'Healthism makes personal health attainment the highest goal, sees poor health outcomes as a result of behaviors, and conflates personal practices of self-care with empowerment and citizenship.'
[18] Bivins, 2020.
[19] Oncini et al, 2023.
[20] Patel, 2022.

21 See Bennett et al, 2009: 168.
22 Willett et al, 2019. For discussion see section 'Political and ethical anxieties: eating for the planet' in this chapter.
23 Bivins, 2020.
24 Nestle, 2007.
25 On eating 'only' food see Pollan, 2008; Rayner, 2016. The concept of UPFs is attributed to Carlos Monteiro in 2009. Chris van Tulleken's (2023) recent enlightening popular and persuasive account, *Ultra-Processed People*, gives an extended account of how 'advances' in food chemistry result in the production of heavily promoted products containing highly processed fats, artificial sweeteners and supplementary additives, and which have addictive properties.
26 Baker et al, 2020: 2.
27 Baker et al, 2020: 4.
28 van Tulleken, 2023: 20.
29 Warde, 1993.
30 Darmon, 2009.
31 Spencer, 2016.
32 Gabaccia, 1998.
33 Boyle, 2011.
34 For example, Beardsworth and Keil, 1997: 235.
35 Darmon and Warde, 2016.
36 Schumacher, 1973.
37 Willett et al, 2019.
38 Willett et al, 2019: 447.
39 Willett et al, 2019: 472–474.
40 Jackson, 2015: 50.

Chapter 8
1 O'Connor (2013 [2006]) listed carrots, turnips and onions as the basic vegetable building blocks of British cookery in the 19th century which are neither the most flavoursome nor the most versatile of ingredients.
2 Grigson, 1980 [1978].
3 Warde et al, 2020b: 222–224. See also Chapter 6, this volume.
4 Gibson, 2024: 102.
5 Grignon, 1993.
6 Gault and Millau, 1977.
7 Still, one of the best way to evaluate both esteem and change in national culinary cultures is through the perceptions of external observers (see Fischler and Masson, 2007: 14–16). However, it should

be remembered that external commentators mostly have to base their opinions on observation of public establishments.
8   Gault and Millau, 1994.
9   Kjaernes et al, 2007: 66.
10 Warde et al, 2020b: 180.
11 For example, Thaler and Sunstein, 2009.
12 See Swinburn et al, 2019.
13 Vogler, 2020.
14 Bennett et al, 2009: 165.

References

Abercrombie, N. (2020) *Commodification and its Discontents*, Cambridge: Polity.

Ahn, Y.Y., Ahnert, S., Bagrow, J. and Barabasi, A.L. (2011) 'Flavor network and the principles of food pairing', *Scientific Reports*. Available at: http://www.npr.org/blogs/thesalt/2011/12/20/144021294/what-a-global-flavor-map-can-tell-us-about-how-we-pair-foods

Allegra (2009) *Eating Out in the UK, 2009: A Comprehensive Analysis of the Informal Eating Out Market*, Allegra.

Appadurai, A. (1990) 'Disjuncture and difference in the global cultural economy', *Theory, Culture & Society*, 7(2–3): 295–310.

Appadurai, A. (1996) *Modernity at Large*, Minneapolis: University of Minnesota Press.

Ashley, B., Hollows, J., Jones, S. and Taylor, B. (2004) *Food and Cultural Studies*, London: Routledge.

Atkinson, W. (2017) *Class in the New Millennium: The Structure, Homologies and Experience of the British Social Space*, London: Routledge.

Atkinson, W. (2021) 'The structure of food taste in 21st century Britain', *British Journal of Sociology*, 72(4): 891–908.

Baker, P., Machado, P., Santos, T., Sievert, K., Backholer, K., Hadjikakou, M., et al (2020) 'Ultra-processed foods and the nutrition transition: global, regional and national trends, food systems transformations and political economy drivers', *Obesity Reviews*, 21(12): e13126.

Barr, A. and Levy, P. (1984) *The Official Foodie Handbook*, London: Ebury Press.

Baudrillard, J. (1998 [1970]) *The Consumer Society: Myths and Structures*, London: SAGE.

Bauman, Z. (1988) *Freedom*, Milton Keynes: Open University Press.

Beardsworth A. and Keil, T. (1997) *Sociology on the Menu: An Invitation to the Study of Food and Society*, London: Routledge.

Beeton, I. (1861) *Mrs Beeton's Book of Household Management*, London: S.O. Beeton.

Bennett, T., Savage, M., Silva, E., Warde, A., Gayo-Cal, M. and Wright, D. (2009) *Culture, Class, Distinction*, London: Routledge.

Bivins, R. (2020) 'Weighing on us all? Quantification and cultural responses to obesity in NHS Britain', *History of Science*, 58(2): 216–242.

Bourdieu, P. (1984 [1979]) *Distinction: A Social Critique of the Judgement of Taste*, London: Routledge & Kegan Paul.

Boyle, J. (2011) 'Becoming vegetarian: the eating patterns and accounts of newly practicing vegetarians', *Food and Foodways*, 19(4): 314–333.

Brannen, J., O'Connell, R. and Mooney, A. (2013) 'Families, meals and synchronicity: eating together in British dual earner families', *Community, Work & Family*, 16(4): 417–434.

Burnett, J. (1989) *Plenty and Want: A Social History of Food in England from 1815 to the Present Day* (3rd edition), London: Routledge.

Burnett, J. (2004) *England Eats Out: 1830 – Present*, Harlow: Pearson.

Cabinet Office (2008) *Food: An Analysis of the Issues*, London: Cabinet Office Strategy Unit. Available at: https://www.carbonindependent.org/files/cabinet_office_food_analysis.pdf

Baumann, S., Johnston, J. and Cairns, K. (2010) 'Caring about food: doing gender in the foodie kitchen', *Gender and Society*, 24(5): 591–615.

Campbell, C. (1987) *The Romantic Ethic and the Spirit of Modern Consumerism*, Oxford: Basil Blackwell.

Charles, N. and Kerr, M. (1988) *Women, Food and Families*, Manchester: Manchester University Press.

Cheng, S.-L., Olsen, W., Southerton, D. and Warde, A. (2007) 'The changing practice of eating: evidence from UK time diaries, 1975 and 2000', *British Journal of Sociology*, 58(1): 39–61.

Cowan R.S. (1983) *More Work for Mother: The Ironies of Household Technology from the Open Hearth to the Microwave*, New York: Basic Books.

Daily Mirror (2015) 'How many meals can you cook?', 26 February.

Daily Mirror (2021) 'More than half of Brits eat just six different meals on a loop, study finds', 21 January.

Daniels, S., Glorieux, I., Minnen, J., Van Tienoven, T. and Weenas, D. (2015) 'Convenience on the menu? A typological conceptualization of family food expenditures and food-related time patterns', *Social Science Research*, 51: 205–218.

Darmon, I. and Warde, A. (2016) 'Senses and sensibilities: stabilising and changing tastes in cross-national couples', *Food Culture & Society*, 19(4): 705–722.

Darmon, I. and Warde, A. (2019) 'Habits and orders of everyday life: commensal adjustment in Anglo-French couples', *British Journal of Sociology*, 70(3): 1025–1042.

Darmon, M. (2009) 'The fifth element: social class and the sociology of anorexia', *Sociology*, 43(4): 717–733.

DEFRA (Department for Environment, Food and Rural Affairs) (2017) *Family Food 2015*, London: DEFRA.

DEFRA (Department for Environment, Food and Rural Affairs) (2019) *Food Statistics Pocketbook, 2018*, London: DEFRA

DeVault, M. (1991) *Feeding the Family: The Social Organisation of Caring as Gendered Work*, Chicago: Chicago University Press.

Dickson Wright, C. (2012) *A History of English Food*, London: Arrow Books.

Dorling, D. (2014) *Inequality and the 1%*, London: Verso.

Dorling, D. (2020) *Slowdown: The End of the Great Acceleration – and Why It's Good for the Planet, the Economy, and Our Lives*, New Haven: Yale University Press.

Douglas, M. (1975) 'Deciphering a meal', in Douglas, M. (ed) *Implicit Meanings: Selected Essays in Anthropology*, London: Routledge and Kegan Paul, pp 249–275.

Driver, C. (1983) *The British at Table 1940–1980*, London: Vintage.

Elder-Vass, D. (2015) 'Free gifts and positional gifts: beyond exchangism', *European Journal of Social Theory*, 18(4): 451–468.

Evans, D. (2014) *Food Waste: Home Consumption, Material Culture and Everyday Life*, London: Bloomsbury.

Evans, G. and Tilley, J. (2017) *The New Politics of Class: The Political Exclusion of the British Working Class*, Oxford: Oxford University Press.

Farrier, A., Dooris, M. and Morley, A. (2019) 'Catalysing change? A critical exploration of the impacts of a community food initiative on people, place and prosperity', *Landscape and Urban Planning*, 192. https://doi.org/j.landurbplan.2019.103663

Fischler, C. (2011) 'Commensality, society and culture', *Social Science Information*, 50(3–4): 528–548.

Fischler, C. ad Masson, E. (2007) *Manger: Francais, Européens et Américains face a l'alimentation*, Paris: Odile Jacob.

Freidberg, S. (2009) *Fresh: A Perishable History*, Cambridge, MA: Belknap/Harvard University Press.

Friedman, S. and Reeves, A. (2020) 'From aristocratic to ordinary: shifting modes of elite distinction', *American Sociological Review*, 85(2): 323–350.

FSA (Food Standards Agency) (various years) *The Food and You Survey: UK Bulletin*, London: FSA Social Science Research Unit.

Gabaccia, D. (1998) *We Are What We Eat: Ethnic Food and the Making of Americans*, Cambridge, MA: Harvard University Press.

Garthwaite, K. (2016) *Hunger Pains: Life Inside Foodbank Britain*, Bristol: Policy Press.

Gault, H. and Millau, C. (various years) *Guide Gault&Millau a Londres*, Paris: Gault-Millau.

GFG (*Good Food Guide*) (various years, various publishers).

Gibson, K. (2024) *Feeding the Middle Classes: Taste, Classed Identity and Domestic Food Practices*, Bristol: Bristol University Press.

Giddens, A. (1991) *Modernity and Self-Identity: Self and Society in the Late Modern Age*, Cambridge: Polity.

Grignon, C. (1993) 'La règle, la mode et le travail: la genèse social du modèle des repas français contemporain', in Aymard, M., Grignon, C. and Sabban, F. (eds) *Le Temps de Manger: alimentation, emploi du temps et rythmes sociaux*, Paris: Maison de Sciences de l'Homme, pp 275–324.

Grigson, J. (1980 [1978]) *Jane Grigson's Vegetable Book*, Harmondsworth: Penguin.

Guthman, J. (2011) *Weighing In: Obesity, Food Justice and the Limits of Capitalism*, Berkeley: University of California Press.

Halsey, A.H. and Webb, J. (eds) (2000) *Twentieth-Century British Social Trends*, London: Macmillan.

Hand, M., Shove, E. and Southerton, D. (2007) 'Home extensions in the United Kingdom: space, time, and practice', *Environment and Planning D: Society and Space*, 35(4): 668–681.

Hardyment, C. (1995) *Slice of Life: The British Way of Eating since 1945*, London: BBC Books.

Harvey, M. (2002) 'Markets, supermarkets and the macro-social shaping of demand: an instituted economic process', in McMeekin, A., Green, K., Tomlinson, M. and Walsh, V. (eds) *Innovation by Demand: An Interdisciplinary Approach to the Study of Demand and its Role in Innovation*, Manchester: Manchester University Press, pp 187–208.

Harvey, M., Quilley, S. and Beynon, H. (2002) *Exploring the Tomato: Transformations of Nature, Society and Economy*, Cheltenham: Edward Elgar.

Haug, W.F. (1986) *Critique of Commodity Aesthetics*, Cambridge: Polity.

Herpin, N. (1988) 'Le repas comme institution, compte rendu d'une enquête exploratoire', *Revue Francaise de Sociologie*, 19: 503–521.

Jackson, P. (2015) *Anxious Appetites: Food and Consumer Culture*, London: Bloomsbury.

Johnston, J. and Baumann, S. (2010) *Foodies: Democracy and Distinction in the Gourmet Foodscape*, London: Routledge.

Julier, A.P. (2013) *Eating Together: Food, Friendship, and Inequality*, Chicago: University of Illinois Press.

Kaufmann, J-C. (2010) *The Meaning of Cooking*, Cambridge: Polity.

Kjaernes, U., Harvey, M. and Warde, A. (2007) *Trust in Food: An Institutional and Comparative Analysis*, Basingstoke: Palgrave Macmillan.

REFERENCES

Kneafsey, M., Cox, R., Holloway, L., Dowler, E., Venn, L. and Tuomainen, H. (2008) *Reconnecting Consumers, Producers and Food: Exploring Alternatives*, London: Berg.

Lane, C. (2014) *The Cultivation of Taste: Chefs and the Organization of Fine Dining*, Oxford: Oxford University Press.

Lane, C. (2018) *From Taverns to Gastropubs: Food, Drink, and Sociality in England*, Oxford: Oxford University Press.

Lane, R.E. (1991) *The Market Experience*, Cambridge: Cambridge University Press.

Lang, T. (2019) *Feeding Britain: Our Food Problems and How to Fix Them*, London: Pelican Books.

Lawrence, J. (2019) *Me, Me, Me: The Search for Community in Post-war England*, Oxford: Oxford University Press.

Leschziner, V. (2015) *At the Chef's Table: Culinary Creativity in Elite Restaurants*, Stanford: Stanford University Press.

Leynse, W. (2006) 'Journeys through "ingestible topography": socializing the "situated eater" in France', *European Studies: A Journal of European Culture, History and Politics*, 22: 129–158.

Lizardo, O. and Skiles, S. (2016) 'After omnivorousness: is Bourdieu still relevant?', in Hanquinet, L. and Savage, M. (eds) *Routledge International Handbook of the Sociology of Arts and Culture*, London: Routledge, pp 90–103.

Marshall, D. and Pettinger, C. (2009) 'Revisiting British meals', in Meiselman, H. (ed) *Meals in Science and Practice: Interdisciplinary Research and Business Practice*, London: Woodhead Publishing, pp 638–661.

Meah, A. and Watson, M. (2011) 'Saints and slackers: challenging discourses about the decline of domestic cooking', *Sociological Research Online*, 16(2). http://www.socresonline.org.uk/16/2/6.html 10.5153/sro.2341

Mellor, J., Blake, M. and Crane, L. (2010) 'When I'm doing a dinner party I don't go for the Tesco cheeses', *Food, Culture & Society*, 13(1): 115–134.

Mennell, S. (1985) *All Manners of Food: Eating and Taste in England and France from the Middle Ages to the Present*, Oxford: Blackwell.

Metcalfe, S. and Warde, A. (eds) (2002) *Market Relations and the Competitive Process*, Manchester: Manchester University Press.

Metcalfe, A., Dryden C., Johnson, M., Owen, J. and Shipton, G. (2009) 'Fathers, food and family life', in Jackson, P. (ed) *Changing Families, Changing Food*, Basingstoke: Palgrave Macmillan, pp 93–117.

Mintel (2017) *Eating Out Review: UK*, Mintel Group.

Mintz, S. (1985) *Sweetness and Power: The Place of Sugar in Modern History*, Harmondsworth: Penguin.

Mintz, S. (2008) 'Food, culture and energy', in Nützenadel, A. and Trentmann, F. (eds) *Food and Globalization: Consumption, Markets and Politics in the Modern World*, Oxford: Berg, pp 21–36.

Moehring, M. (2008) 'Transnational food migration and the internalization of food consumption: ethnic cuisine in West Germany', in Nützenadel, A. and Trentmann, F. (eds) *Food and Globalization: Consumption, Markets and Politics in the Modern World*, Oxford: Berg, pp 129–152.

Murcott, A. (1997) 'Family meals – a thing of the past?', in Caplan, P. (ed) *Food, Health and Identity*, London: Routledge, pp 32–49.

Murcott, A. (2019) *Introducing the Sociology of Food and Eating*, London: Bloomsbury.

Nestle, M. (2007) *Food Politics: How the Food Industry Influences Nutrition and Health*, Berkeley: California University Press.

Neuman, N., Gottzén, L. and Fjellstrom, C. (2017) 'Masculinity and the sociality of cooking in men's everyday lives', *Sociological Review*, 65(4): 816–831.

O'Connell, R. and Brannen, J. (2016) *Food, Families and Work*, London: Bloomsbury.

O'Connor, K. (2013 [2006]) *The English Breakfast: The Biography of a National Meal with Recipes*, London: Bloomsbury.

Oesch, D. (2006) *Redrawing the Class Map: Stratification and Institutions in Britain, Germany, Sweden and Switzerland*, Basingstoke: Palgrave Macmillan.

Oncini, F. (2021) '"It's the noise of the snacks!": school meals on the fringes and frail food pedagogies', *Ethnography*, online first.

Oncini, F., Rödl, B., Triventi, M. and Warde, A. (2023) 'Cultural intolerance, in practice: social variation in food and drink avoidances in Italy, 2003–2016', *Social Indicators Research*, 170: 1075–1096.

ONS (Office for National Statistics) (2019) *Agriculture in the UK 2019*. Assets.publishing.service.gov.uk

ONS (Office for National Statistics) (2020) Family spending in the UK: April 2018 to March 2019. https://www.ons.gov.uk/peoplepop ulationandcommunity/personalandhouseholdfinances/expenditure/ bulletins/familyspendingintheuk/april2018tomarch2019

ONS (Office for National Statistics) (2022) Census estimates of household and family composition', www.ons.gov.uk

ONS (Office for National Statistics) (2023) Retail Prices Index: Long run series: 1947 to 2023. https://www.ons.gov.uk/economy/inflation andpriceindices/timeseries/cdko/mm23

ONS (Office for National Statistics) (various years) *Family Spending*. London: HMSO. www.ons.gov.uk

Otter, C. (2012) 'The British nutrition transition and its histories', *History Compass*, 10/11: 812–825.

Otter, C. (2020) *Diet for a Large Planet: Industrial Britain, Food Systems, and World Ecology*, Chicago: Chicago University Press.

Paddock, J. and Warde, A. (2015) 'Let's eat out more: re-configuring a feminist vision for a sustainable future', *Discover Society*, No. 28, December.

Paddock, J., Warde, A. and Whillans, J. (2017) 'The changing meaning of eating out in three English cities 1995–2015', *Appetite*, 119: 5–13.

Panayi, P. (2008) *Spicing up Britain: The Multicultural History of British Food*, London: Reaktion Books.

Parsons, J. (2015) *Gender, Class and Food: Families, Bodies and Health*, Basingstoke: Palgrave Macmillan.

Patel, R. (2022) 'Top six diet trends in 2022', British Dietetic Association. Available at: https://www.bda.uk.com/resource/top-six-diet-trends-of-2022.html

Peterson, R.A. and Kern, R. (1996) 'Changing highbrow taste: from snob to omnivore', *American Sociological Review*, 61(5): 900–907.

Piketty, T. (2014) *Capital in the Twenty-First Century*, Cambridge, MA: Harvard University Press.

Pirani, D., Harman, V. and Cappellini, B. (2022) 'Family practices and temporality at breakfast: hot spots, convenience and care', *Sociology*, 56(2): 211–226.

Pollan, M. (2008) *In Defence of Food: The Myth of Nutrition and the Pleasures of Eating*, London: Allen Lane.

Purkiss, D. (2022) *English Food: A People's History*, London: William Collins.

Rayner, J. (2016) *The Ten (Food) Commandments*, London: Penguin Books.

Reckwitz, A. (2017 [2012]) *The Invention of Creativity: Modern Society and the Culture of the New*, Cambridge: Polity.

Reckwitz, A. (2020 [2017]) *The Society of Singularities*, Cambridge: Polity.

Rotenberg, R. (1981) 'The impact of industrialization on meal patterns in Vienna, Austria', *Ecology of Food and Nutrition*, 11(1): 25–35.

Rozin, E. (1992) *Ethnic Cuisine: How to Create the Authentic Flavours of 30 International Cuisines*, New York: Penguin.

Runciman, W.G. (2015) *Very Different, But Much the Same: The Evolution of English Society since 1714*, Oxford: Oxford University Press.

Sallaz, J. and Zavisca, J. (2007) 'Bourdieu in America, 1980–2004', *Annual Review of Sociology*, 33: 21–41.

Santoro, M. and Solaroli, M. (2016) 'Contesting culture: Bourdieu and the strong programme in cultural sociology', in Hanquinet, L. and Savage, M. (eds) *Routledge International Handbook of the Sociology of Art and Culture*, London: Routledge, pp 49–76.

Savage, M. (2021) *The Return of Inequality: Social Change and the Weight of the Past*, Cambridge, MA: Harvard University Press.

Schor, J. (1992) *The Overworked American: The Unexpected Decline of Leisure*, New York: Basic Books.

Schumacher, E.F. (1973) *Small is Beautiful: A Study of Economics as if People Matter*, London: Blond and Briggs.

Scitovsky, T. (1976) *The Joyless Economy: An Inquiry into Human Satisfaction and Consumer Dissatisfaction*, New York: Oxford University Press.

Sen, A. (1983) *Poverty and Famines: An Essay on Entitlement and Deprivation*, Oxford: Oxford University Press.

Shapin, S. (2011) 'The sciences of subjectivity', *Social Studies of Science*, 42(2): 170–184.

Short, F. (2006) *Kitchen Secrets: The Meaning of Cooking in Everyday Life*, London: Berg.

Southerton, D. (2003) '"Squeezing time": allocating practices, coordinating networks and scheduling society', *Time & Society*, 12(1): 5–25.

Southerton, D. (2009) 'Reordering temporal rhythms: comparing daily lives of 1937 with those of 2000 in the UK', in Shove, E., Trentmann, F. and Wilk, R. (eds) *Time, Consumption and Everyday Life*, Oxford: Berg, pp 49–63.

Southerton, D. (2020) *Time, Consumption and the Coordination of Everyday Life*, London: Palgrave.

Southerton, D., Díaz-Méndez, C. and Warde, A. (2012) 'Behaviour change and the temporal ordering of eating practices: a UK-Spain comparison', *International Journal of the Sociology of Agriculture and Food*, 19(1): 19–36.

Spencer, C. (2004) *British Food: An Extraordinary Thousand Years of History*, London: Grub Street.

Spencer, C. (2016) *Vegetarianism: A History*, London: Grub Street.

Standing, G. (2011) *The Precariat: The New Dangerous Class*, London: Bloomsbury.

Sulkunen, P. (2009) *The Saturated Society: Governing Risks and Lifestyles in Consumer Culture*, London: SAGE.

Sullivan, O. (2000) 'The division of domestic labour: 20 years of change?', *Sociology*, 34(3): 437–456.

Swinburn, B.A., Kraak, V.I., Allender, S., Atkins, V.J., Baker, P.I., Bogard, J.R., et al (2019) 'The global syndemic of obesity, undernutrition, and climate change: *The Lancet* Commission report', *The Lancet*, 393, 23 February.

Teil, G. and Hennion, A. (2004) 'Discovering quality or performing taste? A sociology of the amateur', in Harvey, M., McMeekin, A. and Warde, A. (eds) *Qualities of Food*, Manchester: Manchester University Press, pp 19–37.

Thaler, R. and Sunstein, C. (2009) *Nudge: Improving Decisions about Health, Wealth and Happiness*, Harmondsworth: Penguin.

Thompson, E.P. (1971) 'The moral economy of the English crowd in the eighteenth century', *Past & Present*, 50: 76–136.

United Nations (2023) *World Happiness Report, 2023*. Available at: https://worldhappiness.report/

van Tulleken, C. (2023) *Ultra-Processed People: Why Do We All Eat Stuff That Isn't Food ... and Why Can't We Stop*, London: Cornerstone Press.

Vogler, P. (2020) *Scoff: A History of Food and Class in Britain*, London: Atlantic Books.

Wansick, B. (2006) *Mindless Eating: Why We Eat More Than We Think*, New York: Bantam Books.

Warde, A. (1993) 'Producers, profits and pictures: an analysis of advertisements for manufactured food', in Kjaernes, U., Holm, L., Ekstrom, M. and Prattala, R. (eds) *Regulating Markets, Regulating People: On Food and Nutrition Policy*, Oslo: Novus Forlag, pp 137–152.

Warde, A. (1997) *Consumption, Food and Taste: Culinary Antinomies and Commodity Culture*, London: SAGE.

Warde, A. (1999) 'Convenient food: space and timing', *British Food Journal*, 101(7): 518–527.

Warde, A. (2000) 'Eating globally: cultural flows and the spread of ethnic restaurants', in Kalb, D., van der Land, M., Staring, R., van Steenbergen, B. and Wilterdink, N. (eds) *The Ends of Globalization: Bringing Society Back In*, Boulder: Rowman & Littlefield, pp 299–316.

Warde, A. (2009) 'Imagining British cuisine: representations of culinary identity in the *Good Food Guide*', *Food, Culture and Society*, 12(2): 149–171.

Warde, A. (2013) 'What sort of a practice is eating?', in Shove, E. and Spurling, N. (eds) *Sustainable Practice: Social Theory and Climate Change*, London: Routledge, pp 17–30.

Warde, A. (2015) 'Towards a complaining sociology', in Fjellstrom, C. (ed) *Klagandets diskurs – matforskare reflekterar [The Discourse of Complaining]*, Uppsala: University of Uppsala, pp 213–220.

Warde, A. (2016) *The Practice of Eating*, Cambridge: Polity.

Warde, A. (2018) 'Changing tastes: the evolution of dining out in England', *Gastronomica: The Journal of Critical Food Studies*, 18(4): 1–12.

Warde, A. and Hetherington, K. (1994) 'English households and routine food practices: a research note', *Sociological Review*, 42(4): 758–778.

Warde, A. and Hirth, S. (2022) 'Evolving antinomies of culinary practice: Britain, 1968–2016', *Food Culture and Society*. https://doi.org/10.1080/15528014.2022.2127069

Warde, A. and Martens, L. (1998) 'Food choice: a sociological approach', in Murcott, A. (ed) *The Nation's Diet*, London: Longman, pp 129–146.

Warde, A. and Martens, L. (2000) *Eating Out: Social Differentiation, Consumption and Pleasure*, Cambridge: Cambridge University Press.

Warde, A. and Yates, L. (2017) 'Understanding eating events: snacks and the British meal pattern', *Food Culture & Society*, 20(1): 15–36.

Warde, A., Wright, D. and Gayo-Cal, M. (2007) 'The meaning of cultural omnivorousness, or the myth of the cultural omnivore', *Cultural Sociology*, 1(2): 143–164.

Warde, A., Whillans, J. and Paddock, J. (2019) 'The allure of variety: eating out in three English cities, 2015', *Poetics*, 72: 17–31.

Warde, A., Paddock, J. and Whillans, J. (2020a) 'Domestic hospitality: as a practice and an alternative economic arrangement', *Cultural Sociology*, 14(4): 379–398.

Warde, A., Paddock, J. and Whillans, J. (2020b) *The Social Significance of Dining Out: A Study of Continuity and Change*, Manchester: Manchester University Press.

Warren, G. (ed) (1958) *The Foods We Eat: A Survey of Meals, Their Content and Chronology by Season, Day of the Week, Region, Class and Age, Conducted in Great Britain by the Market Research Division of W.S. Crawford Limited*, London: Cassell.

Wernick, A. (1981) *Promotional Culture: Advertising, Ideology and Symbolic Expression*. London: SAGE.

Wilk, R. (2006) *Home Cooking in the Global Village: Caribbean Food from Buccaneers to Ecotourists*, Oxford: Berg.

Willett, W., Rockstrom, J., Loken, B., Springmann, M., Lang, T., Vermeulen, S. et al (2019) 'Food in the Anthropocene: the EAT-Lancet Commission on healthy diets from sustainable food systems', *Lancet*, 393: 447–492.

Wilson, B. (2019) *The Way We Eat Now: How the Food Revolution Has Transformed Our Lives, Our Bodies, and Our World*, London: The Fourth Estate.

Wintle, M. (2006) 'Diet and modernization in the Netherlands during the nineteenth and early twentieth centuries', *European Studies: a Journal of European Culture, History and Politics*, 22: 63–84.

Wouters, G. (2008) *Informalization: Manners and Emotions since 1890*, London: SAGE.

WRAP (Waste and Resources Action Programme) (2013) *Estimates of Waste in the Food and Drink Supply Chain*. Available at: http://www.wrap.org.uk/sites/files/wrap/Estimates%20of%20waste%20in%20the%20food%20and%20drink%20supply%20chain_0.pdf

REFERENCES

Yates, L. and Warde, A. (2015) 'The evolving content of meals in Great Britain: results of a survey in 2012 in comparison with the 1950s', *Appetite*, 84(1): 299–308.

Yates, L. and Warde, A. (2017) 'Eating together and eating alone: meal arrangements in British households', *British Journal of Sociology*, 6(1): 97–118.

Zerubavel, E. (2018) *Taken for Granted: The Remarkable Power of the Unremarkable*, Princeton: Princeton University Press.

Zweiniger-Bargielowska, I. (2000) *Austerity in Britain: Rationing, Controls, and Consumption, 1939–1955*, Oxford: Oxford University Press.

Index

References to figures are in *italic* type and references to tables are in **bold** type.

A

access to food 39, 47, 160
addictive properties of foods 139
additives 94, 138
aesthetics 10, 15, 116–118, 163
affluence 2, 11, 44, 46, 62, 87
   and food preferences 135
affordability 45–49, 62
age 13
   see also older people; younger people
agency
   see individuals
agricultural techniques 53–54
Ahn, Y.Y. 65
Ainsworth, Jim 77–78
air freight 54
allergens 134
alternatives to the market 56–62
Amazon 56
American food outlets 52, 66, 110, 165
anxiety 15, 115, 119, 129–131, 159
   dealing with 131–147
   and eating 143–147
   and habit 131–132
   and obesity 137–140
appearance of food 80
apples 55
aristocracy 6
art and culinary culture 118
asylum seekers 46
Atkinson, Will 43–45, 62
aubergines 40
austerity 66, 152, 154, 164
authenticity 76, 104
availability of food 51–56, 62
avocado pears 40, 52
avoidance of specific foods 134–135, 147

B

baby foods 94
bacon 2, 8, 22, 23, 24
Baker, Phillip 138
bakers 9
barbecues 87, 126, 127
Barr, Ann 102–104
Bauman, Zygmunt 119
beans 9, 146
beef 2, 18, 40, 70, 75, 127, 144
   and horsemeat scandal 131
behaviour
   behaviour at restaurants 33, 112, 115
   changing behaviour 132–136, 143–147
biodiversity 50, 146
Birmingham and the balti 74
biscuits 21, 29
bodies, physical
   appearance of 136
   management of 123
   and pleasure 150
Body Mass Index (BMI) 133, 137
Boer war 22
boundary crossing and eating out 110–111
Bourdieu, Pierre 43, 44, 119–120
Boyle, Joseph 141
branding 42, 54, 55
bread 2, 21, 24, 29, 40, 70
breakfast 22–25, 37, 69, 89, 137
Brexit 47, 50, 159

INDEX

British diet
　British cuisine 76–80
　changes in the 149–155, 155–161
　and class 2–7
　the English breakfast 24
　later twentieth century 10–13
　opinions of 1, 2
　origins of 1–7
　Second World War/post-war 7–10
　urban-industrial diet 1, 8, 10–13, 121, 138, 152
burgers 43, 44, 69, 70, 75, 109
Burnett, John 6, 11, 67, 164
　Plenty and Want: A Social History of Food in England from 1815 to the Present Day 3
butchers 9, 55, 141
butter 2, 8, 40
buying food 39–45, 53–56
　see also shops and shopping

C

cafes 28, 32, 69
cakes 9, 21, 29
calories 1, 6, 137, 144
capitalism and waste 59, 60–61, 99
carbohydrates 1, 75
casualisation 33, 70, 150
　casualising eating 26–29, 35, 106–107
celebratory meals 123
celebrities 133
cereals, mass produced 22, 23, 29, 50, 89, 139
ceremonial aspects of eating 35
Charles, N. 88
cheap food 10, 51, 53, 62, 138, 150, 156
cheese 8, 9, 20, 29, 55
chicken 18, 20, 42, 70, 74, 127, 144
　chickens for egg production 40
children 62, 87, 90, 97, 142
　baby foods 94
　eating unusual foods 82, 112
　and rationing 7
　and restaurants 32, 106
　and working mothers 91–92
Chinese restaurants and takeaways 65, 69, 70, 74, 110
chocolate 9, 29
class 2–7, 9, 13, 23, 63, 87, 116, 153–154
　and access to food 160

after Second World War 164
brand loyalty 42
the creative class 118
and culture 119–122
and diet 8
differences between classes 121–122
and ethnicity 15
and food choices 43–45
　see also education; middle class; professional classes; working class
clean and hygienic food 53, 54, 156
climate change 16, 50, 158, 161–162
collective approaches 58, 82, 142, 146
combinations of food 136
comfort when dining out 112, 115, 116
　see also anxiety; pleasure and eating
commercial culture
　see consumer culture; marketing
commercial premises
　see eating out
commodification 15, 85, 117
　alternatives to 56–62
　and convenience 90–97
　and waste 59
common understanding 13, 73, 82
Commonwealth immigration
　see immigration
companionship 32–35, 123
complementary and alternative medicine 134
concern about food 129–131
condensed milk 1, 9
confectionery 9, 21, 139, 140
Conservative governments 46
conservative reactions 122
consumer culture 15, 117, 119, 159
　consumer goods 29, 85–86
consumption **41**
　changes in 40–42
　clusters of food preferences 43–45
　cultural cues for 140
convenience foods 90–97, 128, 130, 157
cookbooks/recipes 6, 10, 22, 72, 73, 98, 105, 152
cook-chill 97
cooking 13
　domestic cookery 10, 84, 89–90, 150
　facilities 47
　learning how to 98–100
　and men 88–89
　professional chefs 52, 69, 78, 89
　satisfaction of 100–101

'from scratch' 72, 86, 92, 93, 94
  see also households and
    household work
cooperation schemes 58
coordination of meal times 25–27
corporate social responsibility 54
cost/expense 96–97
  affordability 45–49, 62
  of buying food 39–42
  of eating out 32, 40
  good value 123
  prices 42, 45, 50, 53, 62, 111
courses, number of 21, 26, 107
COVID-19 46, 47, 49, 97, 131
cuisine styles 110–112, *110*, **111**
culinary culture
  in Britain 1, 6
  'culinary revolution' 11–12
  defining British cuisine 76–80
  in France 7
  multicultural influences 65–66
  in the Netherlands 1
  see also foreign food
culinary omnivorousness 120, 165
cultural capital 12, 118, 120, 151, 154
  cultural omnivores 111, 115,
    122, 154
cultural change 11, 14–16, 162,
  163–164
cultural intermediation 80–83, 159
  cultural intermediaries 12, 15, 67,
    118, 122, 150
  and women's magazines 73
culture and class 119–122
culture and food 110–111
culture and style 116–119
culture wars 119, 122
curry 22, 69, 70, 109, 127

D

Daily Mirror 84
dairy products 50, 139
  cheese 8, 9, 20, 29, 55
  milk 23
DASH 135
DEFRA 32, 40, 133
democratisation 37
deprivation 16, 44–45, 45–49
desserts 6, 18, 70
'de-structuration' of meals 26, 30
DeVault, Marjorie 30
diet
  healthy diet 144–146

the 'nutrition transition' 1, 77
  see also British diet; urban-industrial
    diet; vegetarianism
dieting 14, 134
  see also obesity
dining out 105–116
  see also eating out
dinner 9, 20–22, 37
dinner parties 94, 126
dishes
  new dishes 52
  number of 6, 21, 26, 107
  range of dishes 84
  washing 87
diversification 11, 106, 151, 163
  interest in 107, 109
  origins of 49–51, 64, 112
division of labour 29, 85–90, 100,
  155, 157, 158
divorce 46, 87
domestic cookery 10, 150
  range of dishes 84
  simplification of 89–90
domestic hospitality 58–59, 94, 123,
  126–127
domestic labour 85–91
  see also households and
    household work
dominant standards 12
Dorling, Danny 14
Douglas, Mary 18
drinks 28, 139
duck 42, 44, 45
dumpster diving 60–61

E

earnings/wages
  see incomes
eating, learning 98–100
eating alone 22, 24, 31, 33–35, 147
eating and pleasure 123–129
eating and sociological
  change 163–165
eating between meals 27
eating changes in British
  habits 149–153
  see also British diet
eating disorders 136
eating out 31–33, 40, 43, 123, 151, 164
  at a domestic venue 58–59
  enjoyment of **125**
  as a normal activity 106
  tastes when eating out 67–71

INDEX

eating patterns 9–10, 155
eating practices 13–14
eating together 25, 31
EAT-Lancet diet *145*, 161, 165
economic concerns 7, 10, 16, 93, 96–97
  imports 2, 50, 85, 150
  inflation 7, 50
  international trade 2, 15, 51–53, 138
  markets 39, 56
  post-war period 29
  see also capitalism and waste
education 8, 44, 45, 62, 74, 163
  higher 12, 44, 45, 116, 118, 120, 153
  and preferences 75
  and roast dinners 19
eggs 2, 22, 23, 24, 40, 75, 144
  powdered egg 7, 49
  scrambled egg 9
electricity 47
  electrical goods 85–86
Elias, Norbert 11
elites 2, 6, 7, 122
Elizabethan Poor Laws 2
embarrassment 47, 115, 119, 121
emergency food parcels 47
emotional responses 129
empire and colonialism 1, 141, 153, 159, 164
  Commonwealth immigration 80, 82
  decolonisation 16
  White settler-colonialism 2
employment 91–92, 155, 163
  changes in 25, 31
  in the food sector 85
  manual labour 24
  precarious employment 46–47, 121
  service sector growth 118
  unemployment insurance 8
  of women 24, 88, 90, 97
EMP surveys 18, 28, 31, 74
environment, obesogenic 137–138, 139, 158
environmental concerns 62, 99, 130, 137, 161
  sustainability 143–144
equipment 15, 85–86
ethical eating 44, 45, 132, 135, 140, 143–147
ethnic cuisine 64, 109
ethnic minorities 15, 44, 66, 75, 80, 116, 120
  and deprivation 158

etiquette 13
European Union 16, 50, 150, 159
Evans, David 60
evening meal
  see dinner
everyday life 13, 15, 31, 100, 162
  in the 1950s 117
  and cooking 72
  normalisation of eating out 106
expenditure on buying food 39–42
expenditure on eating out 32, 40

F

familiarisation 106–107, 121
families
  and eating out 32
  expressions of love 87
  family life 100
  nuclear families 35, 87, 90
  and women 30
  see also family meals
Family Food 40
family meals 25, 29–31, 37, 90, 155
  family menus 3–6
  idealisation of 91, 100, 128
  and love 30, 87, 92, 100
farming lobby 159
farm shops 55
fats 1, 2, 8, 29, 94, 138
feminism 87
fertilisers and pesticides 54, 146
Finnish lunches 20
First World War 7
Fischler, Claude 33
fish 6, 20, 22, 43, 74, 75, 144
  and chips 1, 69, 70
fishmongers 9
  sauce 65
flavours 65, 74–75
flour 2
food, cheap 10, 51, 53, 62, 138, 150, 156
food, new in the 1970s 116
food banks 46, 47, **48**, 54, 57
food buying 39–45, 53–56
  see also shops and shopping
food chain 39, 53
food deserts 158
foodies 55, 102–105, **103**, 116
food preferences 8, 9, 43–45, *43*, 65, 70
  and class 10, 12, 62–63, 120, 153
  collective 82
  and education 75
  and individuals 73, 84, 90, 157

195

food production and distribution 2, 7, 50, 146
food safety and quality 53, 54, 130–131, 156
food scandals 131, 157
food security 46, 50, 53, 131, 150
food shortages 8, 45, 130
Food Standards Agency survey 67
food supply 13, 39, 50–51, 150, 157, 158, 164
foreign food 11, 15, 64–67, 151, 164
  and authenticity 76
  and domestic cookery 105
  incorporation by British chefs 78
  normalisation of 80–83
  reception of 74–75
  in women's magazines 71–73
France 6, 20, 50, 77, 80, 104, 142, 156
  and formalised meals 26–27, 30
  and local produce 98–99
  status of cuisine 7, 110, 111
fraudulent behaviour 130, 157
Freeganism 60–61
free range 42
Freidberg, S. 97
frequency of consumption 40–42
fresh food 158
  and air freight 54
  freshness concept 97
fried foods 9
friends/neighbours 18, 127
fruit 2, 10, 21, 23, 29, 42, 43, 44, 146
  grown in UK 50
  rare types of 40
'Fusion-Plus' style 79

G

Gallup survey 67
game 6
garden and tradition, the 77
Garthwaite, Alison, *Hunger Pains* 46
gastronomy 13
gastropubs 70
gender 9, 13, 45, 85, 155, 157
  gender and cooking 86–90
  see also men; women
gentry, the 22
German food 20, 65
Gibson, Kate 12
  Feeding the Middle Classes 153
gifts 30, 57, 58, 59, 124, 127
globalisation 15, 39, 51–52, 116–117, 150

gluten-free produce 54, 134
Good Food Guide (GFG) 36, 76, 79
goose 42, 44
government and politics 8, 119, 122
  British agricultural policy 51
  and food banks 46
  nutritional advice 133
  political alternatives 58
  political anxiety 143–147
  political neglect 15–16
  political protest 45, 60, 163
  and social movements 87, 119, 142
  state intervention 7, 15–16
  sustainable policies 159, 162–163
  trustworthiness of politicians 130–131
  welfare provision 8
gravy 18
grazing 28, 29
Greek food 65
greenhouse gases 60, 162
Grigson, Jane 153
'gut health' diet 135

H

habit 13, 15
  changes in British eating 149–153
  and changing habits 131–136, 139–140, 161–163
happiness and meals 123
health 11, 12, 100, 131, 149–150, 155
  concerns 130, 132–136, 158
  and convenience foods 93
  diet-related illness 16, 50, 139
  free healthcare 8
  healthy diet 144–146
  healthy eating 44, 106
  social change and 3
  the war generation 8
Hennion, A. 64
holidays 68, 109
homegrown food 39, 49, 57
homogenisation 10, 26, 52
horsemeat 131
households and household work
  buying food 39–45, 53–56
  changes in 15, 89
  division of labour 29, 85–90, 100, 155, 157, 158
  menus of 3–6
  self-provisioning 57
  smaller 17, 34
  see also shops and shopping
housewifely virtues 91

INDEX

humour and food 102, 104
Hungarian food 65
hunger and malnutrition 2, 6, 7, 10, 16, 45–49, 130

I

ice creams 29, 70
idealisation of family meals 91, 100, 128
identity 73, 109, 117, 119, 135, 136, 150, 154
 and vegetarianism 141
immigration 11, 15, 116, 132
 influences on UK food 65–67, 80–83
imports 2, 50, 85, 150
incomes 3, 6, 11, 39–40, 44, 47, 62, 116
 and inequality 160
independent shops 9, 55
Indian restaurants and takeaways 66, 74, 109
individuals 117
 agency and uncertainty 13
 changing behaviour 143–147, 161–163
 and cultural change 14–16
 individualisation 35, 36, 47, 73, 137, 157, 163
 and obesity 137–140
 and self-control 154
 social movements of the 1960s 119
 and social position 43–45
 see also bodies, physical
industrialisation/deindustrialisation 1, 2, 118, 163
industrialised food corporations
 and products 1, 10, 28, 51–52, 149, 158
 see also convenience foods; processed foods; ready meals
inequality 8, 37, 40, 87, 154, 158, 159
 food banks 45–49
 growth in 121–122
informalisation 33, 35–37, 106, 126, 156, 163
information and advice 10, 15, 22, 73, 119, 132, 156
ingredients
 cheaper 139
 diversification of 11, 51–53
institutional catering 57, 68
Irish people 65
Italy 65, 77, 156
 Italian food 109
 and school dinners 99

J

Jackson, Peter, *Anxious Appetites* 129–130
Japanese food 106, 110, 156
Jewish people 65

K

kedgeree 22
Kerr, M. 88
ketogenic diet 135
kitchens 85–86, 89
knowledgeability when dining out 112

L

labour in the food sector 85
labour movements 87, 121, 164
lamb 2, 18, 40, 144
land ownership 50, 146, 153
Lang, Tim 50
leftovers 9, 10, 19, 42, 60
legumes 144
leisure opportunities 31
leisure society 103
lentils 146
Levy, Paul 102–104
Leynse, Wendy 98
liberal society 8, 119, 122
life, acceleration of 14–16
lifestyle 117, 120, 130, 135, 136, 160, 164
living alone 34
living standards 154
local shopping and produce 55, 60, 98
love and family meals 30, 87, 92, 100
lunch 20–21, 37, 69, 89
luxuries 10

M

Manchester 76
mangoes 40
manufactured foodstuffs 51–53
margarine 1, 8
marketing 15, 92, 105, 117, 139–140, 157
 marketing of cereals 24
market produce 45, 77
markets 15, 39, 56
marmalade 24
marriage 87, 88
mass markets 53–56, 117
mass media 118, 130, 132, 133, 150
 and foreign food 11, 71–73
Mass Observation 25
Masterchef 89
McDonalds 52

meal, celebratory/elaborate 123
meal arrangements 9–10, 13, 25–31
meal occasions 17, 37–38
  breakfast 22–25, 37, 69, 89, 137
  dinner 9, 20–22, 37, 94, 126
  lunch 20–21, 37, 68, 69, 89
  snacks 27–29, 69, 97
  see also eating out; family meals
meal patterns 9, 26, 28, 37, 155
meal preparation 57, 59, 72, 84–86, 87–89
  collective preparation 58
  and lunch 20
meals, celebratory/elaborate 6
meal times 25–27, 27
meat 1, 2, 6, 9, 10, 40, 50, 74, 135
  cured meats 44
  devilled meats 22
  increasing consumption in 1950s 140–141
  pre-cooked 42
Mediterranean diet 135
men 23, 34, 44, 68, 74
  and domestic labour 85
  and food preferences 75
  in the kitchen 86–90, 100
  male breadwinner demise 15, 29, 87, 91
  and mid-day meals 9, 20
  unfit to fight 22
Mennell, Stephen 10, 11
menus
  for domestic hospitality 127
  household menus 3–6
  pub menu **71**
  restaurant menus 69
  tasting menus 79–80, **81**
microwaves 86
midday meals
  see lunch
middle class 7, 151
  children and unusual foods 82
  domestic hospitality 127
  menus of lower middle class 3–6
  new middle class 12, 15, 118–119, 153–154, 159, 162–163
  and restaurant behaviour 115
  sons and catering careers 89
  see also education
milk 23
mobile phone use while eating 27, 36
'mock' foods 7
Modern British Cooking 77, 152
monotonous diet 3, 6, 10, 47, 84, 151
moral panic 28, 30, 130
moral virtue 91, 92, 93, 96, 155

Mrs Beeton's Book of Household Management 22
multicultural influences 11, 19, 65–67, 119, 152
Murcott, Anne 30
mutton 2
mutual aid 57, 58

N

national diet, a
  see British diet
National Health Service (NHS) 133
neoliberalism 46, 161
Nestle, Marion 137
Netherlands, the 1
new middle class, the 12, 15, 122, 153–154, 159
  creation of the 118–119
  role in policy change 162–163
Norwegian lunches 20
novelty 52, 72, 105, 107, 112, 129, 144
nutrition 2, 11, 13, 23, 93, 133, 149
  'nutrition transition' the 1, 77
  and snacks 27–28
  and social change 3
nuts 29, 144, 146

O

obesity 10, 14, 131, 133, 158, 162
  and anxiety 137–140
  and snack food 28
Ocado 56
O'Connor, K. 22
OECD 129
Ofer, Avner 1
offal 9, 22
Official Foodie Handbook (OFH) 102
older people 19, 34, 75, 82
  'cooking from scratch' 94
omnivorousness 109–112, **113**, 153
organic produce 54
Orwell, George 141
Otter, Chris 1, 2
out-of-date food 43
overcooking 10, 18
overweight, being
  see obesity

P

packaging 94
Panayi, Panikos 2, 11–12, 80, 164
  Spicing up Britain: The Multicultural History of British Food 65–66

INDEX

paprika 65
Paris and Court life 6
Parsons, Julie 104
pasta 40, 69, 70, 75, 109, 127
petrol station forecourts 143
photographing food 157
pies 70
pizza 67, 69, 70, 75
plant diet 146
pleasure and eating 102, 123–129, 147–148, 155
politics
  see government and politics
popular press
  see print media
population replacement 15
pork 18, 40, 70, 75, 135, 144
  sweet and sour pork 67
porridge 22, 23, 128
potatoes 2, 9, 18, 21, 40, 52, 55, 70, 74
poverty 2, 58, 62, 68, 158, 164, 165
  food banks 45–49
  food expenditure 42
  menus from 1901 3–6
prawn cocktail 70
preservation techniques 52, 94, 97, 138
pretentiousness 116
prices 42, 45, 50, 53, 62, 111
print media 10, 82, 104, 105, 118, 133, 150, 157
  foreign food in women's magazines 71–73
processed foods 10, 53, 131, 137–139, 149, 158
  processed fats 1
  snack foods 28
products/items, new 54
  see also novelty
professional chefs 52, 69, 89
  incorporating foreign foods 78
professional classes 6, 45, 116, 118, 120
  in cultural intermediation 12
  living alone 34
professional sports on Sundays 19
protests 45, 60, 163
public health regulation 2, 14
pubs/bars opening hours 69, 70
  pub menu **71**
puddings 9, 18

Q

quality 9, 42, 111, 130–131, 160
  food and class 122
quantity of food eaten 129

R

radical action 16
range of dishes 12, 84, 128
rationing 7–8, 23, 48–49, 152
Rayner, Jay 98
ready meals 43, 44, 53, 92–94, 139
  of differing quality 97
recipes/cookbooks 6, 10, 22, 72, 73, 98, 105, 152
recreation, food as 117, 129, 159, 164
recreational opportunities 31
  recreation on Sundays 19
refrigerators 22, 24, 86, 140
  refrigerated transport 52
regional differentiation 23, 65, 76, 77, 152, 155
  in France 98–99
regularisation of eating out 107
religion 17, 19, 25, 135
  church food banks 46
  religious minorities 44
relishes and spices 77
restaurants 32, 33, 60, 140, 164, 165
  cuisine styles 68–71, *110*, **111**
  foreign 11, 66–67
  improvements in 156
  variety and range of 105–106
rice 40, 75
rich, the 6, 7, 40, 62
  food expenditure 42
roast meat 18, 69, 70, 75, 109, 127
  see also Sundays
routine
  see habit
Rozin, Elizabeth 65
Runciman, Garry 14
Russia 50

S

safety of food 53, 54, 130–131, 156
salads 20, 45, 70
salt 29, 94
sandwiches 20–21, 89, 106
  cheese sandwiches 75
  pre-packaged 43
Saturdays 75
sausages 24, 74
school dinners 68, 99, 133
Schor, Juliet 85
seasonal food 9, 54
Second World War and post-war 7–10, 48, 86, 87
  changes in eating habits since 149–153

self-control 12, 153
self-provisioning 57, 91
self-servicing 85
'servant crisis,' the 7, 86
service sector 25, 118
shame 37, 47, 115
shared experiences 16
shelf-life 97
shellfish 44
shops and shopping 8, 87, 143
  independent shops 9, 55, 60, 98
  online 56
  shops open on Sundays 19
  supermarkets 42, 53–56, 60, 140, 149, 164
shorter meals 24, 26
simplification of meals 25, 33, 89–90, 107
skilled/unskilled workers, menus of 3–6
small meals
  see lunch
Smith, Delia 105
snacks 27–29, 69, 97
sociability 126, 128
social change 161–165, 163–165
social hierarchy 16, 43, 110, 155, 160
  and taste 119–120
  see also class
social media 150
social movements 87, 119, 142
social position 116, 121
sociocultural change 163–165
socioeconomic environment 15
soup 20, 21, 46, 70
Southerton, Dale 25
Spain, meals in 35
special dietary requirements 44
special occasion eating out 112
standards of living 2
state intervention
  see government and politics
steak 69, 70, 109
stir-frys 75
street, eating in the 26, 35
style 10
  style and culture 116–119
  styles of cuisine 110–112
sugar 1, 8, 29, 94, 138
Sullivan 88
Sundays 75
  the role of 19, 25
  Sunday dinner 1, 9, 17–21
supermarkets 42, 53–56, 60, 140, 149, 164

supper 9
supply chains 39, 150, 164
sustainability 51, 143, 146, 158–159, 161–162
  EAT-Lancet diet *145*
symbolic significance 92, 110, 117, 122, 123, 155

T

tables 33, 36
takeaways 11, 64, 66, 69, 94, 140, 164
taste 12, 13, 24, 82, 117, 149, 150
  and class 120, 154
  expanding taste 64–65
  influence of migrants 82
  and style 118
  tastes when eating out 67–71, 105–116
tasting menus 79, 80, **81**, 82
TCP surveys 68, 69, 82, 93, 104, 134
tea 1, 2, 8, 22, 28
  and biscuits 123
tea (the meal) 9, 21
Teil, G. 64
television 118, 150, 157
  cooking programmes 89
  while eating 27, 36
terminology, agreed 73
Thai food 110
Thompson, E.P. 45
three meals a day 9, 26, 28, 155
toast 9, 23, 89
Todmorden, West Yorkshire 58
tomatoes 52, 65
trade, international 2, 15, 51–53, 138
traditional British food 18, 74, 109, 110, 112, 151
transport hubs, eating at 69
travelling, eating while 68
trends 11, 14–15, 52, 149, 151, 157
  see also diversification; familiarisation
Trussell Trust 47, **48**
turkey 42

U

Ukrainian War 50, 131, 150
ultra-processed foods (UPFs) 131, 137–139, 149
United States 53, 60, 110
  food enthusiasts in 104
  food industry 137
  food outlets from 66, 165
  Italian migration to 141

INDEX

urban-industrial diet 1, 8, 10–13, 121, 138, 152

V

van Tulleken, Chris 139
variety 2, 9, 42, 53, 112, 153, 156, 163
veganism 54, 141
vegetables 6, 9, 18, 20, 42, 70, 146, 153
  fresh 93
  grown in UK 50
  rare types of 40
  raw 44
vegetarianism 14, 44, 110, 134, 135, 140–142
Victorian food concerns 14
Vogler, Pen 121

W

Warren 9–10, 18, 20–21, 23, 28
waste 42, 50, 54, 62, 132, 137, 159
  edible food waste 59–60
wealth, redistribution of 8
weekends 37, 75
welfare state 8, 11, 29, 119, 154, 163, 164
  reduction of the 12
wheat 2
white bread/flour 1, 14
White British people 120
  domination of White men 87

wholesome food 1, 10, 152
wild foods 58
women 7, 9, 23, 68, 105, 158
  and domestic labour 29–30, 85, 100, 155
  and eating out 32
  and employment 24, 90, 97
  and food preferences 75
  foreign food in magazines 71–73
  in the kitchen 86–90
  mothers and employment 91–92
  and thin bodies 136
  and vegetarianism 142
  women's magazines 92
working class 2, 3, 7, 10, 35, 62, 87
  culture of the 15
  diet 1, 151–152
  domestic hospitality 127
  see also urban-industrial diet
world wars 2, 7
  see also First World War; Second World War/post-war

Y

yoghurt 23
York 3
Yorkshire pudding 18
YouGov poll 67
younger people 44, 75, 88, 94, 117, 142
  women and thin bodies 136

www.ingramcontent.com/pod-product-compliance
Lightning Source LLC
Chambersburg PA
CBHW051542020426
42333CB00016B/2053